# THE PURPOSE OF AMERICAN POLITICS

## Hans J. Morgenthau
With a new Introduction by
## Kenneth W. Thompson
Director
White Burkett Miller Center
of Public Affairs
University of Virginia

UNIVERSITY
PRESS OF
AMERICA

**University Press of America, Inc.**
P.O. Box 19101, Washington, D.C. 20036

**ISBN (Perfect): 0-8191-2847-3**


**Library of Congress Number : 82-20057**

"Have we, inheritors of this continent and of the ideals to which the fathers consecrated it,—have we maintained them, realizing them, as each generation must, anew? Are we, in the consciousness that the life of man is pledged to higher levels here than elsewhere, striving still to bear aloft the standards of liberty and hope, or, disillusioned and defeated, are we feeling the disgrace of having had a free field in which to do new things and of not having done them? The answer must be, I am sure, that we have been in a fair way of failure,— tragic failure. And we stand in danger of utter failure. . . ."

WOODROW WILSON

*in 1912*

# INTRODUCTION

## Kenneth W. Thompson

In a sense, *The Purpose of American Politics* is the other half of the philosophy of international politics with which Hans J. Morgenthau is often identified. It is sometimes said that Morgenthau's viewpoint is one in which emphasis is placed exclusively on power to the exclusion of purpose and morality. For those most familiar with his work, this interpretation is false and far from the mark. Beginning in 1946 with the publication of *Scientific Man vs. Power Politics,* Professor Morgenthau, in his writings, repeatedly called the attention of American readers to the moral problem. His fellow political philosopher, Walter Lippmann, once said to Morgenthau: "You are greatly misunderstood. You have more concern for morality and politics than anyone I know." His concern with power stemmed in part from the consequences of power for morality.

If anyone has doubts that Morgenthau had a profound interest in purpose as well as politics, the present book should dispel that idea. It was published in 1960 in the wake of renewed interest in national purpose in the United States. Rather early in the Eisenhower administration, the President called on his friend Dr. Henry Wriston, President of Brown University and later of the American Assembly, to explore whether a representative group of Americans might address themselves to a redefinition of the national goals of Americans. Earlier, others at the close of World War II had urged that Americans were failing to articulate the ends of a free society. Half facetiously, certain critics complained that the Russians had been more successful in stating the communist creed by which the Soviet Union was governed. Various bodies were approached to take up the task of formulating American values. One such group was the Social Science Research Council in New York whose members, however, expressed doubts that social scientists could reach a consensus on the national purpose. I recall that the large foundations were asked to assist in the enterprise but no organized center or council came forward to conduct the study until the Wriston Commission on National Goals was created. There followed a second prestigious group established by the *New York Times* and *Life Magazine*. William Bundy was study director for the Wriston Commission and the roster included many establishment figures. Respected and influential Americans such as John Gardner, James Reston and Warren Weaver contributed to the effort.

It was in such a setting and atmosphere that Professor Morgenthau published *The Purpose of American Politics*. The book was an outgrowth of the Albert Shaw Lectures which he delivered in April 1959 at Johns Hopkins University. The publisher, Alfred A. Knopf, had encouraged Morgenthau to write such a book. As an officer of the Rockefeller Foundation, I had been responsible in part at least for some of the funding and the invitations which enabled Morgenthau to spend the academic year 1958-59 at the Institute for Advanced Study at Princeton and the following year at the Washington Center for Foreign Policy Research. We talked at length about his research and his experiences at Princeton and in Washington and a briefer period in residence at Harvard. He had hoped he might have had a second year at Princeton and was disappointed when this did not happen. It was also his dream to be offered a faculty appointment at Harvard and he grieved that this did not happen. He could not restrain his feelings that one or two erstwhile friends had not done what they might have to assist him; he was convinced two prominent scholars at Harvard who were themselves writing about national purpose had opposed his permanent appointment there.

This background is relevant to the profound disappointment Professor Morgenthau experienced at the reaction to his book on national purpose. He told me on several occasions that the book had scarcely caused a ripple. What was doubtless even more painful for him was that the response followed earlier disappointments. I tried to explain then and I would say now that the book was ill-timed and was fated to be swallowed up in reactions to the heavily funded and widely promoted reports of the Wriston Commission and the *New York Times-Life* group. Samuel S. Stratton, Democratic congressman from New York, reviewed *Purpose* in the *New York Times* but there were few important writers who discussed or noticed it. Those American thinkers like Reinhold Niebuhr who recognized the seriousness of Morgenthau's book were busy attacking the shallowness of the commission reports.

Therefore, the republication of *Purpose* in 1982 promises to fill a gap both in the literature deserving discussion of national goals and in the publicly available writings of the late Hans J. Morgenthau. Its publication now will permit Americans to reexamine certain views of a great political scientist which he felt had been significantly overlooked. It may be that readers in the 1980s will be no more prepared than those in the early 1960s for the historical and philosophical demands placed upon them by *Purpose*. They may still prefer wide-ranging commentary on a host of contemporary social problems. It may be true for the 1980s, however, that the insufficiencies and time-bound character of some of the discussions in the 1960s may invite serious consideration of a more integrated and coherent approach. I know Morgenthau hoped for this until his last days.

There are certain unique features to *Purpose*. In contrast to the pundits who contributed to the commission reports, Morgenthau argued that national purpose must be rediscovered, not discovered. It has existed more or less unchanged from the founding of the Republic. Moreover, Morgenthau undertook to integrate the manifold national aspirations of Americans under a single unifying national purpose, that of "achieving equality in freedom." In the days of the Founding Fathers, the national purpose was pursued primarily at home. With Woodrow Wilson, the national purpose was augmented through "offering it by way of example to the world." In part, it was the Wilsonian Crusade that led to the impairment and ultimately the denial of American morality abroad.

Morgenthau did not shy away from the urgent current problems of his time. He discussed McCarthyism, atomic power, foreign aid and the Korean and Chinese problems. Yet a more all-pervasive concern was with certain recurrent and enduring problems including malaise, waste, the decline of the public realm, the loss of the quest for excellence and the paradoxes of democratic government.

For those who see in the American presidency the best hope and gravest challenge facing the republic, he wrote:

> As Chief Executive, the President is the politician-in-chief of the nation. In order to see his decision put into action by his subordinates, he can and must promise and threaten, reward and punish. He needs assistance in the exercise of this power, but he cannot delegate its substance to a Vice President or 'First Secretary,' without risking either its dissipation or its abuse. There is no remedy outside himself for the heaviest burden the President must bear: his loneliness at the pinnacle of decision and power. But there is a compensation. For from that loneliness, calling forth the ultimate reserves of his mind and soul, springs the President's greatness.

# *Preface*

This book grew out of the Albert Shaw Lectures on Diplomatic History which I gave under the title *The Purpose of America* at Johns Hopkins University in April 1959. I am very grateful to Professor C. Vann Woodward of Johns Hopkins University for the intellectual and personal hospitality he extended to me.

Daniel Boorstin, Charles Burton Marshall, and Kenneth W. Thompson read the whole manuscript; Hannah Arendt, Edward C. Banfield, George F. Kennan, Henry A. Kissinger, and Arthur M. Schlesinger, Jr., read part of it. I have greatly—and perhaps not sufficiently—profited from their suggestions and am very much indebted to them for their interest and contribution. However, the lion's share of improving the book is due to Alfred A. Knopf's judgment and taste.

The book was begun during the academic year 1958-9 while I was a member of the Institute for Advanced Study at Princeton, and it was virtually completed during the following academic year while I was associated with the Washington Center for Foreign Policy Research. I am most grateful for the leisure and facilities with which both institutions provided me. I was assisted competently and faithfully in my research by Miss Joan Ogden in Princeton, Mrs. Haynes Fraser in Washington, and Mrs. Yoma Ullman at Harvard, and the staff of the Center for the Study of American Foreign and Military Policy at the University of Chicago.

The following publications and organizations have kindly given permission to use material previously published; *Bulletin of the Atomic Scientists, Commentary,* Committee on Economic Development, Kenyon College, *The New Republic, The New York Times Magazine, The Chicago Review.*

HANS J. MORGENTHAU

*Cambridge, August 1960*

# Contents

*Contents*

*The Purpose*
*of American Politics*

# I

# THE PURPOSE OF AMERICA

## *Equality in Freedom*

### 1. *The Contemporary Crisis*

THE PRESENT CRISIS of American politics is, like its predecessors, essentially a crisis of the national purpose. It is not
primarily the immediate objectives of our policies and the
actions which seek to achieve them that are at fault. It is
rather that these policies have lost the organic connection
with the innermost purposes of the nation. The nation
submits to these policies with passive and uncomprehend-
ing toleration, as in times past people used to submit to
the hardships of nature and the miseries of social life.
They arise as though an impersonal fate had ordained
them, and there seems to be nothing the nation or its
agents can do about it. While the agents of the nation act
on its behalf, settling its fate and in good measure that of
mankind as well, the nation gropes for a meaning and a
purpose and cannot find them. Thus, it draws back upon
itself, filling the public sphere with its private concerns,
using the instruments of government for private gain. The
nation lives, as it were, in two different worlds, the world
of public policy, which it endures, and the private world,

3

which absorbs its intellectual and moral energies. Between these two worlds it establishes an illusory harmony through the ritualistic reiteration of the traditional formulations of the national purpose which in times past gave meaning to private concerns in terms of public purposes and which have become largely irrelevant to the conditions of the modern world.

How can the gulf between these two worlds be bridged? How can we rediscover in the tasks that face the nation and in the policies intended to perform them the purpose which the nation can understand, with which it can identify itself, and upon which it can therefore act with conscious determination? What in the traditional formulation of the national purpose must we remember, and what must we forget, if we want to do justice to the purpose of America in the contemporary world?

If the purpose of America were today as clearly defined, however contested such a definition might be, as it was 180 or 100 or even 50 years ago, it would be sufficient to restate that purpose in one way or another and let it go at that. It is exactly because we are no longer as sure as we used to be of what America stands for, of what distinguishes it from other nations, of what the meaning of its existence is, that we must inquire into its purpose. Our questioning does not arise from controversy, which in the past has pitted Pinckney against Hamilton, Clay against Polk, Bryan against McKinley, Lodge against Wilson, Borah against Franklin D. Roosevelt, each endeavoring to mold the destiny of America to a purpose that he believed to be justified by history and reason. Rather our questioning arises from the lack of relevant controversy; from a vagueness of concept which precludes controversy, for where nothing is clearly stated there is nothing to oppose; from the seeming irrelevance of tradition to contemporary practice, the received ideas being transformed into a ritual

4

which rationalizes practice without influencing it; from the somnambulistic self-deception of a nation which is unaware both of the dangers that threaten it and of the opportunities that await its action, yet marches on as though it knew where it is going. The nation's image of itself is blurred, the awareness of its destiny is dimmed, the knowledge of its interests lacks certainty, and its policies are groping for goals not seen by means half understood. America has become the Rome and Athens of the Western world, the foundation of its lawful order and the fountainhead of its culture. But America does not know this.

Yet the nation's mind, will, and actions are faltering in a world—and in good measure, as we shall see, because of this world—which needs for its own physical survival and for the survival of the human and social achievements of Western civilization the clarity and strength of that nation's purpose. This world presents the United States with novel tasks. These tasks leave behind, both quantitatively and qualitatively, the experiences through which the United States formed, and to which it applied, its conception of the national purpose. The arena within which the United States must defend and promote its purpose has become world-wide. That purpose cannot be accomplished within the limits of the North American continent, since it is challenged by a universal creed that knows no national boundaries and possesses the means of universal destruction. Yet the arena within which the United States developed the conception of its national purpose and tried to achieve it was from the beginning of its history to the end of the Second World War coterminous with the confines of the North American continent. The expeditions into Central America were in the nature of isolated forays, primarily for defensive purposes, and the annexation of the Philippines appears in historic perspective as a temporary aberration. Even the participation in the two world wars was militarily and politically conceived and executed as an isolated effort to extirpate an isolated evil. With this mission seemingly accomplished, the United States actually returned after the First World War, and intended to return after the Second, to that continental arena where it intended to achieve its purpose and where it had tried to achieve it throughout its history.

The instrument which the United States used for the achievement of that purpose was the nation. However different from all other nations that nation was conceived to be and however different it actually was, it was still conceived to be, and actually was, a sovereign, territorially defined entity, isolated from, allied to, competing with, fighting—as the case might be—other similar entities. It was as a nation among nations that the United States was to achieve its purpose.

Thus, the ideas molded by the historic experience of the eighteenth and nineteenth centuries encounter the world-wide tasks of the present and find it hard to give meaning to the thoughts and actions of the nation. The crisis of the national purpose has its roots in this inadequacy of the traditional body of ideas, yet that inadequacy need not by itself have created that crisis. For a nation must continuously re-examine and reformulate the ideas of the past in the light of the experiences of the present and the anticipated demands of the future, always risking failure. The United States, as we shall see, has by and large been successful in that task. What produces a crisis of the national purpose not as an ever present potentiality but as an acute deficiency is the reluctance, if not the outright refusal, to reconcile the old ideas with the new facts. It is as though the creative faculty stands baffled and paralyzed in contemplation of the unprecedented gulf that separates the received ideas from the new experiences, despairing of its ability to bridge it.

## 2. *The Reality of the National Purpose*

The history of the formulation of the national purpose, in America as elsewhere, is the story of bad theology and absurd metaphysics, of phony theories and fraudulent science, of crude rationalizations and vulgar delusions of grandeur. All great nations have blasphemously identified their mission with a divine purpose; if one were to believe the claims of all the "chosen peoples," monotheism itself would become suspect. All great nations of the Western world have claimed at one time or other to have the mission of defending civilization against one another. The national purpose has been derived from the superiority of race or the laws of history or economic necessity. Books such as Albert K. Weinberg's *Manifest Destiny* and Robert Michel's *Der Patriotismus* testify to the persuasiveness of such and similar follies. According to Professor Pratt, "manifest destiny . . . became a justification for almost any addition of territory which the United States had the will and the power to obtain."[1] Thus, it is small wonder that sober observers have doubted the validity of concepts such as national purpose and national interest and have concluded that behind them there is at best nothing more than the interests of particular groups, which are identified with the nation and rationalized and justified as such in ideological terms. In this view, the idea of the national purpose is a political ideology to which nothing corresponds in verifiable experience.

However, to reason thus is to confound the abuse of reality with reality itself. It is to fall into the error of logical positivism, which denies the validity of philosophy

[1] Julius W. Pratt: "The Ideology of American Expansion," in *Essays in Honor of W. E. Dodd,* ed. Avery Craven (Chicago: University of Chicago Press; 1935), p. 345.

7

because philosophic knowledge is uncertain and subject to abuse. It is to fall into the error of atheism, which denies the validity of religion on similar grounds. Yet philosophy and religion, however given to error and subject to abuse, are not figments of the imagination or artifacts of deception, but express in rational or symbolic terms the reality of an inner experience, which is not less real for not being of the senses. The same holds true of the idea of the national purpose. As in philosophy and religion, the task here, too, is to maintain and restore the validity of the idea while avoiding the pitfalls of error and abuse.

In order to comprehend the reality of the national purpose it is not necessary to listen to the ideologues of nationalism. It is only necessary to consult the evidence of history as our minds reflect it. We know that a great nation worthy of our remembrance has contributed to the affairs of men more than the successful defense and promotion of its national interests. That defense and that promotion are the objects of foreign policy, seeking to maintain or increase the power of the nation, acquire territory, conclude alliances, wage victorious war, and conclude advantageous peace.

In order to be worthy of our lasting sympathy, a nation must pursue its interests for the sake of a transcendent purpose that gives meaning to the day-by-day operations of its foreign policy. The empires of the Huns and the Mongols, eminently successful in political and military terms, mean nothing to us; but ancient Greece, Rome, and Israel do. We remember ancient Greece, Rome, and Israel with a sense of personal involvement—in contrast to the many states of the ancient world whose existence and deeds are recorded only in history books—because they were not just political organizations whose purpose was limited to their survival and physical growth but civilizations, unique realizations of human potentialities that we have in common with them. And their achievements appear to us in retrospect, as they appeared to their contemporaries, not just as isolated contributions of some great men, but as the collective work of generations in which a collective purpose was revealed. Posterity understands the nature of that purpose as its contemporaries did.

We see in Greece, and more particularly in Athens, the model of perfection in art and literature, in the theory and practice of government, to be emulated, but not to be surpassed, by future generations; we see in the Greeks the providers of standards of excellence by which the achievements of the ages will be judged. And it was thus that Pericles saw his city when he accounted for her place and mission in his funeral speech. "Our form of government does not enter into rivalry with the institutions of others. We do not copy our neighbors, but are an example to them. . . . I say that Athens is the school of Hellas. . . . In the hour of trial Athens alone among her contemporaries is superior to the report of her."[2] We see in Rome the cradle of rational government, of the rule of law, and of empire; and so did the Romans. "But, Romans," declaims Virgil,

> *never forget that government is your medium!*
> *Be this your art:—to practice men in the habit of peace,*
> *Generosity to the conquered, and firmness against aggressors.*[3]

We look to Israel as the repository of the religious experience of monotheism, and so does the Bible. In the words of Isaiah:

[2] Thucydides: *The History of the Peloponnesian War*, trans. B. Jowett (Oxford: At the Clarendon Press; 1881), III, 37, 41.

[3] *The Aeneid of Virgil*, trans. C. Day Lewis (Garden City: Doubleday Anchor Books; 1956), p. 154.

### The Purpose of America: Equality in Freedom

*I will give you as a light to the nations,*
*that my salvation may reach to the end of the earth.*[4]

In the contemporary world we look to nations such as
Great Britain and France, as they look to themselves, for
specific contributions to the affairs of man which only they
can make. With similar expectations millions of men look,
as they have in the past, to China, Russia, and the United
States. As this is not a matter of national power, they look
also to Italy and Spain. But they do not look to a great
many other nations. They do not look, for instance, to Jor-
dan, "a country," to quote the *Manchester Guardian,*
"without a purpose or a meaning."[5] The existence of purpose and meaning or lack of them is an objective fact of
experience which either carries or excludes a commitment
to future performance. We expect of certain nations certain deeds, for we have read in their past deeds a purpose
to which we expect future deeds to conform.

The reality of the national purpose, then, resides in the
political and social history of the nation—that is, in a continuum of actions that reveal a common and unique pattern pointing to a common and unique purpose. That purpose may well be implicit in the action, only to be discovered in retrospect. In all nations but one the awareness
of the national purpose in conscious thought—evolved by
way of articulation, self-interpretation, justification, and
rationalization—followed upon its achievement in action,
confirming again Hegel's observation that philosophy "appears only when actuality is already there cut and dried
after its process of formation has been completed. . . .
The owl of Minerva spreads its wings only with the falling
of the dusk."[6] Greece and Rome, Great Britain and

4 Isaiah, 49:6.
5 James Morris, in *Manchester Guardian Weekly*, July 24, 1958.
6 Georg Wilhelm Friedrich Hegel: *Philosophy of Right*, trans.
T. M. Knox (Oxford: At the Clarendon Press; 1945), pp. 12, 13.

France became aware of the national purpose and developed a philosophy of it only after it had been achieved, after the pattern had been set in deeds by which both philosophy and future deeds were to be judged. Thus, in the search for the national purpose, action takes precedence over reflection, the implicit meaning over the explicit interpretation, and only in so far as the latter is borne out by the former do reflection and interpretation help rather than hinder understanding.

## 3. *The American Experience*

The rule that action precedes reflection in the discovery of the national purpose suffers but one complete exception. The United States is the only nation that has reversed the sequence by reflecting upon its purpose before it had come into existence. The awareness of its purpose was not an afterthought. The United States was founded as a nation with a particular purpose in mind. And at the very threshold of American history appeared two contradictory conceptions of the national purpose whose tension was to dominate the first great crisis of the American purpose. One conception limits the purpose of America to the promotion of happiness at home and defines the task of government as the development of domestic institutions and policies assuring that happiness. Charles Pinckney formulated that conception on January 25, 1787, in the Federal Convention:

> Our true situation appears to me to be this.—a new extensive Country containing within itself the materials for forming a Government capable of extending to its citizens all the blessings of civil & religious liberty—capable of making them happy at home. This is

the great end of Republican Establishments. We mistake the object of our government, if we hope or wish that it is to make us respectable abroad. Conquest or superiority among other powers is not or ought not ever to be the object of republican systems. If they are sufficiently active & energetic to rescue us from contempt & preserve our domestic happiness & security, it is all we can expect from them,—it is more than almost any other Government ensures to its citizens.[1]

The other conception maintains that the very purpose of assuring the happiness of the citizens requires strength abroad. As Alexander Hamilton put it on June 29 of the same year:

> It had been said that respectability in the eyes of foreign Nations was not the object at which we aimed; that the proper object of republican Government was domestic tranquillity & happiness. This was an ideal distinction. No Governmt. could give us tranquillity & happiness at home, which did not possess sufficient stability and strength to make us respectable abroad.[2]

And the Yates version of Hamilton's remarks contains the following significant addition: ". . . even to observe neutrality you must have a strong government."[3]

It would, however, be much too simple to assume that this conception of the national purpose and others advanced throughout American history were in themselves original with American thinkers and statesmen. What is original and even unique in the purpose of America does not lie in the realm of intellectual invention. Quite the

---

[1] *The Records of the Federal Convention of 1787*, ed. Max Farrand, Vol. I (New Haven: Yale University Press; 1911), p. 402.

[2] Ibid., pp. 466, 467.

[3] Ibid., pp. 473.

contrary: if one takes the ideas by themselves, one is struck by their lack of originality. The ideas that have articulated the purpose of America are the ideas of Europe, ancient and modern. The intellectual components of Pinckney's conception stem from the classical philosophy of Greece with its emphasis upon the good life and its neglect of foreign policy, from the apolitical individualism of the Roman Stoa, and from the same element of eighteenth-century rationalism. The English and Continental liberals of the nineteenth and twentieth centuries, proclaiming the primacy of domestic over foreign policy to the point of looking forward to the abolition of foreign policy altogether, drew on that same tradition.

On the other hand, Hamilton's conception of the national purpose, defending the indispensability of foreign policy if not its primacy, simply applies the European tradition of the reason of state to the American scene. The conceptions of the national purpose which were advanced in the United States during the nineteenth century are but an echo—and frequently a vulgarized one—of the European litany of nationalism. None of the fifteen ideas through which, according to Dr. Weinberg, the idea of manifest destiny was expressed is original with America. Woodrow Wilson's is virtually the first voice that gives to the idea of the purpose of America an intellectual content that can be called distinctly American. And going back from Pinckney and Hamilton to the very beginnings of American thought, the idea of America as the "chosen people" having a unique and divinely ordained mission to fulfill can of course be directly traced to Puritan England, to which an identical mission was attributed in identical terms. The Pilgrims brought that idea to America and used it unchanged in the American environment. What was new was not the idea but the environment, and from the impact of a new environment upon old ideas grew the originality and uniqueness of American political philosophy, of which the idea of the national purpose forms a part.

The distinctive character of the new environment— empty spaces of fertile land without political rule or competition—was clearly perceived at the very beginning of American history. "And forasmuch as we have been certainly given to understand by divers of our good subjects," says the Charter of James I of 1620,

> that have for these many years past frequented those coasts and territories, between the degrees of forty and forty-eight, that there is no other the subjects of any Christian King or State, by any authority from their sovereigns, Lords, or princes, actually in possession of any of the said lands or precincts, whereby any right, claim, interest, or title, may, might or ought by that means accrue, belong, or appertain unto them, or any of them. And also for that we have been further given certainly to know, that within these late years there has by God's visitation reigned a wonderful plague, together with many horrible slaughters, and murders, committed amongst the savages and brutish people there, heretofore inhabiting, in a manner to the utter destruction, devastation, and depopulation of that whole territory, so that there is not left for many leagues together in a manner, any that do claim or challenge any kind of interests therein, nor any other superior Lord or sovereign to make claim thereunto, whereby we in our judgment are persuaded and satisfied that the appointed time is come in which Almighty God in his great goodness and bounty towards us and our people, has thought fit and determined, that those large and goodly territories, deserted as it were by their

natural inhabitants, should be possessed and enjoyed by such of our subjects and people as heretofore have and hereafter shall by his mercy and favor, and by his powerful army, be directed and conducted thither.

And John Locke discerned the opportunity that empty spaces of fertile land offered to purposeful cultivation:

There cannot be a clearer demonstration of anything than several nations of the Americans are of this, who are rich in land and poor in all the comforts of life; whom nature having furnished as liberally as any other people with the materials of plenty—i.e., a fruitful soil, apt to produce in abundance what might serve for food, raiment, and delight—yet, for want of improving it by labour, have not one-hundredth part of the conveniences we enjoy. And a king of a large and fruitful territory there, feeds, lodges, and is clad worse than a day-labourer in England. . . .

Thus in the beginning all the world was America, and more so than that is now, for no such thing as money was anywhere known.[4]

The ideas that the immigrants brought with them from Europe had one quality in common: they were considered expressions of the objective order of things to be realized in America. That order was conceived in religious or secular terms; it was deemed to have been ordained by God or by reason. The religious order ran the gamut from English High Church through puritanism to the Quakers, and the rational order was received through the teachings of the Romans, Locke, and the French Encyclopedists. Yet,

[4] John Locke: *The Second Treatise on Government: An Essay Concerning the True Original Extent and End of Civil Government*, ed. J. W. Gough (New York: The Macmillan Co.; 1956), No. 41, 49, pp. 22, 26.

however that objective order was understood, America was built in the image of such an order and in the light of the objective truths to which both the cosmic order and human society were thought to owe their existence. A land empty of history and of people offered the opportunity for building a society in the image of such an objective order—or rather, as it turned out, a multiplicity of such societies, differing according to the images of order in which they were built.

These ideas about the nature of man and society which the immigrants brought with them were not so much transformed in substance as infused by a new spirit and endowed with a new quality by two peculiarly American experiences: the equalitarian conditions of society and the absence of serious competition from abroad. Before Tocqueville gave the classical account of American equality and before in our time Professor Louis Hartz interpreted the same experience and its political consequences in terms of "the liberal tradition in America," Jean de Crèvecoeur, Benjamin Franklin, and Charles Pinckney called attention to equality as "the leading feature of the United States."[5]

A "modern society," wrote Crèvecoeur in the *Letters from an American Farmer,*

> offers itself to his contemplation, different from what he had hitherto seen. It is not composed, as in Europe, of great lords who possess everything, and of a herd of people who have nothing. Here are no aristocratical families, no courts, no kings, no bishops, no ecclesiastical dominion, no invisible power giving to a few a very visible one; no great manufacturers employing

[5] Pinckney, in *The Records of the Federal Convention of 1787,* Vol. I.

thousands, no great refinements of luxury. The rich
and the poor are not so far removed from each other
as they are in Europe. Some few towns excepted,
we are all tillers of the earth, from Nova Scotia to
West Florida. We are a people of cultivators, scattered over an immense territory communicating with
each other by means of good roads and navigable
rivers, united by the silken bands of mild government, all respecting the laws, without dreading their
power, because they are equitable. We are all animated with the spirit of an industry which is unfettered and unrestrained, because each person works
for himself. If he travels through our rural districts
he views not the hostile castle, and the haughty mansion, contrasted with the clay-built hut and miserable
cabin, where cattle and men help to keep each other
warm, and dwell in meanness, smoke, and indigence.
A pleasing uniformity of decent competence appears
throughout our habitations. . . . We have no princes,
for whom we toil, starve, and bleed; we are the most
perfect society now existing in the world. Here man
is free as he ought to be; nor is this pleasing equality
so transitory as many others are.[6]

"The truth is," Franklin advised would-be immigrants,

that though there are in that country few people so
miserable as the poor of Europe, there are also very
few that in Europe would be called rich; it is rather
a general happy mediocrity that prevails. There are
few great proprietors of the soil, and few tenants;
most people cultivate their own lands, or follow some

[6] John de Crèvecoeur: *Letters from an American Farmer* (New
York: E. P. Dutton and Co.; 1912), pp. 39-41.

handicraft or merchandise; very few rich enough to live idly upon their rents or incomes. . . .[7]

"The people of the U. States," to quote Pinckney again,

are perhaps the most singular of any we are acquainted with. Among them there are fewer distinctions of fortune & less of rank, than among the inhabitants of any other nation. Every freeman has a right to the same protection & security; and a very moderate share of property entitles them to the possession of all the honors and privileges the public can bestow: hence arises a greater equality, than is to be found among the people of any other country, and an equality which is more likely to continue—I say this equality is likely to continue, because in a new Country, possessing immense tracts of uncultivated lands, where every temptation is offered to emigration & where industry must be rewarded with competency, there will be few poor, and few dependent—Every member of the Society almost, will enjoy an equal power of arriving at the supreme offices and consequently of directing the strength & sentiments of the whole Community. None will be excluded by birth, & few by fortune, from voting for proper persons to fill the offices of Government—the whole community will enjoy in the fullest sense that kind of political liberty which consists in the power the members of the State reserve to themselves, of arriving at the public offices, or at least, of having votes in the nomination of those who fill them.

And Walt Whitman draws the moral conclusion from this experience of equality:

[7] "Information to those who would remove to America," in *The Works of Benjamin Franklin* (London: J. Johnson, etc.; 1806), III, 399.

By God! I will accept nothing which all men cannot have the counterpart of on the same terms. . . .

The other fundamental experience, the absence of serious competition from abroad, is too obvious a fact to require much elaboration. Washington, in the Farewell Address, referred to "our detached and distant situation" and asked: "Why forego the advantages of so peculiar a situation?" Looking at so peculiar a situation from England, John Bright could write on March 10, 1884, to Augustin Jones, a Friend: "On your continent we may hope your growing millions may henceforth know nothing of war. None can assail you; and you are anxious to abstain from mingling with the quarrels of other nations."[8]

These two experiences, equality at home and safety abroad, have one quality in common which is uniquely American: the absence of a specific political content. That is to say, the permanent threat of political domination from within and without, which has molded the political experiences of all other nations, is absent from them. No citizen of the United States was slated to be permanently the subject of the political domination of others. He may be ruled over by them today only to have a chance to rule over them tomorrow. There were, and there are today, no permanent rulers and no permanent subjects in America. Political equality means equal access to political rule. In contrast to totalitarian equality, which reduces all individuals except the rulers to the same level of impotence before the power of the state, the political equality of the American tradition raises all citizens to the level of potential rulers. American equality is equality in freedom. In it, equality, freedom, and power are one; for American equality denies both the permanent possession of political

[8] *The Public Letters of the Right Hon. John Bright, M.P.*, ed. H. J. Leech (London: Sampson, Low, etc.; 1885), p. 296.

power and the permanent subjection to it. By making power equally accessible to all, it makes all both potentially powerful and free.

The meaning of political equality at home—that is, the opportunity for the individual to rule as a matter of principle—is duplicated by the meaning that the absence of a permanent threat from abroad carries for the nation: the opportunity to rule without permanent hindrance. Both experiences converge in the experience of freedom from permanent restraint, which is tantamount to a permanent opportunity to exercise power. Freedom, equality, opportunity, power are different manifestations of the same single experience. Hamilton, in the speech quoted before, pointed to this organic relationship of equality, freedom, and power when he remarked: "It has been sd. that if the smaller states renounced their equality they renounce at the same time their *liberty*. The truth is it is a contest for power not for liberty."[9] He might have called it more correctly a contest both for liberty and for power, power being the result of liberty and a denial of liberty resulting in the denial of power.

Not only is a specific political content absent from the American experience, but it is peculiar to that experience that it is devoid of any specific substantive content whatsoever. Its content is provided by the conceptions of an objective order which the settlers sought to realize in America and which were infused with the spirit of equality and freedom. They became the substantive concepts from which equality and freedom receive their meaning. For equality and freedom are incomplete and formal concepts. They point to a relation with some other substantive concept or concepts, and they receive their full meaning only from that relationship. They are correlational concepts, not terminal ones. Equality, to be meaningful,

[9] Loc. cit., p. 466.

requires an answer to the question: equal with regard to what? The meaning of freedom is revealed by the answer to the question: freedom from what? And the meaning of both is completed by the answer to the question: equal and free for what?

We have already seen that the answer to the first two questions must be given in political and identical terms. Freedom in the original American sense means freedom from permanent political rule; equality in that sense means equal access to political rule. It is the answer to the third question—equal and free for what?—that concerns us here. What is the transcendent purpose for the sake of which equality and freedom are sought and which modifies equality with a qualitative principle of merit and freedom with a political principle of order? It is characteristic of the American purpose and illuminates its formal and procedural as well as its pluralistic nature that no single answer can be given to that question. America has no single substantive purpose, but can have any number of them. Their variety derives from those conceptions of objective order which the various groups of early settlers brought from abroad. The persistence of that variety is accounted for by the natural environment and the principle of equality in freedom. The natural environment made for a diffusion of power which precluded the victory of one conception of order over all others, and the very principle of equality in freedom, applied to the realms of religious faith and philosophic conviction, encouraged and sanctioned their variety.

The American purpose is in consequence peculiarly intangible, shapeless, and procedural. It consists not in a specific substantive ideal and achievement but in a peculiar mode of procedure, a peculiar way of thinking and acting in the social sphere, in a peculiar conception of the relations between the individual and society. That procedure, that way of thinking and acting, and that conception were at the service of an objective order to be realized in America.

What the early settlers brought to America was the conception, or rather a variety of conceptions, of an objective order and the purpose to realize that order here. What brought these men to America was the expectation that they could undertake this task in the conditions of equality in freedom. What they found in America was a natural and social environment that provided these conditions. What is essential, then, is the existence of substantive, transcendent purposes, derived from what is believed to be an objective order, and the environment of equality in freedom within which the realization of that purpose is sought. The assumption of such a substantive, transcendent, and objective order, however conceived, gives meaning to the American experience of equality in freedom. Renounce that assumption, and the American experience itself, as we shall see, changes its nature.

## 4. *Equality in Freedom*

Out of this unique and exhilarating experience of being free, as it were, vertically and horizontally, without a permanent master from within and without a permanent enemy from abroad, the specifically American state of mind arises. To Rousseau's statement that "Man is born free, but everywhere he is in chains," that mind might well have replied: man may or may not be born free, but in America he is without chains. Man in America is free to rise within the nation as high as merit and opportunity will carry him, and the American nation is free to expand as far as its power will carry it. These two kinds of mobility—the vertical and the horizontal—were experienced as being interconnected, the latter serving as a supplement to the former.

Vertical mobility is the direct result of the equal and free condition of American existence. A society in which no man has a fixed station into which he is born and which he can leave at best under extraordinary circumstances is of necessity a society of equal opportunity. A man's station is determined by his merit, and he rises and falls with that merit. This is the distinctive quality of American society. Benjamin Franklin saw it clearly when he said:

> Much less is it advisable for a person to go thither who has no other quality to recommend him but his birth. In Europe it has indeed its value; but it is a commodity that cannot be carried to a worse market than to that of America, where people do not inquire concerning a stranger: *What is he?* but: *What can he do?*[1]

Of the vertical mobility of American society, Abraham Lincoln has given two telling accounts.

> . . . there is not, of necessity, [he said in his message to Congress of December 1861] any such thing as the free hired laborer being fixed to that condition for life. . . . The prudent, penniless beginner in the world labors for wages a while; saves a surplus with which to buy tools or land for himself, then labors on his own account another while, and at length hires another new beginner to help him.[2]

And he elaborated on this theme in a more speculative fashion in 1863:

[1] Loc. cit., p. 400.

[2] *Collected Works of Abraham Lincoln,* ed. Roy P. Basler (New Brunswick: Rutgers University Press; 1959), V, 52.

That some should be rich shows that others may become rich, and hence is just encouragement to industry and enterprise. Let not him who is houseless pull down the house of another, but let him work diligently and build one for himself, thus by example assuring that his home should be safe from violence when built.

As a matter of principle, a straight path was supposed to lead from the log cabin to the millionaire's mansion and the White House: Yet log cabins were more numerous than millionaires' mansions, and the White House can accommodate but one occupant at a time. Furthermore, some colonial societies, such as Virginia, were from the beginning highly stratified on aristocratic lines and virtually excluded "the lower classes" from advancement. While every American boy was given a chance to travel that path, only a few could expect to arrive at the destination. Thus, the competition was bound not only to be fierce but also to deny the final achievement to the great majority of the competitors. The equality of domestic opportunity came to be experienced as a mass race in which all male Americans had a chance to start and which only a few were able to finish. The great majority dropped out because they were defeated or because they were satisfied to have reached an intermediate goal or because they decided to seek opportunity elsewhere. Freedom to expand beyond the borders provided that opportunity.

That freedom prevented the actual denial of domestic achievement from being experienced as a denial of opportunity itself. Those who had failed to rise to the top in the established society, instead of being reduced to a frustrated and resentful class, could form a new society or, rather, a succession of new societies which provided them with still other and ever renewed opportunities to rise to the top. "Migration has become almost a habit, in the West," writes a contemporary observer in a penetrating analysis, reminiscent of Tocqueville, of the formation and class structure of the new societies. "Hundreds of men can be found, not fifty years of age, who have settled for the fourth, fifth, or sixth time on a new spot."[3] This territorial expansion of the area of freedom of opportunity transformed the quality of the American experience in two significant respects. It accentuated the experience of equal opportunity and the apolitical character of the experience.

Full equality of opportunity existed at home only at the start of the race and became limited to fewer and fewer people as the race neared the goal. In the wide arena of America's continental expansion, that race remained open longer and for more people, and those to whom it seemed no longer open enough in one spot could move to another that still afforded equal opportunity for all. That opportunity appeared to be as unlimited as were the expanses of empty territory which made it possible. It must, however, be noted that this experience of endless opportunity was predicated upon the availability of limitless empty land. For in the measure that a territory became settled and integrated into the nation, the equality of opportunity it provided became more or less subject to the domestic restrictions which we have mentioned and to escape which the territory had been settled in the first place.

In truth, of course, the supply of empty land was not unlimited. Its limits were set by geography, the power of other nations, and America's own absorptive capacity. Yet during the period in which the idea of the American purpose was formed, the only limit sporadically experienced was the power of another nation, such as British power in Canada, and that limit did not affect either expansion or

[3] J. M. Peck: *A New Guide for Emigrants to the West* (Boston: Gould, Kendall and Lincoln; 1837), p. 121.

the consciousness of its purpose. For if seeking opportunity through expansion to the north appeared too risky, the limitless expanses of the west offered more opportunity than even the most enterprising of men could use.

Within the boundaries of the United States the experience of equal opportunity occurred primarily in two fields of endeavor: politics and business, and the spirit and the modes of action of the latter tended to intermingle with and permeate the former. "The passions that agitate the Americans most deeply," Tocqueville observed, "are not their political, but their commercial passions; or, rather, they introduce the habits of business into their political life."[4] And Ostrogorski noted: "In that world, awaiting cultivation, the love of power aims less at men than at things."[5] What was but a tendency on the domestic plane became the distinctive character of territorial expansion. The mode of acquisition tells the story. Most of the territories acquired by the United States were not conquered but were bought for a money consideration. The United States expanded not through a series of victories over its enemies—the Mexican War being the sole exception—but through a series of real-estate transactions. While the political and military purpose was not always absent from these transactions, the economic purpose never was, and more often than not it was the predominant or the only one.

Yet more important for our argument is the fact that the individuals who settled in the new territories did not come as conquerors or colonizers; they did not come to establish political dominion over others. Rather they came in order to restore their own freedom from political

[4] *Democracy in America* (New York: The Vantage Press; 1945), I, 308.
[5] M. Ostrogorski: *Democracy and the Organization of Political Parties* (New York: The Macmillan Co.; 1902), II, 592.

dominion and use it for private gain. Freedom here has an apolitical meaning; it connotes both anarchy and a chance for unhampered acquisition. Freedom signifies freedom from being ruled and from ruling others and freedom to make a living and gain wealth without competition. It is no exaggeration to say that the ideal type of pioneer has left political civilization behind and has restored that state of nature, which before may have existed nowhere but in the longings of the imagination or the lives of isolated adventurers, where man is nobody's slave and nobody's master and nobody's competitor either. He is all by himself, having nobody above or beneath or beside him. He wants to be free not in the relative sense of political freedom, which he has already experienced and from which he has just escaped. The conditions of the frontier push the domestic conditions of freedom and equal opportunity to their logical extreme: freedom becomes anarchy, and equal opportunity becomes absence of competition. Thoreau has given literary expression to that ideal of freedom, and John Adams has described its actual condition:

> In the present state of society and manners in America, with a people living chiefly by agriculture, in small numbers, sprinkled over large tracts of land, they are not subject to those panics and transports, those contagions of madness and folly, which are seen in countries where large numbers live in small places, in daily fear of perishing for want. We know, therefore, that the people can live and increase under almost any kind of government, or without any government at all.[6]

[6] "Defense of the Constitutions of Government of the United States of America," in *The Works of John Adams* (Boston: Charles C. Little and James Brown; 1851), IV, 587.

This, then, is the essence of the American experience: freedom from permanent political domination, which has as its corollary the opportunity for all to compete in equality for power and wealth and, under the conditions of the frontier, opens up the possibility of absolute freedom from involvement in politics and competition. The awareness of that experience and the resolve to perpetuate it mold the conception of the purpose of America. Yet, as we have indicated, this conception is not a mere retrospective summary and articulation of something already experienced; it molds the experience even as it is molded by the experience. One must go further and say that the experience itself is preceded by, and almost requires in view of its very nature, a conscious, active will and rational awareness of purpose and likely consequence. In this relationship to the national experience, antedating and conditioning it, the conception of the American purpose is unique. Lincoln was aware of that relationship when he said on February 22, 1861, in Independence Hall in Philadelphia:

> I have never had a feeling politically that did not spring from the sentiments embodied in the Declaration of Independence. . . . I have often inquired of myself, what great principle or idea it was that kept this Confederacy so long together. It was not the mere matter of the separation of the colonies from the mother land; but something in that Declaration giving liberty, not alone to the people of this country, but hope to the world for all future time. It was that which gave promise that in due time the weights should be lifted from the shoulders of all men, and that *all* should have an equal chance. This is the sentiment embodied in that Declaration of Independ-

ence. . . . I would rather be assassinated on this spot than to surrender it.[7]

Other nations have reflected upon their unique contribution by contemplating their past and have drawn inspiration and standards for action from that contemplation. Yet no other nation has ever decided at the very moment of its birth, by way of a rational choice among alternatives, what its unique contribution was going to be, what would distinguish it from all other nations, for the sake of what purpose it was being founded. Other nations have developed myths of their founding, justifying after the event their existence and history and endowing them typically with a divine purpose. The United States did not emerge from the mists of pre-history in search of rationalization and justification of its existence and history. Before it existed and could have a history, it decided, as it were, what kind of history it was going to have. That decision, consistently adhered to throughout American history, has given American society an extraordinary unity, both in time and in space, to which Tocqueville has called attention:

> In America all laws originate in some way in the same thought. The whole society is, as it were, founded on one single fact; everything derives from one unique principle. One could compare America to a big forest, cut through by a multitude of straight roads which end at the same point. One only needs to find that point of convergence, and everything becomes clear at one glance.[8]

[7] *Collected Works of Abraham Lincoln,* ed. Roy P. Basler (New Brunswick: Rutgers University Press; 1959), IV, 240.

[8] Letter of August 1835 to Count Molé. *Oeuvres Complètes d'Alexis de Tocqueville, Publiées par Madame de Tocqueville* (Paris: Michel Levy Frères, Libraires Editeurs; 1866), VII, 135. Translation by author.

## 5. *The American Revolution*

In a sense, then, it can be said that the revolution which
gave birth to the United States is the only true revolution
in history, because it is the only one in which men as
creatures of history rationally chose to become its creators,
to start history afresh by ridding themselves of its burdens
and heeding its lessons, to give their nation a novel purpose.

The English revolutions of the seventeenth century, like
the French revolution of 1789, were attempts at restoring
an ancient order of things, an ancient "constitution,"
which the powers-that-be were despoiling. The American
revolution was an attempt not at restoring an ancient order
that was supposed to have existed previously, but at creating a new order of things the like of which had never been
seen before. The American revolution was radical in the
literal sense of going to the roots and pulling them out.
It was radical in the sense in which Marx imagined the
proletarian revolution to be radical, drawing a line under
all previous history and starting the historic process *de
novo.*

If this understanding of the way in which the purpose
of America was formed is correct, then the real American
revolution did occur not in 1776 but began in 1620. It
was the decision, taken in England, to establish beyond
the sea a new society conforming to certain principles and
the fact of its establishment in accordance with these principles which constitute the real American revolution. The
nature of that revolution was social rather than political.
The Puritans who went to America set out to create a new
society, while the Puritans who remained in England endeavored to transform the old one. The latter used political revolution and civil war to achieve their end; that is,

they sought to break the political power and destroy the political institutions that stood in their way. The men of the *Mayflower* and their successors turned their backs on the old society and its politics and established by a single act of will a new society that was free, if not of politics altogether, at least of the politics of the old world and of its confining restraints.

The voyage of 1620 from London to Cape Cod, then, appears as but the first in a series of migrations, undertaken for a similar purpose, which either duplicated that first voyage or extended, to paraphrase the title of Professor Perry Miller's book, the errand of that voyage into ever farther reaches of the wilderness. The pattern of the transoceanic migration of 1620, separating, as it were, the founding revolutionaries from the fighting ones, the fugitives from the old politics from its would-be destroyers, is repeated in the transoceanic migration of 1848, as it was in less spectacular ones before and after. Similarly, the succession of continental migrations was carried to the Pacific confines of the continent by the same purpose to which the first settlement in Massachusetts owed both its existence and its character.

The real American revolution was not only social rather than political, but was also, and was bound to be in view of the function it performed, a permanent one. It has been an endless process rather than an isolated act consummated at a particular time, a restless and dynamic search for a state of society that could at best be approximated, never fully attained. For, as we have seen, it is in the very nature of that ideal state of society—equality of opportunity with a minimum of political control—that the chances for its realization decrease with the stabilization of society itself. A stable society after the Continental model which uses political and economic controls to allow but isolated individuals and marginal groups to move up or down from their assigned places is the very antithesis of what the American revolution stands for. In view of the intrinsic tendency of society to stabilize itself, the American revolution was bound to be a ceaseless struggle, ever renewing its vigor from the ever present denial of its goal.

Within this process of unceasing social revolution the political revolution of 1776 is a mere incident. As a possibility, it was implicit in the social revolution from the very beginning; the actual attempt at stifling the social revolution by British political and economic controls, ever present as a threat, made it inevitable. "I have always laughed," wrote John Adams to Benjamin Rush on May 21, 1807, "at the affectation of representing American independence as a novel idea, as a modern discovery, as a late invention. The idea of it as a possible thing, as a probable event, nay, as a necessary and unavoidable measure, in case Great Britain should assume an unconstitutional authority over us, has been familiar to Americans from the first settlement of the country. . . ."[1] The war for independence, John Adams wrote to Dr. Morse on January 1, 1816, was "not a revolutionary war, for the revolution was complete, in the minds of the people, and the union of the colonies, before the war commenced in the skirmishes of Concord and Lexington on the 19th of April, 1775."[2] "Who, then," he asks in his letter to William Tudor of September 18, 1818, "was the author, inventor, discoverer of independence? The only true answer must be the first emigrants, and the proof of it is the Charter of James I. When we say that Otis, Adams, Mayhew, Henry, Lee, Jefferson, etc., were authors of independence, we ought to say they were only awakeners

---

[1] *The Works of John Adams* (Boston: Little, Brown and Co.; 1854), IX, 596.
[2] Loc. cit., X (1856), 197.

and revivers of the original fundamental principle of colonization."[3]

## 6. *The Threefold Purpose*

The distinctive character of the American experience and the unique purposeful awareness of it, which the American mind contained from the outset, make the nature of the American purpose almost a foregone conclusion. The conjunction of these two factors makes the purpose of America identical with the American experience. The early settlers came to America with the purpose of building a certain kind of society, and they built it. Purpose and achievement were one, and succeeding generations emulated both purpose and achievement. As the first achievement reflected the purpose that preceded it, so the achievement, seen in the light of that first purpose, created a tradition committed to that first purpose and its achievement: the establishment of equality in freedom in America. Both the liberal conservatism and the revolutionary liberalism of the American political tradition are enclosed in that extraordinary identity of purpose and achievement and their mutual stimulation. To maintain that achievement of equality in freedom within the United States has, then, been the fundamental and minimal purpose of America.

This purpose is fundamental, since the distinctiveness of America as a nation among nations is predicated upon it. It is minimal in that anyone who is committed to the American tradition must embrace it. Without that purpose, America would be nothing more than a complex of power and wealth without specific meaning. Without the achievement of that purpose, America would share with

[3] Ibid., p. 359.

other nations both aspiration and failure. What makes America unique among the nations is that it has achieved at least in a certain measure what other nations—by no means many—have aspired to. It has created a society that is still today radically different from the other societies of the modern world.

And not only is it different; it is also superior if equality in freedom in the American sense is a good to which other nations aspire without achieving it. Thus, the very uniqueness of the American purpose and its achievement —that is, the establishment of freedom conceived as equality of opportunity and minimization of political control— brings into being another purpose that does not by itself require additional action but endows the action required by the fundamental purpose with a special dignity and responsibility: to maintain equality in freedom in America as an example for other nations to emulate. America is not required by this purpose to do for other nations what it would not do for itself. Rather, what it does for itself it does not only for itself, but for the sake of other nations as well. The American purpose carries within itself a meaning that transcends the national boundaries of America and addresses itself to all the nations of the world. By pursuing its own purpose and in the measure that it achieves it, America gives meaning to the aspirations of other nations and furthers the awakening and achievement of their purpose. In the words of Jefferson:

A just and solid republican government maintained here, will be a standing monument and example for the aim and imitation of the people of other countries; and I join with you in the hope and belief that they will see from our example that a free government is of all others the most energetic, and that the inquiry which has been excited among the mass of mankind by our revolution and its consequences will ameliorate the condition of man over a great portion of the globe.[1]

And in the words of Lincoln:

> . . . the Declaration of Independence . . . [gave] liberty, not alone to the people of this country, but hope to the world for all future time. It was that which gave promise that in due time the weights should be lifted from the shoulders of all men. . . .[2]

---

[1] Letter to John Dickinson, March 6, 1801, in *The Writings of Thomas Jefferson,* ed. A. Lipscomb (Washington, D.C.: Thomas Jefferson Memorial Association; 1905), X, 217.

[2] Speech in Philadelphia, February 22, 1861, in *The Collected Works of Abraham Lincoln,* ed. Roy P. Basler (New Brunswick: Rutgers University Press; 1959), IV, 240. Cf. this passage from Washington's First Inaugural Address:

> . . . and since the preservation of the sacred fire of liberty and the destiny of the republican model of government are justly considered as deeply, perhaps as finally staked, on the experiment entrusted to the hands of the American people.

See also Jefferson's letter to John Hollins of May 5, 1811:

> And when we reflect that the eyes of the virtuous all over the earth are turned with anxiety on us, as the only depositories of the sacred fire of liberty, and that our falling into anarchy would decide forever the destinies of mankind, and seal the political heresy that man is incapable of self-government, the only contest between divided friends should be who will dare farthest into the rank of the common enemy." [Loc. cit., XIII, 58.]

For a foreign reaction to the same problem see Turgot's letter of March 22, 1778, to Dr. Price:

> All right-thinking men must pray that this people may arrive at all the prosperity of which they are capable. They are the

However, as we have seen, the conjunction of the dynamic liberalism of American society and the availability of empty land called forth a series of repetitions of that first migration from London to Cape Cod. The fundamental American purpose of maintaining equality in freedom in America is assumed to require for its achievement a continuous and contiguous expansion of the area in which Americans can enjoy equality in freedom beyond the original boundaries of the United States. This is the third purpose of America: to expand the area of equality in freedom in order to maintain equality in freedom at home. Yet this expansionism has posed a problem both for philosophy and for statecraft and, hence, has become an object for controversy.

From the assumption that the achievement of equality in freedom in the American sense is a worthy purpose for a nation, the conclusion follows as self-evident that it

---

hope of the human race. They should be the model. They must prove to the world, as a fact, that men can be both free and peaceful and can dispense with the trammels of all sorts which tyrants and charlatans of every costume have presumed to impose under the pretext of public safety. They must give the example of political liberty, of religious liberty, of commercial and industrial liberty. The asylum which America affords to the oppressed of all nations will console the world. The facility of profiting by it, in making escape from the consequences of bad governments, will compel the European powers to be just, and to see things as they are. The rest of the world will, by degrees, have its eyes opened to the dispersion of the illusions amidst which politicians have been cradled. But, for that end, America herself must guarantee that she will never become (as so many of your ministerial writers have preached) an image of our Europe, a mass of divided powers disputing about territories or the profits of commerce, and continually cementing the slavery of peoples by their own blood. [*The Life and Writings of Turgot,* ed. W. Walker Stephens (London and New York: Longmans, Green and Co.; 1895), p. 303.]

ought to be maintained for its own sake and as an example for other nations. The self-evident character of this conclusion has never been doubted throughout American history. And the proposition that territorial expansion is necessary for the achievement of equality in freedom at home has not been seriously doubted either in so far as it took the form of expansion into the empty spaces of the West by the primary means of real-estate transactions. The manifest destiny of that expansion, which Professor Bemis has called "manifest opportunity," appears as but an organic extension of the manifest opportunity whose achievement at home has been the purpose of America. The necessity and legitimacy of that expansion were as self-evident as the American purpose itself.

## 7. *The Denial*

The American purpose met its first great doubt, finally putting into question the very existence of America as a nation, when territorial expansion chose as its object not empty spaces but established political entities, such as Canada, Cuba, or Texas. As the self-evident necessity and legitimacy of territorial expansion into empty spaces was a reflection of the self-evident quality of the American purpose at home, so the doubt about the other kind of territorial expansion was a reflection of the doubt about the American purpose at home. That crisis concerned the very meaning of freedom, interpreted differently by two sectors of American society in view of their differing conceptions of the objective order from which freedom receives its meaning. The self-evident necessity and legitimacy of territorial expansion in the name of freedom depends upon a consensus as to the kind of freedom territorial expansion will promote. Yet the issue of slavery split American society into two groups, each committed to a different kind of freedom and intent upon promoting its own kind through territorial expansion. For the North, freedom meant equal political and economic opportunity for all men regardless of color; for the slave-holding states that opportunity applied to white men only. Both the North and the South saw the purpose of America in the preservation and expansion of their respective kinds of freedom. Expansion into politically unorganized territories was judged by each section in terms of the effect it was likely to have upon its own kind of freedom. The South opposed the annexation of Canada because the area of free soil would have been extended, while it promoted the annexation of Texas because of the effect upon the extension of slavery.

These and similar controversies foreshadowed the great crisis of the Civil War, arising from the very same issue of the extension of slavery and being fought on the fundamental issue of whether America could continue to exist as one nation dedicated to one purpose or would permanently break up into two different nations standing for different purposes developed from different interpretations of what freedom meant. The outcome of the Civil War settled the fundamental issue of union once and for all by establishing the military and political supremacy of the Federal government. It was able to settle the fundamental issue of the purpose of that union only in abstract constitutional terms. America was to be again what it had been at its inception: one nation dedicated to one purpose, and that purpose was again defined as freedom for all men. However, the social forces, especially in the form of political and economic interests, which had given birth to the restrictive interpretation of freedom continued, beneath the "great generalities" of the Constitution, to withhold the actual enjoyment of equal opportunity from those who, according to the declared purpose of the new union, are supposed to enjoy it.

The contrast between the legal and moral commitment to equal opportunity for all and the actual denial of that opportunity to a collectively defined group of citizens constitutes a tragic denial of the American purpose. Its tragic quality stems from its inescapability, its imperviousness to the good intentions of either the reformer or the paternalist, its rootedness in two sets of interests and principles which are both incompatible and legitimate. The attempt at translating the legal and moral commitment into practice comes up against the stubborn if not unyielding facts of experience, and the impossibility of remaining faithful to the American purpose becomes part of the American experience itself.

That experience is reflected in an endemic crisis of conscience which endeavors to reconcile purpose and achievement by either reformulating the purpose or, more generally in our time, making practice conform to it. Yet reformulation is bound to be tantamount to denial since anything less than equal opportunity for all as a matter of principle runs counter to what has been recognized at home and abroad as the purpose of America; thus, reformulation cannot help but sharpen the crisis of conscience. The attempt to make practice conform to the purpose, in turn, must lead to an endemic social crisis, erupting from time to time into acute political conflict, since a recalcitrant social reality does not allow the attempt to succeed. Thus, we have been able to achieve nothing more than an uneasy *modus vivendi* between purpose and achievement, shifting the points of acute conflict and with them the experience of failure from one area to another, tilting the balance here toward achievement, standing still or retreating elsewhere. Aware of over-all failure in spite of partial success, the national conscience remains ill at ease, and the sharpened formulation of the national purpose through constitutional interpretations only serve to sharpen the experience of failure.

Nowhere else has the purpose of America come up against so intractable a problem, struggling with it without being able to overcome it, and nowhere has the national conscience, by virtue of the failure to fulfill the national purpose, suffered permanently, to quote Jefferson's letter to Edward Coles of 1814, "a moral reproach," a "condition of moral and political reprobation."[1] The national purpose has time and again been challenged and denied realization both by government and by people; yet in historic perspective these challenges and denials appear as nothing more than painful lapses, retarding detours, temporary retreats before new advances.

The Alien and Sedition Laws of 1798, impeding the settlement and absorption of immigrants and stifling popular criticism of the government, abridged political freedom and set up a barrier against those dynamic renewals through successful waves of immigration which were to become the human source of the American social system. If these laws had remained on the books, America could not have lived up to its purpose; its very existence as a nation could no longer have been justified by it. As George Nicholas, one of the framers of the Kentucky Resolutions opposing the Alien and Sedition Laws, wrote in 1798 to his friend in Virginia: "What will it avail us, if we can preserve our independence as a nation, nay if we can even raise our country to the highest pitch of national glory, provided we at the same time lose our own liberties? . . . We ought to consider it as a truth of the most important nature—that independence abroad is of no real value, un-

[1] *The Works of Thomas Jefferson,* ed. Paul Leicester Ford (New York and London: G. P. Putnam's Son; 1905), XI, 416.

less it is accompanied with liberty at home."[2] Whenever the government undertook thereafter to abridge liberty at home in order to defend independence abroad with similar legislative enactments or administrative practices, it was called to order within a few years' time either by public opinion or by one of its own branches, such as the courts; its deviations from the American purpose are remembered as mere incidents, temporary aberrations that had no lasting effect upon American life.

Popular movements, such as the Native American Party, hardly fared better. Their main aim was to protect the United States from alien persons and ideas, and opposition to immigration was therefore one of their main planks. Immigration having been, as we have seen, one of the essentials for the achievement of the American purpose, it is worthy of note that while the Native American Party was organized in 1835 and the Know-Nothing Order in 1850, the Homestead Act of 1862 made the western territories accessible to immigrants, Congress passed on July 4, 1864, "An Act to Encourage Immigration," and the platform of the Republican party of the same year declared: "Foreign immigration which in the past has added so much to the wealth, resources, and increase of power to this nation—the asylum of the oppressed of all nations—should be fostered and encouraged by a liberal and just policy." Other laws, enacted before and after, provided incentives for immigrants through the provision of land, the regulation of contract labor, and other measures.

Popular agitation against aliens already immigrated, which was nourished by each new wave of immigrants, was no more effective in the long run. The impairments of equal opportunity which the new immigrants suffered

[2] *A Letter from George Nicholas of Kentucky to a Friend in Virginia* (Lexington and Philadelphia: James Carey; 1799), p. 4.

were by and large temporary, and it was, significantly enough, the next wave of immigrants which provided the preceding ones with the dual opportunity of freeing themselves from their disabilities and imposing them on those who arrived after them. The principle of unrestricted immigration was drastically and permanently abridged only in 1924. Yet here we are in a period that in the aspects most vital to the achievement of the American purpose differs radically from the preceding two and a half centuries during which the concept of the American purpose was formed and its achievement experienced.

# II

# THE FIRST CRISIS
## (1890-1940)

## A. *Impairment of Mobility at Home*

### 1. *Impairment of Mobility*

THAT PERIOD BEGINS roughly in 1890 and ends, again roughly speaking, in 1940. It begins with the closing of the frontier and ends with the consummation of the New Deal and the American involvement in the Second World War. Its distinctive character in terms of our discussion is marked by six momentous experiences on the domestic plane: the closing of the frontier; the emergence of a stratified society with extreme contrasts in economic and political power; the cessation of numerically unlimited immigration; the crash of 1929 and its aftermath; alienation from the American purpose; restoration through social reform. On the international plane that period is dominated by four experiences: America as a colonial power; America as a crusading power; America as a world power without a purpose; the involvement of America in the Second World War.

43

One can summarize the impact that these experiences— save the last-mentioned in each series—made upon the American awareness of the national purpose by saying that they appeared to obliterate the earlier experiences from which the purpose of America arose and to deny the validity of that purpose. No master within, no enemy without; equality, opportunity, freedom, power for the individual—what was left of them after the nation had undergone the first crisis of its purpose? Little, if anything, was left of them in terms of the historical configuration in which they emerged in the seventeenth and eighteenth centuries and asserted themselves in the nineteenth. However, their essence reappeared and reasserted itself, sometimes with faltering steps and in intellectual and political disarray, yet intact. It emerged out of the new experiences of the last decade of the nineteenth century and the first four decades of the twentieth in a new formulation commensurate with these experiences, only to be put into question again by the experiences of the forties and fifties. How the purpose of America emerged from these novel experiences is the story of the vitality of a pattern of attitudes and ideas, capable, on the one hand, of withstanding the shock of new experiences and absorbing their impact and, on the other, of imposing itself upon those experiences, transmuting itself and the experiences in the process.

The six domestic experiences which mark the period of the first crisis of the American purpose are interconnected. They are either different manifestations of the one overriding experience, the loss of mobility at home, or institutional and psychological reactions to that loss. The four experiences which constitute that crisis on the international plane are projections of the domestic ones onto the international scene. They follow one another in time, being successive responses to the loss of mobility experienced on the domestic scene.

44

### Impairment of Mobility

This interconnection of the domestic and international responses to the first crisis of the American purpose is but a reflection of the intimate and necessary relationship between the domestic and international manifestations of the American purpose in the period of its flowering. The purpose of mobility at home—that is, mobility in the vertical direction—required for its consummation mobility abroad —that is, a horizontal mobility. When the limits of horizontal mobility had seemingly been reached, the American purpose faced a crisis that was by definition domestic and international at the same time. Thus, the closing of the frontier constitutes a turning point in the realization of the American purpose, the decisive event that led to its crisis in practice and to the need for its reformulation in the consciousness of the nation.

With the appropriation of all available empty spaces on the North American continent, the mechanism through which American society was able to renew again and again its achievement of domestic freedom became unavailable. With that horizontal mobility gone, the vertical mobility, for the sake of which the former had functioned, was threatened with impairment, if not extinction, too. The man who felt himself deprived of his opportunity now had, as it were, no place to go where the race was still open to all who were willing and able to run. He could try to force his way up if he felt strong enough; he could stay, reconciled or resentful, in the place where he was; but he could no longer break out of the shackles that threatened to tie him ever more closely to a particular lowly place in an ever more stratified society.

That stratification was, as we have seen, a natural process that no society could escape for any length of time. What is peculiar to America is the principle of selection by which the highest strata of society were set up against the lower ones. In the absence of the traditional principles of

45

selection, such as birth, military merit, bureaucratic distinction, intellectual achievement, and in view of the necessarily fleeting nature of political power that was bestowed and withdrawn by the vagaries of the democratic process, the possession of wealth became the chief mark of social distinction and source of social and political power in America. American society, devoid of a stable structure and of identifiable groups permanently deprived of, or vested with, power, found in wealth the instrument by which power could be acquired, maintained, and transferred.

Wealth, if wisely managed, provides its holder and his heirs with a permanent source of power. Its easy negotiability and the vast opportunities for the creation of new wealth which a virgin country offered in a period of rapid industrialization gave wealth and the power derived from it a mobility that was congenial to American society. For that society, as we have seen, regarded mobility as its peculiar achievement and was dedicated to its perpetuation. In the societies of the Continent, wealth as a source of power had to compete with other sources of social distinction, primarily of aristocratic origin and hallowed by age and exclusiveness, and it had to compete against them with the severe handicap of novelty and vulgarity. For wealth is the democratic principle of social distinction *par excellence*. Anybody can acquire it, and its mere possession gives its owner a potential source of power, regardless of any other qualities he may or may not possess. This is the meaning of Tocqueville's observation that the Americans "introduce the habits of business into their political life."

The period following the Civil War witnessed a radical departure from the pattern of relative economic and political equality in which earlier observers, such as Pinckney, had seen the distinctive characteristic of America and the preservation of which Jefferson considered to be essential for the preservation of American democracy. The accumulation of enormous fortunes and, more particularly, the acquisition of monopolistic control over key industries and resources brought in their wake proportionate concentrations of political power. Railroads, mining companies, public utilities came to exercise political control over whole regions of the country, and those who had the money could buy votes, political office, and public officials.

However, freedom of competition remained in principle intact; for the poor and powerless of today retained the chance of becoming rich and powerful tomorrow. Thus, the denunciation of the "malefactors of great wealth" and of political corruption was in good measure the protest of the temporarily dispossessed who resented their exclusion from the circle of the rich and powerful. In practice, however, permanent concentrations of wealth and, more particularly, monopolistic controls impaired permanently the operation of equal competition for wealth and power. That competition still operated on the low and medium levels of the social ladder, yet the top positions of wealth and power had by and large become exempt from it. A man could still rise in society by competing successfully for wealth and power, but the terms of the competition became less equal the higher he rose. Wealth and monopolies had become vested interests by using the mechanics of economic and political competition to entrench themselves, escaping from the risks of competition. As such, they had an initial advantage that the ability and luck of the man in the street had little chance of overcoming.

The man in the street could not compete on equal terms, and could hardly compete at all, with railroads, mining companies, and public utilities. Politicians, beholden to the vested interests, would come and go, exercising ostensibly the functions of government; yet the vested interests would retain control of the levers of power. The man in the street could still compete on equal terms with his fellows for economic and political position, as long as he was content to compete within the pattern of power established by the vested interests; but if he was bold enough to challenge that pattern itself, he had little chance of succeeding. Thus, the American achievement of equal opportunity and vertical mobility as its result still survived, but they survived only within a pattern of power virtually exempt from competition. Vertical mobility as the social and political achievement of the American purpose of equality had on the highest level given way to economic and political stratification based on wealth. Americans now had permanent rulers and were permanent subjects.

A society thus constituted could not help seeing unrestricted immigration in a different light from that in which its predecessors had viewed it. An intimate and necessary relationship tied unrestricted immigration to the foundation of ever new societies in the empty spaces. One was complementary to the other. Unrestricted immigration made westward expansion both necessary and possible. Without it, the territories beyond the original frontiers of the United States might have been settled by isolated pioneers, and there would not have been enough settlers to establish political organization.

This organic relationship between American expansion and unrestricted immigration was clear to the Founding Fathers. One of their grievances was the British limitation on immigration and the acquisition of land, and, significantly the Declaration of Independence mentions them together. It complained that the King "has endeavored to prevent the population of these states; for that purpose obstructing the naturalization of foreigners; refusing to pass others to encourage their immigration hither, and

raising the conditions of new appropriations of lands."
Alexander Hamilton used religious freedom as an incentive to immigration. "A perfect equality of religious
privileges," he wrote in 1792 in his Report on Manu-
factures, "will probably cause them [the immigrants] to
flock from Europe to the United States."

Since the United States seemed to have reached the natural limits of its territorial expansion, unrestricted immigration seemed to have lost its rationale. And with American
society in the process of stratification, mass immigration
appeared as a threat to the achievement of the American purpose, at least in the economic sphere. The closing
of the frontier had transformed the ideal of freedom from
competition into a utopian dream. The stratification of
American society was making freedom of competition an
instrument by which the privileged classes maintained
and expanded their advantage. The mass immigration of
cheap labor appeared to put native Americans at a decisive disadvantage in the competition for a livelihood and
for social advancement. Thus, opposition to immigration
was a natural concomitant of the closing of the frontier
and of the stratification of American society, and it is not
by accident that the three factors appeared on the American scene simultaneously toward the end of the nineteenth
century.

The attempts at limiting immigration which began in
the 1880's and culminated in the Immigration Act of
1924 are in both intent and effect different from those
which preceded them. The earlier measures excluded certain categories of immigrants, defined in religious or racial
terms—viz., Catholics or Orientals—or based on physical,
mental, moral, or educational defects, but did not intend
to limit the total number of immigrants. This was exactly
the intent of the immigration acts of 1921 and 1924, which
did limit the total number of immigrants by means of the

quota system. The effects of this legislation were drastic. During the decade 1841–50 the number of immigrants was 1,700,000, and in no subsequent decade up to 1930 was the number smaller; the maximum number during this period was almost 8,800,000 for the first decade of this century. Yet from 1931 to 1940 immigrants numbered only 528,000—fewer even than the almost 600,000 who immigrated during the decade ending in 1840. Thus, while it seemed as though both the horizontal and the vertical mobility and, with it, the absorptive capacity of American society had been permanently impaired, the United States denied the chance of being absorbed to millions of would-be immigrants whose predecessors had given dynamic content to the mobility inherent in the American system. That succession of massive immigrations, starting with the voyage of 1620, ebbed to a succession of trickles, not very significant in absolute numbers and even less so in comparison with the total American population. American society, in search of a new mobility, had to look elsewhere.

## 2. *The Economic Crisis of 1929*

The doubt that the concentration of wealth and power had cast upon the American achievement during the half-century following the Civil War was transformed into doubt about the American purpose itself by the economic crisis that followed the crash of 1929. For that crisis did not just exempt the command posts of economic and political power from the equal opportunity promised by the American purpose, leaving it intact on the middle and lower levels; rather it appeared to deny the validity of the American purpose throughout the whole social fabric. It seemed to exclude large sectors of the population not only from political and economic competition on equal terms, but also from the opportunity to lead a purposeful life. Previously, the man in the street had still a chance, with much ability and luck, to rise at least a considerable distance toward the top; now the best he could hope for was to stay where he was and not to sink below that station. The dynamics of American society now seemed to point downward rather than upward. Opportunity no longer beckoned; instead stagnation and destitution threatened.

Previous economic crises had been, and were experienced as, cyclical phases within an irresistible upward trend, interludes between two phases of prosperity of which the latter was bound to be superior to the preceding one. The economic crisis of the thirties made a different impact upon the American mind. Its length and seeming incurability made it appear to many contemporaries as the *reductio ad absurdum* of the capitalistic system itself. The paradoxes of idle men without access to idle machines, of hunger in the midst of plenty of food, of idle money separated from opportunities for investment seemed to provide empirical proof of the inner contradictions with which Marxism and its crypto-Marxist derivatives, popular in the United States, had found the capitalistic system incurably afflicted. Those ills appeared not as mere interludes between periods of prosperity, but rather as symptoms of a chronic disease which was bound to get worse with every new crisis and which could not be cured with the capitalistic remedies.

The impact of that crisis upon the consciousness of its actual and prospective victims—a substantial majority of the American people—was a dual denial of the American purpose. The effects of that crisis appeared as the destruction of the American achievement, and that crisis was experienced as the outright denial of the experience of three centuries which the nation had come to accept as typically American. Vertical mobility there still was, but it was now experienced as a tendency to move below the economic and social level previously attained. Equal opportunity there still was, but it was now experienced as the equal chance to get on the dole. Freedom there still was, but it was now experienced as a freedom to sell apples on the street. Power there still was, but it was now experienced as the meaningless gesture of casting a ballot. Large masses of Americans experienced for the first time without escape or obvious remedy the economic stagnation, social immo- bility, political impotence, and the ever present threat of worse to come which had been the traditional condition of the masses of Europe. The economic crisis, by remaking America in the image of Europe, seemed to have made a mockery of the American purpose and put an end to the American experiment itself.

Thus, the impact of the economic crisis upon American consciousness was not limited to denying the ability of America to achieve its purpose; it put into question the validity of the purpose itself. The experiences of the clos- ing of the frontier, of social stratification in the form of concentration of wealth and power, of the cessation of un- restricted immigration had prepared the ground for that denial. The intellectual tools for that denial were at hand in the economic interpretation of American history.

Seen from the perspective of the economic crisis of the thirties, these experiences appear as mere preparation for the ultimate collapse of the American purpose, successive steps in a drama of disillusionment and frustration. The closing of the frontier seemed to have made escape impos- sible. The concentrations of wealth and power seemed to have prepared the ground for the final assault upon the individual's position and opportunities. The attempt to save this position and these chances by limiting immigration had obviously failed. Yet these experiences, as interpreted by the literature and the social sciences of the twenties and thirties, only provided added proof for the basic proposition of that school of thought: that the purpose of America was nothing more than a political ideology masking the economic interests of privileged groups. In this view, the very concept of the national purpose had no more reality than had the idea of the national interest. The War for Independence and the American Constitution were thought to be nothing but instruments of class interests, and so was the Civil War. The United States was believed to have intervened in the First World War only to secure profits to the munitions makers and save the investments of the house of Morgan. In those qualities which really count in this philosophy—that is, the economic ones—American society appeared never to have been really different from the societies of Europe.

In the light of that economic interpretation of American history, the experiences of the late nineteenth century and first decades of the twentieth, culminating in the economic crisis of the thirties, appeared not so much as deviations from the American purpose and achievement as but the latest and most spectacular manifestations of their fictitious character, to which all of American history testified. To put the then prevailing thought bluntly: the idea of the American purpose and achievement was a fraud perpetrated by the American ruling class for economic gain, and while the fraudulent character of that idea had been concealed during the first two and a half centuries of American history, these experiences made it obvious for all to see.

In order to grasp the devastating impact these experiences, as interpreted by the then prevailing school of thought, had upon the popular understanding of the American purpose, it is necessary to consider the peculiarly intangible and shapeless nature of that purpose. The distinctiveness of the American purpose does not consist, as we have seen, in a particular substantive idea, a specific concrete arrangement, some single achievement, the consummation of which could be pinpointed in time. Rather it consists in the achievement of a particular mode of procedure, of a particular way of thinking and acting in the social sphere, of a particular conception of the relations between the individual and society. The American purpose seeks the maintenance and intensification of social movement for its own sake, mobility regardless of where it moves to, dynamism as an end in itself. The achievement of so shapeless and intangible a national purpose in terms of individual freedom and equal opportunity is bound to leave always something to be desired. The very extent of the achievement will be open to doubt and subjective interpretation, in so far as it is not defined in terms of the only tangible, objective standard available: the possession of wealth. According to their station and expectations, those who judge the American achievement will differ about its measure and point with pride or reproach to the distance that of necessity separates achievements from purpose.

This shapeless and intangible concept serves not only as the purpose of the nation, but also as the integrating principle of American society. American society does not coalesce around any immemorial national tradition of dynastic loyalties, ethnic affinities, class distinctions. What binds it together is that to which it owes its existence: its purpose. America as a living society is identical with its purpose and the awareness of its achievement. Do away with the belief in the validity of that purpose and in the possibility of its achievement, and you have cut the umbilical cord that joins America to her children. From 1620 to our day the waves of immigrants which make up the American people came in search of equality in freedom, and they either stayed where they had first settled because they found it there or moved westward until they did find it. "What attachment," asks Crèvecoeur, "can a poor European emigrant have for a country where he had nothing? The knowledge of the language, the love of a few kindred as poor as himself, were the only cords that tied him: his country is now that which gives him land, bread, protection, and consequence: *Ubi panis ibi patria,* is the motto of all emigrants."[1] If freedom and equality can no longer be found in America, there is no reason for America to exist. "When it comes to this [the Know-Nothings getting control]," Abraham Lincoln, most American of Americans, could write to Joshua Speed on August 24, 1855, "I should prefer emigrating to some country where they make no pretence of loving liberty—to Russia, for instance, where despotism can be taken pure, and without the base alloy of hypocrisy."[2]

America has not known, as have other nations, the phenomenon of the temporary émigré, the voluntary exile who does not like a phase of his country's history, who waits it out abroad, who may try to stimulate the process of change from his exile, and who returns when the phase has passed. America had no Jacobites, no émigrés like the French aristocrats who during the revolution waited in Coblenz for the restoration of the Bourbons, or like the anti-fascists who worked for the downfall of fascism and returned after its demise. America has only expatriates, people who cut themselves loose once and for all, who leave never to return. The American exile does not leave a household temporarily unpleasant and wait abroad for the

[1] St. John de Crèvecoeur: *Letters from an American Farmer* (New York: E. P. Dutton and Co.; 1912), p. 43.

[2] *Collected Works of Abraham Lincoln,* ed. Roy P. Basler (New Brunswick: Rutgers University Press; 1959), II, 323.

disturbance to pass. Rather he leaves a beloved by whom he has been betrayed; there can be no turning back.

The United States was founded upon loyalty not to a monarch or a piece of territory, but to a purpose. We pledge allegiance to a flag that is the symbol of certain principles: "liberty and justice for all." Loyalty that attaches to a man or a territory may not be affected by the violation of principles perpetrated by that man or within that territory. A nation which was built upon a common loyalty to a certain purpose, whose citizens have come together voluntarily to share in the achievement of that purpose, which owes its very existence to a revolt against arbitrary impediments to the achievement of that purpose —such a nation stands or falls, as a nation, with its loyalty to that purpose.

The man who chooses the United States as his nation concludes, as it were, a silent compact with himself, his fellow citizens, and his government to co-operate in the achievement of that purpose; of that compact the Constitution is the symbol and the American political system the living manifestation. This man will reconcile himself to the achievement falling short of the ideal, he will forgive sporadic violations of that purpose. What he cannot reconcile himself to and cannot forgive is the denial of the purpose itself in theory or practice. Such a denial denies his obligation to remain loyal to a government and a society that are no longer loyal to the common purpose. Thus, it is in the nature of things that the denial of the American purpose will alienate the people from America itself.

This was indeed the effect of the successive partial denials of the American purpose in the economic and political spheres, culminating in the economic crisis of the thirties. Alienation as reaction to that crisis took the forms of a general malaise about America, which was believed either to have reached "maturity"—that is, stagnation—or to be ripe for revolution after the Fascist or Communist model; of the spread of Marxist and crypto-Marxist philosophies; of the development of class consciousness in theory and practice; of the rise to prominence of the internal and external expatriate. Yet while the economic crisis brought these attitudes of alienation to the fore, their roots lie deep in American society. Three qualities of American society have made alienation an ever present threat: the looseness of the American social structure; the foreign origin of large sectors of American society; the possession of wealth as the main objective and tangible criterion of social distinction.

All politically civilized societies—in contrast to tyrannies—owe their continuing existence to a consensus concerning at least the foundations of society and to the power of the government to enforce that consensus against recalcitrant minorities. The possible objectives of that consensus range from the general character of society and government, its personnel and procedures, to the concrete objectives of policy; typically, the consensus emerges out of a struggle between antagonistic and frequently incompatible conceptions of what the consensus should be.

### 3. *Alienation*

It is characteristic of the United States that it owes its existence to a consensus both minimal and unanimous; and it was only because it was minimal that it could be unanimous. The object of that consensus is defined by the American purpose: equality in freedom—that is to say, equality of competition for undefined goals with a minimum of political interference or, to put it the other way around, a political order just strong enough to give all members of society an equal chance to do as they please. How could the intended pluralism of such a society be prevented from degenerating into separatism and dissolving American society into its component parts? How could the dynamics of a multiplicity of sub-societies, many of which were physically remote from the central authority, be kept united by so loose a common framework? Tocqueville noted that the center of political and social gravity was in the states and local communities, not in the federal government, and it is worthy of note that the issue of whether there should be one American society with a central government deserving of the name was definitely decided only in 1865. And the spectacular success of so unlikely a venture in the conscious making of society and government has obscured the specter of failure which haunted the founders and their immediate successors.

The prospect of failure, inherent in the very looseness of America's social structure and in the weakness of its government, was increased by the complexion that American society took on during the nineteenth century as the result of successive waves of mass immigration. How could a society that appeared to be so fragile to begin with absorb large heterogeneous masses without losing its identity, if not its unified existence? How could, more particularly, the Western states and territories remain an integral part of American society controlled by the Federal government? According to the census of 1880, the inhabitants of foreign birth or extraction (natives with at least one foreign-born parent) of Washington territory numbered 38 per cent; of Montana, 49 per cent; of Wyoming, 50 per cent; of Utah, 52 per cent; of Idaho, 53 per cent; of Arizona, 55 per cent; of the Dakotas, 66 per cent; of Nebraska, 43 per cent; of California, 60 per cent; of Nevada, 63 per cent; of Minnesota, 72 per cent. According to the census of 1900, the inhabitants of foreign birth or extraction of the eleven Mountain and Pacific states amounted to 47.6

per cent of the total population. The percentage for Utah was 61.2, for Montana 57.3, California 54.9, North Dakota 77.5, South Dakota 61.1, Minnesota 74.9.

The possibility of alienation appeared here as a natural result of alien settlement, and it did so in two different respects. Could these large alien settlements be expected to be faithful to the American purpose and to the American government? Was the common purpose of having equality in freedom strong enough to resist the temptation to develop on American soil stratified societies after the Continental model and to override the ancient loyalties to nations and kings? The spectacular success of the American experiment in this respect, too, has tended to obscure the reality of the risk and the seeming justification for the anxieties caused by it.

These two potential sources of alienation—the amorphousness of American society and its strong alien component—have existed throughout American history. The awareness of the third potential source—wealth as the main objective and tangible standard for social distinction—is concomitant with the actual stratification of American society according to wealth, which followed the Civil War. No civilization had ever considered the possession of wealth as the main or highest standard of excellence, and even many American owners of wealth have justified that possession implicitly or explicitly in terms of achievement, service, or power and have atoned for it by public service and philanthropies commensurate with it. The popular attitude toward wealth as the dominant standard of social distinction has been ambivalent. Of this ambivalence, the movements of social protest and reform are characteristic. They oppose the dominance of wealth, but in good measure because legal and social arrangements curtail equal competition for it. Yet there was no ambivalence about the all-persuasiveness of that standard as manifested in those conspicuous aspects of popular culture which go by the name of materialism. The triumph of that materialism went hand in hand with a general vulgarity and coarseness and lack of understanding of, if not contempt for, those refinements in manners and appreciation for things of the mind which the Western tradition has cherished above wealth.

These traits could not but repel a small group of sensitive and well-educated Americans, as they repelled many foreigners. Those Americans who admired the genteel tradition, fragments of which still survived on the Atlantic coast, experienced those traits as a profanation and betrayal of what they thought America ought to stand for. They despaired of America and found in Europe what they missed here. They became external or internal expatriates. H. L. Mencken, iconoclast, was no less an expatriate for staying home than was Henry James, Anglophile, who went away. Both prototypes refused to identify themselves with America as they found it. They viewed it with disgust and judged its purpose, as they understood it, at best a failure and at worst a fraud. While this group was small in numbers, it was large in influence. The snob appeal that things foreign and, more particularly, British continue to exert upon the American mind is a tribute both to the groups representative role and to its persistent influence. Some of the most talented American writers set the climate of opinion for, and their prestige gave respectability to, the doubt and denial of the American purpose which we witnessed at the end of this period.

These doubts about the validity of the American purpose and the reality and possibility of its achievement have come to the fore of the American mind whenever the unity of America seemed to be threatened by mass alienation from within—that is, by social disintegration. In order to meet that threat, America had to come to terms with a dual, typically American paradox. The only remedy available, curtailment of freedom, was tantamount to a denial of the original formulation of the American purpose. America was threatened by the degeneration of freedom into anarchy and could save itself only by curtailing freedom. By thus impairing the achievement of the American purpose, however, it risked strengthening the forces of alienation wihch it sought to keep in check. Yet as the threat of alienation and disintegration is endemic in the American social system, so is the reaction to it of doing violence to the American purpose of equality in freedom. The dilemma which George Nicholas defined as choice between liberty and survival on the occasion of the Alien and Sedition Laws has been a persistent theme of American history.

## 4. *Conformity*

The instrument that American society has used to counter the endemic threat of alienation has been the enforcement, by unorganized society, of conformity in opinion and attitudes. The instruments it has used to deal with the acute threat of alienation have been exclusion and repression of minorities and the instigation of social reforms.

Enforced conformity of opinions and attitudes is the cement that holds together the structure of American society, a society lacking in those hierarchical structures, with the exception of that of wealth, to which other societies owe their stability. Conformity is of course the egalitarian instrument of social cohesion *par excellence* and thus carries within itself the first of the two paradoxes to which we have referred; for while it denies freedom, its achievement of equality is complete. Nobody in particular sets its standards or enforces them since all do, and nobody in particu-

lar is subject to them since all are. The wise and the foolish, the rich and the poor, the powerful and the weak—they
are all in differing degrees legislators, judges, executors,
and subjects at the same time. All social agents and institutions are constantly on the alert to protect so brittle a social structure against its congenital vulnerability to attacks
from within. Conformity originates and ends with anonymous society. It creates a gregarious society whose members are happy and secure, sharing equality of status and
sameness of opinion. Thus, the amorphousness of American society still puts its stamp upon the very remedy that
cures its congenital ill. It does so not only with respect to
the general nature of the remedy but also with respect to
its content.

Conformity requires standards to which to conform. It
requires an answer to the question: conformity to what?
Freedom in the American sense means freedom from political control, and, as a utopian ideal, from competition;
equality means equality of opportunity and, more particularly, of competition. But what does conformity mean? In
terms of substantive standards, it can mean anything.
Whatever unorganized society, as public opinion, and organized society, as the rule of the majority, are willing to
enforce is a fit standard to conform to. Mr. Justice
Holmes' dictum: ". . . I have no practical criticism [with
regard to laws] except what the crowd wants"[1] points to
the potential for extreme relativism and subjectivism inherent in American conformity, a potential that, as we
shall see, has been realized in our time.

This conformity is characterized by extreme permissiveness in the choice of content and rigorous enforcement of
the content chosen. Absurd and disreputable practices in

[1] Letter to Pollock, April 23, 1910, in *The Pollock-Holmes Letters,*
ed. Mark De Wolfe Howe (Cambridge: Cambridge University Press;
1942), I, 163.

business and education, for instance, will be strictly enforced as long as they are approved by society, to be replaced by others, better or worse, when they have found favor with society. The incompetent and the fraud are tolerated as long as they abide by the rules of the game. In the absence of one objective standard of judgment and with social acceptance being the ultimate criterion, to secure and keep social acceptance becomes the main goal of social competition, and promotion in all fields of social life—religion and scholarship, for instance, no less than business—as a means to that end tends to replace the search for one objective truth believed to be both indiscernible and illusory.

Yet the very permissiveness of the American consensus in terms of content requires the commitment to a definite *modus operandi*. That *modus operandi* is but the reflection of the American purpose in the unorganized social sphere. Equality in freedom here becomes freedom of competition for social approval. Here again Mr. Justice Holmes is the authentic voice of the American spirit: ". . . the best test of truth is the power of the thought to get itself accepted in the competition of the market. . . ."[2] Today's truth, then, becomes tomorrow's error, once it has lost out in that competition. The only permanent commitment of the American consensus is to the freedom to compete on equal terms for the opportunity to determine the content of that consensus. That commitment requires that all competitors observe the rules of competition which seek to safeguard the equality of competitive chance. This, then, is the fundamental law of the American consensus: everybody may compete on equal terms, and everybody must compete according to the rules of the

[2] Dissenting opinion in *Abrams vs. United States,* 250 U.S. 616 (1919) at 630.

game. Fair play, wherever it may lead, is the rule by which unorganized American society lives.

The American consensus, devoid of one objective substantive standard and committed to freedom of competition, creates of necessity a society that is pluralistic both in space and in time. Within its framework, any number of sub-societies will simultaneously develop around any kind of integrative principle, and all kinds of integrative principles will follow one another in time. The very dynamics of such a permissive society, indifferent as a matter of principle to the content of its consensus, carries within itself the propensity toward self-destruction. As individual freedom carries within itself the seeds of anarchy, so pluralism carries within itself the seeds of social disintegration. The threat of disintegration, actual or imaginary, has been experienced by American society in three different forms according to its sub-national, other-national, and supranational origin. Parochial sub-societies—especially economic, ethnic, and sectional ones—have tried, or have appeared to try, to substitute themselves for the whole of American society. Ethnic groups in particular have from time to time tended, or have appeared to tend, to perpetuate the ways of, and loyalties to, the society of their origin at the expense of American society. Religious sub-societies and those identified with an international political philosophy or movement, such as Marxism, or an international organization, such as the United Nations, have been suspected of subjecting loyalty to America to a supranational test.

The awareness of these specific threats, actual or imaginary, was sharpened by the awareness of the endemic precariousness of the American consensus, caused by lack of substantive agreement and its resulting pluralistic character. American society had always to be on guard against deviations from conformity and had to take special measures against what appeared to be mass deviations constituting a special threat to the American consensus. In the absence of such a threat, the normal unorganized and spontaneous social pressures sufficed to keep disintegrating tendencies in check. Against such a threat and denials of its purpose in general, American society reacted in three typical and fundamentally different ways: by imposing liabilities upon those from whom the threat appeared to emanate; by retreating into utopianism or pessimism; by attacking in the pragmatic spirit of social reform the internal conditions upon which the threat appeared to feed. That is to say, America denied its purpose, or it remained but ineffectually committed to it, or it reaffirmed its purpose through effective action. The first alternative led to the exclusion and suppression of religious and political groups thought to be especially liable to constitute such a threat. Sporadic xenophobia and religious and political intolerance have been typically American defenses against acute dangers to the American consensus. From the second alternative issued utopian schemes and a pessimistic literature. The last alternative brought into being attempts at social reform which continued the American revolution by attacking within American society deviations from the American purpose.

## 5. *Utopianism, Pessimism, and Pragmatism*

If America was created for the purpose of founding a society on equality in freedom, then the economic and political stratification that transformed American society after the Civil War was a denial of that purpose. The full achievement of that purpose was possible only under the marginal near-anarchic conditions of the frontier. As a general principle consistently applied to a mature society, it was of course a utopian dream. For a favorable environment can minimize the relations of power and mitigate their burden by keeping them loose and shifting, but it cannot exercise the fact of power from society. The Founding Fathers knew this, for they knew Calvin and Hobbes, and many were themselves living in stratified societies. But the original conditions of the frontier society lent plausibility to the American dream of a society without distinctions of power by offering in horizontal and vertical mobility escapes from subjection to power and opportunities for exercising it.

The emergence of a stratified American society in the second half of the nineteenth century cast doubt on the plausibility of the American dream. It thus planted the seeds, which were long in germinating, of a more profound understanding of the nature of man and society. The early settlers expected in America to escape the evil of power which the societies of Europe had inflicted upon them. They were shocked when they encountered that evil gaining ascendancy in the very society they had founded. The road is long from that shock to the recognition that that evil is not in society but in ourselves and that we take it with us wherever we go. The westward migrations were in a sense flights from evil. When the closing of the frontier forced America to face the evil in its midst, the flight from evil became the hunt for it. Since it could no longer be escaped, it had to be hunted down and done away with. Thus, the pioneer who had gone from London to Cape Cod, from Cape Cod to the Ohio, from the Ohio to Kansas, from Kansas to the Pacific coast, in order to escape evil, now transformed himself into Captain Ahab, who roams the seven seas to hunt down and kill Moby Dick, the whale of evil.

Here, then, are the roots both of American utopianism and of American pessimism. Once the frontier was closed, escape from evil either became flight from reality or yielded to the sorrowful contemplation of a reality that could not be redeemed. Thus, America reacted to the closing of the frontier and the accompanying transformation of American society by substituting for an unacceptable reality blueprints of a brave new world. If the stratified society and the evils attending it could no longer be escaped by leaving them for a new society conceived in equality and freedom, they could still be transcended by an act of thought and will. Freedom bordering on anarchy and equality bordering on freedom from competition in an organized society were now regarded not as ideals but as utopias, and it is not by accident that when that truth started to sink in—that is, during the last decade of the nineteenth century—America found release from its frustration in the publication of almost fifty utopian romances.[1] While in the 1830's and 1840's the utopianism of complete equality and freedom was still a practical proposition, leading to the actual establishment of utopian communities, the conditions of the last decade reduced it to a literary exercise. The utopian escape became a substitute for the incessant renewal of American society, no longer to be achieved through territorial expansion.

Pessimism is America's other reaction to the ubiquity of evil. Hawthorne, Poe, and Melville testify to its presence even in the heyday of American expansion. They uncovered in America the human condition, drastically at variance with the American dream. However different American society was from other societies, Americans had not escaped, and could not escape, the evil in which all men share. That tragic sense of life, expressed in a few masterpieces unrepresentative of the popular mood, had to wait half a

[1] Samuel Eliot Morison and Henry Steele Commager: *The Growth of the American Republic* (New York: Oxford University Press; 1942), II, 369.

century till it found a popular echo in the disillusioned generation of the inter-war period. It is significant that *Moby Dick* sold less than a thousand copies in Melville's lifetime. Only in the 1920's was it recognized for what it is.

It is characteristic of both the literary and the popular expression of that mood that it remained entirely private. It did not cause the creation of a public tragedy as an American art form bringing the individual face to face with organized society. It is concerned with private tragedy —i.e., the inability of even American man to escape evil. It is as apolitical as American society from which it springs, and as the American purpose to whose denial it is a reaction. *Moby Dick* is indeed its classic expression.

Popular pessimism in America feeds on the contrast between social reality and the American dream. Literary pessimism in America is nourished by the loneliness to which American society relegates the intellectual in a specifically American way. The genuine intellectual has, of course, always been lonely, for he must be "the enemy of the people" who tells the world things it either does not want to hear or cannot understand. This existential loneliness is brought home to the American intellectual with peculiar poignancy because he is placed in a society that, being conformist, gregarious, and pragmatic, finds the lonely thinker not so much dangerous and incomprehensible as incongruous and irrelevant. The American intellectual is not only lonely but also forsaken.

He has reacted by retreating from American life altogether, like Henry James, by negating American life, like Henry Adams, or by using the popular misunderstanding of his work for the glorification of conformity and gregariousness, like Mark Twain. Only when the intellectual is misunderstood or plays a popular act is he able to come to terms with society. Otherwise, he must stop being a genuine intellectual by being practical—which at bottom is just another way of being misunderstood and playing an act. It is as a helper in social causes, as the uplifter of the spirit, as the "social engineer" that the American intellectual comes into his own. By forcing these roles upon him, society misunderstands the intellectual's proper role, which is to think for the sake of thinking, and transforms him into a doer of sorts. By accepting these roles, the intellectual becomes at best a practitioner and at worst an ideologue of social action. Thus the intellectual ceases to be the conscience of society and becomes its agent. His congenital pessimism is overwhelmed by the congenital optimism of a conformist, gregarious, and pragmatic society.

At least in its domestic concerns, American society has never indulged for long in the utopian and pessimistic escapes. What has held it back from facing social problems with purposeful resolution has been not so much utopianism and pessimism as fear of government. Once that fear was overcome, American society has attacked social problems with the inventiveness, ingenuity, and pragmatic experimentation, that are the hallmarks of the American mind in action. The pragmatic approach to social problems is congenital to a society that is not committed to a particular substantive purpose but finds its purpose in a specific *modus operandi*. Such a society can afford to deal with each problem on its merits, in terms not of preconceived philosophic tenets but of the results desired and to be expected from a particular course of action; for American society is still spacious and mobile enough to be able to tolerate a number of alternative solutions to a given problem without risking social disintegration. Thus, whatever action promises results will be tried, and dogmatic consistency is not allowed to stand in the way of trying something else that promises better results. When American society comes face to face with failure, its typical mood is optimistic; its typical intellectual attitude, pragmatic; its typical action, social reform.

## 6. *Social Reform*

The success of social reform in reformulating and revitalizing the American purpose, restoring the sense of its achievement, and thereby reintegrating American society tends to obscure in retrospect the reality of the crisis. The movements of social reform—Populism, the Progressive Movement, Theodore Roosevelt's New Nationalism and Square Deal, Woodrow Wilson's New Freedom, Franklin D. Roosevelt's New Deal—appear in retrospect as different phases of a single endeavor, born of and nourished by one experience and seeking the same goal by essentially identical means. That experience was the exploitation of human and material resources for private gain, which tended to negate the American purpose of vertical social mobility. That goal was the restoration of the American purpose under the new conditions of an urban and industrial society. The means employed was the Federal government's assumption of responsibility for the achievement of the goal.

Movements of social reform dominated the scene in the Western world throughout the better part of the nineteenth century, and most of them antedate the American movements. Yet the experiences from which the former arose differ fundamentally from that to which the latter owe their existence. Conscience and expediency—that is, universal moral and rational considerations—stimulated the European movements of social reform. The American movements, on the other hand, are conceived in a specific sense of failure, in the sense of a specifically American failing. Certainly the exploitation and degradation of man by man, the impairment of his life, liberty, and pursuit of happiness by a wealthy minority are universal outrages, yet they are in a peculiar sense outrages against the American purpose. All men ought to be ashamed of a society thus constituted, but Americans have a peculiarly American reason for being ashamed. This specifically American experience is implicit in the moral fervor of the platform of the Populist party of 1892 and explicit in its reference to America's degeneration "into European conditions":

> We meet in the midst of a nation brought to the verge of moral, political, and material ruin. Corruption dominates the ballot-box, the legislatures, the Congress, and touches even the ermine of the bench. The people are demoralized. . . . The urban workmen are denied the right of organization for self-protection; imported pauperized labor beats down their wages, a hireling standing army, unrecognized by our laws, is established to shoot them down, and they are rapidly degenerating into European conditions. The fruits of the toil of millions are boldly stolen to build up colossal fortunes for a few, unprecedented in the history of mankind; and the possessors of these in turn, despise the republic and endanger liberty. From the same prolific womb of governmental injustice we breed the two great classes—tramps and millionaires.[1]

Twenty years later Woodrow Wilson translated the mood of that indictment into explicit terms by raising the question of whether America had remained faithful to its purpose and giving a negative answer:

> . . . are we preserving freedom in this land of ours, the hope of all the earth?
> Have we, inheritors of this continent and of the

[1] Quoted after Morison and Commager: op. cit., II, 241.

ideals to which the fathers consecrated it,—have we maintained them, realizing them, as each generation must, anew? Are we, in the consciousness that the life of man is pledged to higher levels here than elsewhere, striving still to bear aloft the standards of liberty and hope, or, disillusioned and defeated, are we feeling the disgrace of having had a free field in which to do new things and of not having done them?

The answer must be, I am sure, that we have been in a fair way of failure,—tragic failure. And we stand in danger of utter failure yet except we fulfil speedily the determination we have reached, to deal with the new and subtle tyrannies according to their deserts.[2] . . . America is not a place of which it can be said, as it used to be, that a man may choose his own calling and pursue it just as far as his abilities enable him to pursue it; because to-day, if he enters certain fields, there are organizations which will use means against him that will prevent his building up a business which they do not want to have built up; organizations that will see to it that the ground is cut from under him and the markets shut against him. . . .

And this is the country which has lifted to the admiration of the world its ideals of absolutely free opportunity, where no man is supposed to be under any limitation except the limitation of his character and of his mind; where there is supposed to be no distinction of class, no distinction of blood, no distinction of social status, but where men win or lose on their merits.

I lay it very close to my conscience as a public man whether we can any longer stand at our doors and

[2] Woodrow Wilson: *The New Freedom* (New York and Garden City: Doubleday, Page and Co.; 1913), pp. 284-5.

welcome all newcomers upon those terms. American industry is not free, as once it was free; American enterprise is not free; the man with only a little capital is finding it harder to get into the field, more and more impossible to compete with the big fellow. Why? Because the laws of this country do not prevent the strong from crushing the weak. That is the reason, and because the strong have crushed the weak the strong dominate the industry and the economic life of this country.[3]

Theodore Roosevelt gave that indictment a positive turn by proclaiming that

. . . our task as Americans is to strive for social and industrial justice, achieved through the genuine rule of the people. This is our end, our purpose. . . .

We, here in America, hold in our hands the hope of the world, the fate of the coming years; and shame and disgrace will be ours if in our eyes the light of high resolve is dimmed, if we trail in the dust the golden hopes of men. If on this new continent we merely build another country of great but unjustly divided material prosperity, we shall have done nothing; and we shall do as little if we merely set the greed of envy against the greed of arrogance, and thereby destroy the material well-being of all of us. To turn this government either into government by a plutocracy or government by a mob would be to repeat on a large scale the lamentable failures of the world that is dead.[4]

If the state of the individual in America was as Wilson

[3] Ibid., pp. 14,15.
[4] *Collected Works* (New York: Charles Scribner's Sons; 1926), XVII, 170-1.

described it and if the American purpose had been correctly defined by Theodore Roosevelt, how could that purpose of providing the individual with equal opportunity in freedom be redeemed? There was no going back to the natural equality of the frontier. That very equality, giving the strong, the ruthless, the power-hungry, the clever the same chance as everybody else and, hence, a better chance, engendered its denial. The stratified inequality of the America of 1912 was the upshot of the equality of the American purpose. Equality of competition, by dint of the natural inequality of the competitors, had destroyed competition itself, and freedom of competition had become for the monopolies freedom from competition. As Henry D. Lloyd, the author of *Wealth versus Commonwealth,* put it: "Liberty produces wealth, and wealth destroys liberty." The experience of an age that had seen equality destroyed in consequence of its consistent application was fundamentally different from Pinckney's and Lincoln's experience of actual equality. "There is one great basic fact," to quote Wilson again,

> which underlies all the questions that are discussed on the political platform at the present moment. That singular fact is that nothing is done in this country as it was done twenty years ago.
>
> We are in the presence of a new organization of society. Our life has broken away from the past. The life of America is not the life that it was twenty years ago; it is not the life that it was ten years ago. We have changed our economic conditions, absolutely, from top to bottom; and, with our economic society, the organization of our life. The old political formulas do not fit the present problems; they read now like documents taken out of a forgotten age. . . . We are facing the necessity of fitting a new social organi-

zation, as we did once fit the old organization, to the happiness and prosperity of the great body of citizens; for we are conscious that the new order of society has not been made to fit and provide the convenience or prosperity of the average man. The life of the nation has grown infinitely varied. It does not centre now upon questions of governmental structure or of the distribution of governmental powers. It centres upon questions of the very structure and operation of society itself, of which government is only the instrument. Our development has run so fast and so far along the lines sketched in the earlier day of constitutional definition, has so crossed and interlaced those lines, has piled upon them such novel structures of trust and combination, has elaborated within them a life so manifold, so full of forces which transcend the boundaries of the country itself and fill the eyes of the world, that a new nation seems to have been created which the old formulas do not fit or afford a vital interpretation of.

We have come upon a very different age from any that preceded us. We have come upon an age when we do not do business in the way in which we used to do business,—when we do not carry on any of the operations of manufacture, sale, transportation, or communication as men used to carry them on. There is a sense in which in our day the individual has been submerged. In most parts of our country men work, not for themselves, not as partners in the old way in which they used to work, but generally as employees, —in a higher or lower grade,—of corporations. There was a time when corporations played a very minor part in our business affairs, but now they play the chief part, and most men are the servants of corporations.

. . . Your individuality is swallowed up in the individuality and purpose of a great organization.

It is true that, while most men are thus submerged in the corporation, a few, a very few, are exalted to a power which as individuals they could never have wielded. Through the great organizations of which they are the heads, a few are enabled to play a part unprecedented by anything in history in the control of the business operations of the country and in the determination of the happiness of great numbers of people.

Yesterday, and ever since history began, men were related to one another as individuals. To be sure there were the family, the Church, and the State, institutions which associated men in certain wide circles of relationship. But in the ordinary concerns of life, in the ordinary work, in the daily round, men dealt freely and directly with one another. To-day, the everyday relationships of men are largely with great impersonal concerns, with organizations, not with other individual men.

Now this is nothing short of a new social age, a new era of human relationships, a new stage-setting for the drama of life.[5]

Yet fifteen years later, in the heyday of Prohibition and prosperity, a foreigner took this picture of America with him:

A European returns from America with the memory, no doubt, of a thousand kindnesses received and a thousand friends made, but also, if he is honest, with the feeling, perhaps defined, perhaps undefined, that here is a Continent gone wrong.

[5] Loc. cit., pp. 3-7.

76

A hundred and fifty years ago the fathers of the American Commonwealth set out to build a nation upon the two foundations of human liberty and human equality. It is impossible not to feel to-day that the American is free just where he should be equal, and equal just where he should be free. By the argument of liberty he defends a capitalism which has placed in the hands of wealth power, monstrous and irresponsible, and, by that of equality and a jumble of bunkum metaphysics about One Man One Vote and the State the Expression of the Citizen's Real Will, a series of insolent interferences with the ordinary activities of ordinary men, which, in any other country and in any other age, would have been condemned as impossible and inartistic, if they had been created, for the purpose of romance, by the imagination of a professional satirist. He has allowed a tenth-rate, sectarian, police-regulation to be imported into his Constitution. Whatever eccentricities the law has forgotten to prohibit, are prohibited by a public opinion, more tyrannous even than the law.[6]

## 7. *The Intervention of Government*

Society, left to its own devices in accordance with the American purpose, had through the interplay of its own autonomous forces given the lie to that purpose. American society, fashioned in the image of the American purpose of equal opportunity and freedom of competition with a minimum of political control, had ended by abrogating both equal opportunity and freedom of competition. What fatal flaw in the original conception of the Ameri-

[6] Christopher Hollis: *The American Heresy* (London: Sheed and Ward; 1927), p. 7.

can purpose had brought about so paradoxical a result? It was found in the founders' confidence in society and mistrust of government. Society was expected, if left to develop according to its own inner laws, to perpetuate the equality with which it started. Government was dreaded as the political organization *par excellence,* the institutionalization of the domination of man by man—that is, of inequality and lack of freedom.

The falsity of that simple juxtaposition of government as the institutionalized denial of equality in freedom and society as equality's natural abode was experienced in the radical transformation that American society had undergone since the Civil War. That experience led the movements of social reform to a radical departure from the traditional conception of the proper relationship between government and society. Society had betrayed the American purpose by destroying equality and curtailing freedom. The evils of society were a part of the American experience; they could be seen in the dispossessed farmers trekking back east, in the misery of the workingman, in laboring women and children, in the degradation of poverty, in the shame of the cities. By contrast, the evil of government as the main threat to individual equality and freedom was on the American scene mainly speculative, a part of the American philosophic tradition from which derives the structure of American government. What the American experience showed to be wrong with government was not that it was strong enough to impair the individual's equality and freedom, but that it was weak enough to allow an oligarchy of wealth, the proved enemy of equality in freedom, to use government as an instrument of its own. It was the alliance between weak government and unchecked wealth which was responsible for the apparent failure of the American purpose.

*The Intervention of Government*

This being so, the cure was as obvious as was the cause of the disease. All movements of social reform were agreed upon the need for a government strong enough to restore the American purpose of equality in freedom by limiting the political and economic power of wealth. The intervention of the government took five different directions relevant to the subject of our discussion: protection of the human resources of the nation in the form of social legislation; restoration and protection of the natural resources of the nation in the form of reclamation and conservation; regulation and control of concentrations of economic power; use of credit and taxation for social purposes; active participation in economic activity.

While these types of government intervention, especially the first and the last, were fully developed only in the last decade of the period under discussion—that is, by the New Deal—as intellectual and political desiderata they dominated the scene from the beginning of the period. In retrospect, the New Deal appears to have added to the techniques of social reform and to its quantitative realization rather than to its intellectual conception. That conception was consummated in Wilson's political thought, which brought forth with unexcelled lucidity the necessary relationship between the restoration of the American purpose and social reform. Wilson, in turn, was not so much the creator of new ideas and the inventor of new devices as the mouthpiece of popular aspirations and the codifier of legislative proposals that for decades had been debated and enacted throughout the country.

The great Federal reform legislation of Wilson and the two Roosevelts is in good measure the codification and elaboration of state laws, enacted particularly in the Middle West and West. The movements of social reform were truly grass-roots movements, especially in their agrarian

79

manifestations; they grew not primarily from humanitarian impulses or philosophic postulates but from the experience of the man in the street and, more especially, in the fields who had been deprived of what he considered to be the essence of America and was resolved to recover it. The reports of the moral fervor of these popular movements and the moral tone and arguments of their manifestos and of the speeches of leaders such as Bryan, the two Roosevelts, and Wilson make it clear that we are here in the presence of still another phase of that permanent American revolution which, like previous phases, sought to restore the American purpose of equality in freedom.

Yet this phase differed from all its predecessors in that it could escape the negation of equality and freedom in the form of political domination, but had to come to terms with it. Toward the close of the nineteenth century, Americans were for the first time unable to turn their backs on the problem of power and go into the wilderness which is supposed to know nothing of it. For the first time they were obliged to turn around and face it not in the narrow confines of constitutional arrangements or professional politics, but as a ubiquitous social fact. The nature of their response was, in view of the circumstances, a foregone conclusion. There was only one power that could hope to match the private power of wealth and to keep in check the private government of wealth, and that was the public power, the Federal government.

Yet by vesting in the Federal government powers that were supposed to be superior to the power of wealth and by charging it with functions that were supposed to be more comprehensive than those of any private organization, the United States abandoned one main tenet of the American political tradition and entangled itself in an intellectual and political dilemma. The American tradition assumes, and the American Constitution and the American political system are predicated upon the assumption, that the main enemy of individual equality and freedom is the public power, the government, which is the most conspicuous and potentially the strongest organization dedicated to the domination of man by man. Since it did not occur to the political philosophers of the eighteenth and nineteenth centuries that society might generate concentrations of private power denying equality in freedom, all that appeared to be needed was to reduce the powers of the government to a minimum and guard against abuses of power through constitutional safeguards. The spontaneous emergence of concentrations of private power, as destructive of equality in freedom as the public power was expected to be, found the United States intellectually and politically unprepared. It brought the nation face to face with a dilemma which is inherent in all political situations and indeed in the human situation itself, but which was novel to the American experience.

America could expect to cope with the evil of private power only by unchaining what appeared to be the lesser evil of public power. Now, for the first time in the American experience, it became obvious that it was impossible to escape the evil of power altogether. America, like all other nations and, for that matter, like all men, had to choose between two evils, and inescapably it chose the evil of public power to restrain, control, compete with, and destroy the evil of private power.

How did the American purpose of equality in freedom emerge from this contest between public and private power? The outcome was of course obscured by the involvement of the United States in the Second World War, but even so it is clear that the American purpose emerged victorious as a moral force moving men to action, while its achievement remained impaired by an organized society whose stratification was determined by the possession of wealth. The movements of social reform failed most spectacularly in their attack on concentrations of wealth *per se*. If economic bigness is a curse, we still live under it. The same holds true of the political influence of wealth. Reform legislation forced the concentrations of wealth to regroup themselves and refashion their legal arrangements; it did not touch the substance of their social and political power. However, it affected the exercise of that power in four significant respects: through regulation and control, through taxation, through government competition, especially in the fields of credit and utilities, and through labor legislation. These measures limited the freedom of action of the concentrations of wealth. Prevented from proceeding in the traditional ways, they had to develop new outlets for their social and political power. The social and political power of wealth was tamed and civilized, but not abolished. The government took charge of the rules of the game, revising, strengthening, and enforcing them; yet, as it were, the New York Yankees were still playing the rest of the league and winning.

These measures contributed to the restoration of the American purpose in that they blunted the sharp edges of economic inequality and improved the chances for successful competition. A more fundamental contribution was made by the measures of the Federal government (to which certain facets of labor legislation belong) which seek to preserve and develop the human and material resources of the nation. By discharging successfully this newly assumed responsibility, the government made use of the three elements of American society which in the main provide the reason why the purpose of America emerged victorious from its first great crisis: the natural interior frontier; the interior frontier as social artifact; the equality and libertarian dynamics of American society.

## 8. *The Restoration of Vertical Mobility*

When the territorial—that is, the exterior—frontier was closed in 1890 (according to the Bureau of the Census), it was closed only in the specific sense of the disappearance of free land. But it was by no means closed in the sense of Americans having no place to go. While Americans could no longer go forward into the unknown and unappropriated, they could still go backward into the unexplored and unexploited. Empty spaces had been apportioned but not yet filled. The wilderness had been appropriated but not yet conquered; it had been left behind. Those who had reached the territorial frontier and had not found what they were looking for would simply turn around and look for it in back of that frontier. As William Allen White said of the farmers who in the early nineties headed back east with "In God we trusted, in Kansas we busted" written on their wagons: "They had such high hopes when they went out there; they are so desolate now—no, not now, for now they are in the land of corn and honey. They have come out of the wilderness, back to the land of promise."[1]

The trenchant irony of that last phrase reveals a fundamental truth about the lasting opportunity to achieve the American purpose. The westward movement could be reversed without loss of purpose. Horizontal mobility could move backward as well as forward and still perform its function for American society. The territorial frontier, far from being nothing more than the quantitative availability of free land, was but a spectacular instance of a general quality of American society: equal opportunity in freedom. The dispossessed farmer of the nineties was no more condemned to stay where he was, waiting for better

[1] Quoted after Morison and Commager: loc. cit., II, 238.

times, than was the Okie of the thirties or the unemployed of the fifties. The abundance and variety of natural resources and the economic and social tasks waiting to be performed provided opportunities for the venturesome and the able which were commensurate with, and in terms of material rewards superior to, those the territorial frontier had offered.

The territorial frontier of the seventeenth, eighteenth, and nineteenth centuries was replaced by the interior frontier of resources to be exploited and tasks to be performed. As a matter of fact, the opening of that interior frontier coincided with territorial expansion. For while the pioneers moved west, the more enterprising of those who stayed behind or had just arrived from Europe sought and found opportunities within the territory already settled. On the political plan, the destruction of the aristocratically stratified society of the Federalist period by the Jacksonian revolution is the most spectacular instance of the dynamism of the interior frontier before the territorial one was closed.

Superimposed upon that natural frontier is still another one: the frontier as social artifact. Not only were the spaces behind the territorial frontier underdeveloped and ready to be developed, but American society had also established social contrivances conducive to such development by those able and willing to undertake it. Three such artifacts are important for our discussion: the equalitarian mobility inherent in wealth; functional stratification combined with personal mobility; and competition provided by technological innovation.

We have pointed before to the central function that the possession of wealth performs for American society as the dominant standard of social distinction. While the unequal distribution of wealth and the unequal distribution of social and political power resulting therefrom were responsible for the crisis of the American purpose, a peculiar quality of wealth, what might be called its equalitarian quality, has worked as an antidote to that crisis. Wealth in the form of money changing hands in a capitalistic system, is accessible to all who are able and willing to take advantage of the rules of capitalistic distribution. It is not attached to, nor is it withheld from, a particular class of persons. Money is no respecter of persons; before it, as it were, all men are equal. As the economic crisis of the period and especially the crisis of the 1930's demonstrated, today's millionaire may be a pauper tomorrow, and today's millionaire may have been a penniless immigrant only yesterday. Thus, the rise and fall of monetary fortunes carries within itself an element of hope and even of expectation which stimulates effort. As anybody's son could become President, so he might become a millionaire, and many knew those who had. This empirical evidence of the possibility of its achievement sustained faith in the reality of the American purpose and stimulated the effort to achieve it.

The social stratification derived from the possession of wealth shows in America a peculiarity that strengthens the mobility inherent in monetary wealth itself: the combination of functional stratification with personal mobility. The big corporation is a force of great social and political power, and it is so in relative permanence. It may dominate the economic and political life of a municipality or of a state and may influence policies of the Federal government through the control of members of Congress and of executive officials and administrative agencies.

Yet while the social and political functions of the corporation are fixed in relative permanence—that is, while it performs these functions as long as its relative power allows it to perform them—the persons exercising these functions are by and large not predetermined in any way.

It is true that relatives of top officials and owners of great wealth have in certain circumstances a special chance to rise to the top. However, by and large what we found to be true of the acquisition of wealth and of political power is also true of the selection of the officials of corporations: the principle of vertical mobility applies. As anybody's son has a chance to become President of the United States or a millionaire, so he has a chance to become president of a great corporation.

According to a summary of the studies in this field, the percentage of workers' sons who have risen to executive positions in industry has actually increased during the last generation. In the 1870's, of 303 top executives in the largest textile, steel, and railroad companies 25 per cent were the sons of farmers and 8 per cent the sons of workers. In 1952, of 8,300 executives of the largest enterprises 15 per cent were the sons of workers. And while the share of the sons of the poor in the very top positions has slightly declined in recent years, the share of the wealthy has declined more sharply.[2]

It is this divorcement of the person performing the function from the institutionalized function itself which creates within a system of stratified power an equal opportunity for all to exercise that power. The concentrations of economic power have given America its permanent political and economic masters, yet the purpose of America gives all Americans an approximately equal chance to rise to that mastery. While this is not equality in freedom, it is still equality in freedom impaired.

Not only is the exercise of corporate power determined by the vertical mobility of the American system, but cor-

[2] Clyde Kluckhohn: "Have There Been Discernable Shifts in American Values During the Past Generation?" in *The American Style,* ed. Elting E. Morison (New York: Harper & Bros.; 1956), pp. 155 ff.

porate power itself is, at least in the long run, exposed to competition from within the corporate world. This is the result of technological innovation, which continuously creates new centers of corporate power competing with, and ultimately replacing, old ones. A century ago certain railroads controlled the political and economic life of whole states and certain segments of Federal legislation; no railroad holds such power today. Instead, the oil interests have risen in the scales of corporate power, as have the industries that provide the Federal government with the instruments of defense. And the relative power of the different defense industries rises and falls, and does so rather rapidly, with changes in weapons technology.

This technological competition induces yet another element of vertical mobility. Whoever is able to put a technological innovation to economic use has a chance to compete with the existing centers of corporate power for economic and political advantage. The competition among individuals as the dominant aspect of American economic life was ended by concentrations of corporate wealth, and the competition among corporate entities of the same productive type, at least on the basis of the quality and price of the product, was superseded by monopolistic or oligopolistic control. Price and quality competition now takes the form of the competition of different technologies, embedded in different corporate empires. This is indeed a far cry from the freedom of competition of the American purpose, yet it is at least the fragment of a man-made new frontier, a partial redemption from the denial of the American purpose by a monopolistic and oligopolistic economic system.

However, the three frontiers that have determined the development of American society—the territorial, the natural, and the frontier as social artifact—do not by themselves explain that development. Frontiers provide the objective opportunities for social achievement; they do not provide the achievement itself. Other societies have had frontiers to conquer and have carried on as though they did not exist. Why is it that Americans have never ceased looking for them, discovering them, and developing their potentialities? The answer to that question leads us beyond rational explanation into the mysterious realm of the spirit and character of a nation. How do we explain the fact that on March 5, 1959, thirty-seven Detroiters, by all appearances not driven by economic necessity, migrated to Alaska, re-enacting, as it were, almost three and a half centuries later, the first migration of 1620? How do we explain that these two events are linked by an unbroken tradition of collective restlessness, a collective seeking out of the new, the challenging, the better, of a life of equality in freedom?

It was by way of the two new frontiers and of the equalitarian and libertarian ethos and dynamics of American society that the movements of social reform did their work of restoration. They tried to make the new frontiers accessible to the American masses, and they gave an example of faith in action. The demonstration of that faith banished the fatalism of despair and provided the aimless energies of the people with a goal. This goal was identical with the American purpose and, hence, could command the loyalties of the people. The movements of social reform radically transformed the relationships between government and society and imposed upon the concentrations of wealth social and political responsibilities of considerable magnitude. These tangible achievements have tended to overshadow the profound and lasting influence the movements of social reform have had upon the ethos and the dynamics of America. By proving to the people in deeds that the purpose of America was not dead but only stunned and ready to be revived, by demonstrating through action that something could be done and that "the only thing we have to fear is fear itself," by providing opportunities for action, by reviving the American revolution—to use John Adams's phrase—"in the minds of the people," these movements destroyed in fact the ground for that alienation from the American purpose which, as we have seen, is an endemic threat to America.

Thus, by the time the Second World War broke out, drawing America step by step into its vortex, America had undergone three novel and lasting experiences. It had come face to face with the problem of power, not as a compartmentalized thing to be carefully confined and neatly balanced, but as a ubiquitous thing that could be neither confined nor evaded. It had come face to face with the unchecked social and political power of wealth and had experienced the moral and physical degradation that comes in the wake of such unchecked power. These experiences cast a doubt not only upon the practical feasibility of the American purpose but also upon its philosophic and moral validity. Finally, it saw the American purpose emerge from this crisis stunned and mutilated but alive, opening within a complex network of social, economic, and political relationships new opportunities for which Americans could compete if not in complete freedom, at least on fairly equal terms. America had lost her innocence about her purpose, but she had not lost enough of it to perceive clearly and completely the nature of the social forces that stand in the way of its achievement. The first domestic crisis of the American purpose, caused by the economic transformation of American society and interrupted by the Second World War, blends into the second crisis, which is predominantly political in nature and in the midst of which we find ourselves today.

# B. *Impairment of Mobility Abroad*

## 1. *Territorial Expansion*

The closing of the frontier had a symbolic rather than a real significance for horizontal mobility within the United States; for, as we have seen, the two interior frontiers provided unexhausted opportunities for movement. The appropriation of the last piece of land east of the Pacific had, however, an enormous impact upon the horizontal mobility of the United States beyond its borders. The westward and southward expansion of the United States, step by step from the Atlantic coast to the Gulf of Mexico and the Pacific, had a kind of inner logic and natural necessity that underlay the different versions of manifest destiny. Expansion into Cuba and Canada could similarly be justified on plausible grounds of geographic contiguity, strategic interests, or ethnic and cultural affinity. Thus, throughout the nineteenth century, successive generations of Americans looked longingly upon these two pieces of real estate which seemed to fall naturally within the sweep of manifest destiny. Only the unwillingness of the population of Canada to be absorbed and the power of Great Britain, on the one hand, and the relative remoteness of Cuba and the character of its population, on the other, stood in the way of a destiny otherwise manifest. Southward expansion, while geographically as "natural" as the westward one and advocated as such, was impractical because it would have taxed the capacity of the nation to absorb large ethnically, culturally, and linguistically alien populations.

The closing of the frontier, then, posed for the United States what William Graham Sumner called during the election campaign of 1900 "the predominant issue." Had the United States reached the natural limits of its territorial expansion at the Pacific coast or should it expand beyond the limits of the North American continent? The Spanish-American War raised that issue in an acute form, and its aftermath gave an answer that is familiar. It must, however, be pointed out that it was a mere accident of history that the issue was thus raised and that this particular answer was given. The United States would have had to come to terms with the issue even if the Spanish-American War had not occurred, and actually it has been coming to terms with it ever since.

The occupation of the westernmost limits of the continent confronted the United States with the choice between standing still and going ahead, and in that choice is enclosed a decision about the purpose of America. The issue to be decided by that choice was not the acquisition of territory *per se*. For two and a half centuries, since James I issued the charter to the Plymouth Company in 1620, Americans had not ceased to acquire territory, but it had been empty territory or territory so sparsely settled that the native population presented no serious impediment to American settlement. Thus, the annexation of a string of Pacific islands in the 1850's and 1860's had created no issue.

The settlers of these empty spaces could hope to achieve America's purpose: equality in freedom. Yet expansion beyond these empty spaces into populated territories was bound to put into question the achievement of the American purpose by raising the issue of whether and how equality in freedom could be established among conquered populations and between them and the American conqueror. In other words, was this new kind of expansion compatible with the American purpose? This was the issue which was raised in 1898 by the annexation of Hawaii, the Philippines, and Puerto Rico, and by the establishment of a protectorate over Cuba. Of those who answered that question in the negative, nobody saw more clearly the relation between "the predominant issue" and the American purpose than William Graham Sumner: "The question at stake is nothing less than the integrity of this state in its most essential elements."[1] He based his position on two arguments, one taken from the traditional conception of the American purpose, the other pointing to the practical consequences of its violation. The argument from tradition is a restatement of Pinckney's position:

This confederated state of ours was never planned for indefinite expansion or for an imperial policy. We boast of it a great deal, but we must know that its advantages are won at the cost of limitations, as is the case with most things in this world. The fathers of the Republic planned a confederation of free and peaceful industrial commonwealths, shielded by their geographical position from the jealousies, rivalries, and traditional policies of the Old World and bringing all the resources of civilization to bear for the domestic happiness of the population only. They meant to have no grand statecraft or "high politics," no "balance of power" or "reasons of state," which had cost the human race so much. They meant to offer no field for what Benjamin Franklin called the "pest of glory." It is the limitation of this scheme of

[1] William Graham Sumner: "The Conquest of the United States by Spain," in *War and Other Essays* (New Haven: Yale University Press; 1919), p. 314.

the state that the state created under it must forego a great number of the grand functions of European states; especially that it contains no methods and apparatus of conquest, extension, domination, and imperialism. The plan of the fathers would have no controlling authority for us if it had been proved by experience that that plan was narrow, inadequate, and mistaken. Are we prepared to vote that it has proved so? For our territorial extension has reached limits which are complete for all purposes and leave no necessity for "rectification of boundaries.[2]

By conquering subject peoples, the United States betrays its distinctive purpose and becomes just another imperialistic nation like Spain. By betraying its own purpose, it adopts the purpose of Spain.

During the last year the public has been familiarized with descriptions of Spain and of Spanish methods of doing things until the name of Spain has become a symbol for a certain well-defined set of notions and policies. On the other hand, the name of the United States has always been, for all of us, a symbol for a state of things, a set of ideas and traditions, a group of views about social and political affairs. Spain was the first, for a long time the greatest, of the modern imperialistic states. The United States, by its historical origin, its traditions, and its principles, is the chief representative of the revolt and reaction against that kind of a state. I intend to show that, by the line of action now proposed to us, which we call expansion and imperialism, we are throwing away some of the most important elements of the American symbol and are adopting some of the most

[2] Sumner: "The Fallacy of Territorial Expansion," ibid., pp. 291-2.

important elements of the Spanish symbol. We have beaten Spain in a military conflict, but we are submitting to be conquered by her on the field of ideas and policies.[3]

This departure from the American purpose brings the nation face to face with an inescapable dilemma.

The Americans have been committed from the outset to the doctrine that all men are equal. We have elevated it into an absolute doctrine as a part of the theory of our social and political fabric. It has always been a domestic dogma in spite of its absolute form, and as a domestic dogma it has always stood in glaring contradiction to the facts about Indians and negroes and to our legislation about Chinamen. In its absolute form it must, of course, apply to Kanakas, Malays, Tagals, and Chinese just as much as to Yankees, Germans, and Irish. It is an astonishing event that we have lived to see American arms carry this domestic dogma out where it must be tested in its application to uncivilized and half-civilized peoples. At the first touch of the test we throw the doctrine away and adopt the Spanish doctrine. We are told by all the imperialists that these people are not fit for liberty and self-government; that it is rebellion for them to resist our beneficence; that we must send fleets and armies to kill them if they do it; that we must devise a government for them and administer it ourselves; that we may buy them or sell them as we please, and dispose of their "trade" for our own advantage. What is that but the policy of Spain to her dependencies? What can we expect as a conse-

[3] Sumner: "The Conquest of the United States by Spain," ibid., p. 299.

94

quence of it? Nothing but that it will bring us where Spain is now.

But then, if it is not right for us to hold these islands as dependencies, you may ask me whether I think that we ought to take them into our Union, at least some of them, and let them help to govern us. Certainly not. If *that* question is raised, then the question whether they are, in our judgment, fit for self-government or not is in order. . . .

It follows, then, that it is unwisdom to take into a State like this any foreign element which is not congenial to it. Any such element will act as a solvent upon it. Consequently we are brought by our new conquests face to face with this dilemma: we must either hold them as inferior possessions, to be ruled and exploited by us after the fashion of the old colonial system, or we must take them in on an equality with ourselves, where they will help to govern us and to corrupt a political system which they do not understand and in which they cannot participate. From that dilemma there is no escape except to give them independence and to let them work out their own salvation or go without it.[4]

The predominant issue that the new expansion raised for the American purpose, then, was really "how to let go of what we had seized."[5] Sumner was unqualifiedly pessimistic about the prospect.

I do not believe that, if the United States undertakes to govern the [Philippine] islands, it will ever give them up except to superior force. . . .[6]

[4] Ibid., pp. 309-12.
[5] Ibid., p. 337.
[6] Ibid., p. 301.

It is as safe as any political prediction can be that we shall never again give up the jurisdiction over Cuba.[7]

How could Sumner have been so right in his analysis of the problem and so wrong in his prognosis? The answer must be found in the same underestimation of the dynamic strength of the American purpose which vitiated the prophecies of despair brought forth by the domestic crisis of the 1930's. The United States had hardly acquired its colonial empire when it searched for ways to disembarrass itself of it, and within a few decades the empire had been given up. The acquisition of that empire was indeed, in the words of Professor Bemis, "the great aberration," a historic incident that had no organic connection with the purpose and interests of America. As Sumner put it:

Upon a positive analysis, therefore, the case of recent expansion is shown to be different from all the earlier cases which are cited to justify it precisely in the most essential fact, the interest of the American people as the efficient motive.[8]

What Talleyrand said in 1808 to Tsar Alexander with regard to the territorial expansion of France applies here: "The Rhine, the Alps, and the Pyrénées are the conquests of France; the rest, of the Emperor; they mean nothing to France." "Oregon, California, Texas," one might say, overstating the case somewhat, "are the conquests of America; the Philippines, Puerto Rico, and Cuba are the conquests of the President; they mean nothing to America."

How tenuous the connection was between these conquests and what the American people regarded as their

[7] Sumner: "The Predominant Issue," ibid., p. 343.
[8] Ibid., p. 344.

permanent interests is clearly revealed in the hesitant and halfhearted mode of acquisition. This is true even of the acquisition of Hawaii, which otherwise is a case apart; for Hawaii was placed by the Reciprocity Treaty of 1875 definitely within the American sphere of influence and was dominated to an ever increasing extent, very much after the model of the western states, by white settlers using as labor the rapidly disappearing natives and immigrants, especially from the Orient, and these settlers staged in 1893 a revolution that in aspiration and result resembled the Texan revolt of 1836. Yet even here, where territorial expansion had followed in a certain measure the continental pattern and, hence, could easily be construed as a natural extension of the latter, it took the United States five and a half years, from the signing of the treaty of annexation in February 1893 to the actual transfer of sovereignty in August 1898, to complete the process of annexation. These years were dominated by congressional inactivity and presidential hesitation. The new treaty of annexation which McKinley signed in June 1897 was not acted upon by the Senate, and the President felt compelled in March 1898 to urge congressional approval of annexation by a joint resolution requiring only a simple majority. Yet it was the impact of the Spanish-American War which in July of that year moved the majority of Congress to approve the annexation of Hawaii.

What is striking in the annexation of the Philippines is not only the slowness and hesitancy of the process, but also the inconclusiveness of the supporting arguments and the narrowness of senatorial approval. Annexation of the Philippines was not an original war aim of the United States. It was not in order to conquer them that the United States made war on Spain. As Professor Bemis put it:

Before the war there had not been the slightest demand for the acquisition of the Philippine Islands. The average American citizen could not have told you whether Filipinos were Far Eastern aborigines or a species of tropical nuts. The American people had no more interest in the islands than they have today in Madagascar. At the time of Dewey's victory, President McKinley himself had to look them up on the globe; he could not have told their locality, he said, within two thousand miles.[9]

At the end of the war the United States was committed to nothing more than the cession of the island of Luzon. Both the President and the Peace Commissioners were without an objective standard that would have enabled them to decide how much more of the Philippines they should demand. Thus it was that McKinley, according to his famous account, had to fall back on divine intervention in order to decide that since the United States could not give the Philippines back to Spain, since it could not turn them over to a rival power, since it could not leave them to themselves, "there was nothing left for us to do but take them all. . . ." The Senate approved annexation with one vote above the constitutionally required minimum of two thirds and by the casting vote of the Vice-President rejected a resolution promising independence to the Philippines. Yet while the United States annexed without qualification the Philippines, in which it had no concrete interest, at the outset of the war it promised independence to Cuba and kept that promise although both the general geographic conception of manifest destiny and concrete military interests had for almost a century previ-

[9] Samuel Flagg Bemis: *A Diplomatic History of the United States* (New York: Henry Holt and Co.; 1936), p. 469.

ously been recognized to include American control over Cuba!

Rarely, if ever, can a great power have embarked upon a policy of conquest with less conviction, determination, and sense of purpose. For the United States, conquest beyond the limits of the North American continent was from the outset an unavoidable embarrassment rather than the achievement of a national purpose. The United States fell heir to the last American and Asian fragments of the Spanish empire, and there seemed to be no alternative to keeping them for the time being. Once it had acquired what the defeat of Spain had left without a master, the United States undertook not to expand its acquisitions but, in Sumner's trenchant phrase, "to let go of what we have seized." The self-set task of liquidating the American empire almost as soon as it was acquired, while safeguarding the interests of the United States and of the inhabitants of the conquered territories, implies the recognition by the United States itself of the aberration from the American purpose in which transoceanic territorial expansion had involved the nation.

## 2. *The American Mission Abroad*

However, the faltering steps beyond the boundaries of the North American continent and, more particularly, their retraction almost as soon as they were taken have also a positive significance for the purpose of America. We recall that this purpose does not exhaust itself in the achievement of equality in freedom for Americans, but comprises this achievement as a model to be emulated by all mankind. The American purpose was intended not only to bestow the happiness of equality in freedom upon Americans but also to give through the American achievement an example of the happiness that is within the grasp of all men. This promise of universal happiness obviously did not mean that all men could achieve it by simple imitation, but it did mean that no group of men was *a priori* excluded from achieving it and that, as a matter of principle, given favorable circumstances, all men could achieve it. Such circumstances were of two kinds: the objective conditions of existence—that is, empty spaces and natural wealth such as had favored the Americans—and the ability of a people ingenious and partial to innovation to make use of these objective conditions.

From this conception of the American purpose and of its relation to the world at large it was only a step to the acceptance, on the part of America, of the positive obligation to assist less favored peoples, subject to American influence, to achieve the happiness enjoyed by Americans. Thus, the territorial expansion of America, hesitating and embarrassed, beyond the boundaries of the continent at the turn of the century goes hand in hand with the self-confident and vigorous expansion of the American principles and practices of government. In that fashion territorial expansion could be justified as serving the American purpose, and so could its liquidation after that purpose seemed to be achieved. It then appeared that America had not just stumbled upon the Philippines, Cuba, and Puerto Rico without knowing what it was doing, but that these historic accidents became, if they were not from the beginning, instruments through which America used its power to achieve its purpose for the benefits of other peoples. And it relinquished that power when that purpose seemed to have been achieved or when it seemed that that purpose could not, for the time being, be realized. The hyperbolic moralisms with which American expansion has been traditionally justified, then, contain elements not only of subjective sincerity but also of objective truth. The idea of the American mission to the less fortunate peoples of the world is certainly a political ideology, a rationalization and justification of policies that were undertaken for other and primarily selfish reasons. But that idea expresses also a serious commitment to a purpose that is merely the American purpose projected beyond the territorial limits of America and circumscribed only by the reach of American influence.

In view of this relationship between the American purpose and territorial expansion, McKinley's and Theodore Roosevelt's policies toward the former Spanish possessions do not differ materially from Taft's and Wilson's policies toward Haiti, Honduras, Mexico, Nicaragua, Panama, and Santo Domingo. The new tradition of American foreign policy, initiated by the Spanish-American War, remained unbroken from 1898 to 1917. Paradoxically in view of what happened after 1917, the Wilsonian phase, in contrast to McKinley's and Roosevelt's, is marked by a more clearly defined relationship between temporary territorial expansion, on the one hand, and the American purpose and the concrete national interests of the United States, on the other. Intervention for a particular purpose now replaced annexation.

All Wilsonian interventions were responses to threats to American interests—political, military, economic—emanating from one or another of the Central American republics, and the nature and the intensity of the interventions were commensurate with the threat. The measures taken or enforced in the cause of intervention—political and fiscal reform, economic and social improvements, sanitation —sought to provide circumstances conducive to the achievement of at least a certain measure of equality in freedom among the peoples concerned. To refer to the expansionist policies of this period as imperialism, dollar or otherwise, is to completely misunderstand their objective nature. We are at this point not concerned with their moral quality, especially as compared with that of the expansionist policies of other nations. We are concerned here only with their distinctive character and the reason for it. The expansionist policies of the United States were different from those of other nations because these policies were a projection of the American purpose into the world.

The historic significance of the completion of America's continental expansion toward the end of the nineteenth century, which ushers in this phase of American foreign policy, lies in that it presented the United States with three choices, each of which in a different way required a reconsideration of the American purpose. The United States could accept its continental limits both as definitive and as coterminous with the limits of the American purpose and could rely for the latter's continuing achievement upon the availability of the interior frontiers; in other words, it could accept Pinckney's abstentionist and restrictive conception of America. Or the United States could continue its territorial expansion beyond the limits of the North American continent, facing other nations in political rivalries and military contests that, if successful, would force it to reconcile the conquest of subject peoples with its equalitarian and libertarian principles and practices. Finally, the United States could transform the conception of its purpose as a model to be emulated by other nations into an ideal that would liberate other nations and make them happy through American influence and power. Either accompanied by, or divorced from, territorial expansion, the American purpose would thus become the objective of a crusade whose actual limits would be the limits of American influence and power and whose potential limits would be the limits of the globe.

These three choices were implicit in the American purpose from the beginning and in the reality of American power as it developed during the first century of American history. Calhoun, for instance, saw them clearly when he said:

> It has been lately urged in a very respectable quarter that it is the mission of this country to spread civil and religious liberty over all the globe, and especially over this continent—even by force, if necessary. It is a sad delusion. . . . To preserve it [liberty], it is indispensable to adopt a course of moderation and justice toward all other countries; to avoid war whenever it can be avoided; to let those great causes which are now at work, and which by the mere operation of time, will raise our country to an elevation and influence which no country has ever heretofore attained, continue to work. By pursuing such a course, we may succeed in combining greatness and liberty . . . and do more to extend liberty by our example over this continent and the world generally, than would be done by a thousand victories.[1]

The period which started with the Spanish-American War and ended with America's entrance into the First World War saw America turn its back on the first of these choices, the isolationist one, try the second, imperialist one, and then commit itself to the third, crusading one, strictly circumscribed by the limits of American interests and power. At the end of that period the second choice had proved to be a mere historic interlude which was in the process of liquidation and which had not been able to deflect the United States for any length of time from its primary concern with providing domestic conditions favorable to the achievement of the American purpose. That remained true of the third choice as well. In so far as the

[1] *The Works of John C. Calhoun,* ed. by Richard K. Crallé (New York: Appleton and Co., 1854), IV, 416, 420.

United States committed itself to the third choice, it did so either in order to give meaning to the process of liquidation or else in order to protect interests centered in the North American continent. During that period the center of gravity of both Roosevelt's and Wilson's administrations was at home, and the election campaign of 1912 was fought by both men on behalf of the American purpose at home and against Taft's administration, which was accused of being indifferent to it.

### 3. *The Wilsonian Crusade*

The year 1917 constitutes a turning point in the history not only of American foreign policy but of the American purpose as well; for it witnessed the radical and systematic severance of the connection that had in the past tied the American purpose abroad to the territorial home base of American interests and power. No longer simply a model to be emulated by willing foreign nations, the American purpose now was transformed into a formula of universal salvation by which right-thinking nations would voluntarily abide and to which the others—that is, the enemy— must be compelled to submit. Once the enemy was disarmed, the formula would prevail by the inner force of its own rationality.

This transformation of the American purpose was similar to that of 1898 in two respects: it was both a radical and a temporary departure from tradition. By 1920 the crusade for democracy was liquidated. Yet while the departure of 1917 was even more short-lived than the departure of 1898 and left less to be liquidated, it was much more deeply rooted in the ethos of America, and, hence, its influence upon America's consciousness of its purpose was more lasting and profound. As Wilson was more clearly aware of the nature of the American purpose and of its implications than were his predecessors of 1898 and 1901, so does his work show an inner affinity to, and logical coherence with, the core of the American purpose which are absent from the halfhearted and embarrassed forays beyond our continental boundaries of the turn of the century.

Wilson appeared on the national scene as the restorer of the American purpose at home. It was as the most persuasive crusader for that restoration that he was elected in 1912, and he campaigned for re-election in 1916 primarily on the strength of his success in keeping the process of restoration from being interrupted by the First World War. He became the crusader for the American purpose abroad not by his own choice but by dint of circumstances over which he had no control and which left him no choice, just as the role of conqueror was thrust upon Mc-Kinley in 1898 and that of the leader of the non-Communist world upon Truman in 1945. There is deep significance, to which we shall return, in the fact that the American conqueror, crusader, and world leader fulfilled their tasks in spite of their preferences, as instruments rather than molders of history.

Yet history did not foreordain that Wilson should react to the circumstances of 1917 by way of a democratic crusade; it only provided the opportunity for the American reaction to take that form. That American reaction did take that form is due to the Wilsonian conception of the American purpose as the First World War brought it face to face with the friendly or hostile but in any event alien purposes of the great powers of the world. To avoid this confrontation had been, as we have seen, the purpose of America abroad. We wanted to expand without incurring the political and military liabilities that generally go with territorial expansion. When we reached the western limits of the North American continent, we could maintain our apolitical purpose only by standing still. The world had caught up with the fugitives from politics, and the crisis of the American purpose abroad was at hand. In terms of political and military power, that crisis became acute in the Spanish-American War and its aftermath in a rather innocuous way; for at the end of the nineteenth century Spain was hardly a more formidable antagonist than any of its former American colonies. In terms of the ethos of America's awareness of its purpose, the crisis consisted of nothing more than a temporary deviation, and the very experience of that deviation, of the incongruity of an American colonial empire, served to sharpen that awareness and strengthen that ethos. The very process of liquidation became a manifestation of the vitality of the redefined American purpose in action.

The crisis to which the First World War subjected the American purpose was entirely different in character and results. It was different in character because it denied the apolitical assumptions upon which the American purpose abroad was built and confronted the United States with a dilemma that was insoluble within the framework of these assumptions. For almost a century and a half the United States had expanded in the back yard of the European balance of power and behind the screen of the British Navy. Its security was assured when it could keep the ambitions and rivalries of European powers out of the Western Hemisphere and exploit them for the purpose of its own expansion. America had to make a choice, so it appeared, between playing the game of power politics and using the game played by others to help it achieve its purpose, and it had chosen the latter alternative.

Now, overnight, the United States had become one of the chief players in the game, committing its blood and treasure on the other side of the Atlantic in a cause that on the face of it seemed no different from the traditional rivalries of European powers. Had the United States been just a power among others and had its purpose not been to keep aloof from the struggle for power outside the Western Hemisphere, its involvement in the First World War would not have confronted it with an insoluble dilemma. It would have done as other powers do: look to its own advantage and compete with its allies for the spoils of victory. By doing this, it would have departed from its purpose in a more profound, extensive, and irrevocable way than it had done in the aftermath of the Spanish-American War.

Wilson was too deeply committed to the American purpose and too clearly aware of its implications to take so simple a view and to choose so painless a course. In order to remain faithful to the American purpose and lead the United States into the war, he had to view the war in terms of the American purpose. Thus, for Wilson it was not America that was being contaminated by European power politics in Europe and deflected from its purpose; rather it was power politics in Europe and everywhere which was being cleansed of its odium by American participation in the war. The First World War became the instrument through which America would achieve its purpose by bringing equality in freedom to all the world. America, far from betraying its apolitical purpose by participating in the war, would free all the world, as it had freed itself, from the scourge of power politics, the balance of power, armaments races, alliances, spheres of influence, and the rest. The purpose of the war was not only to end war, but to end power politics as well.

Not only was the seeming contradiction between the American purpose and American participation in the war thus eliminated, but American participation in the war also revealed itself as the very consummation of the American purpose. America would remain faithful to its purpose in a negative way by not seeking any advantage, territorial or otherwise, for itself; and it would remain faithful to its purpose in a positive way by not only offering its own equality in freedom as a model to be emulated, but also spilling its blood and spending its treasure to make the world safe for democracy—that is, to enable the world to emulate America. In Wilson's thought and action the democratic crusade was thus a logical extension of the American purpose, adapted to the circumstances of the twentieth century.

Yet by thus avoiding one horn of the dilemma, the contamination of the American purpose with power politics, Wilson found himself hoisted on the other, the impotence of a universal formula of salvation, armed with nothing but its own inner rationality, to alter the conditions of man. For a fleeting historic moment, while all that was required was the pronouncement of the formula without action implementing it, the Wilson of the Fourteen Points was in fact accepted by the world as the apostle of the American purpose; for the world, unaware of the Wilsonian dilemma, expected American power to be at the service of the Wilsonian principles. Yet the world was bound to be disappointed in this expectation. In view of Wilson's choice, there could be no action in support of the American purpose. When Wilson had to protect concrete American interests in the Western Hemisphere, he had joined the power of America to its purpose. Confronted with the world that he had promised to free from the burden of power, he had nothing but words to support the purpose. As Lloyd George put it: "The Americans appeared to assume responsibility for the sole guardianship of the Ten Commandments and for the Sermon on the Mount; yet when it came to a practical question of assistance and responsibility, they absolutely refused to accept it."

There is no gainsaying the grandeur and nobility of the Wilsonian conception of the American purpose, but there is no gainsaying, either, its utter failure in practice. This failure was due to Wilson's attempt to interpret the reality of foreign policy in terms of the American purpose instead of reformulating the American purpose in the light of that reality. Wilson proposed to bridge the gap that has always and of necessity existed between the American achievement and the conditions of other nations by giving the principles of the American achievement universal applicability. In the process he not only widened the gap but also inflicted a crippling blow upon the plausibility of the American purpose.

The very plausibility of the American purpose and the possibility of its achievement were from the beginning dependent upon the objective conditions of American existence which drew out certain qualities of the Americans and rewarded them with success. This unique concatenation of objective and subjective conditions, bringing forth unique results, could plausibly be held up as a model for others to emulate only if conditions elsewhere were not totally different from those prevailing in the United States. Even in conditions not completely dissimilar, American principles could apply only as ideal guideposts, not as blueprints to be imitated to the letter. America was not a paradise to be duplicated elsewhere, it was a paradise open to all who wanted to enter it. It was as a light to attract strangers, not as a flame to be spread throughout the world, that America fulfilled its purpose. The Statue of Liberty is indeed its proper symbol.

This manifestation of the American purpose was thus modified in actual performance. It was pared down, as it were, and revised in the light of the American experience, and its universal claim paled before its achievement for America. Wilson radically reversed the direction of that revision. He lifted the American purpose up to the skies, divorced from the concrete conditions of American existence. It was to mean political salvation for the world and, only through this, for America as well. Wilson was moved, as we have seen, by the depth of his commitment and by America's confrontation with the outside world. He was moved also by the domestic crisis of the American purpose. If the American experiment had been a failure, as he said in 1912, how could it serve as a model for others to emulate? And if America was unable to give equality in freedom to her own children, how could she keep open her door for strangers to share her children's humiliation? In terms of the Wilsonian assumptions, the domestic experience of America had nothing to offer the world. But the principles of America, divorced from that experience, still had. Yet while Wilson could divorce the American purpose from the American experience, he could not divorce it from the experience of the world. From the former he took it, to the latter he sought to apply it. And in this he failed, as he was bound to fail.

## 4. *The Denial*

The United States reacted to Wilson's failure to make the world over in the image of an American purpose, redefined into universality and separated from American interests and power, as it had reacted to the redefinition of the American purpose in terms of colonialism: it liquidated the policies that reflected the new purpose. It liquidated Wilson's crusading purpose in one dramatic act by rejecting the League of Nations in 1920, and it finished liquidating colonialism in a long-drawn-out process consummated only in the mid-thirties. Yet it put an end also to the interventionist policies that Taft and Wilson had pursued in Central America, replacing them in the thirties with Franklin D. Roosevelt's Good Neighbor policy. Thus, the two decades following Wilson's crusade found the United States in full retreat into its continental boundaries. Of the three choices with which the encounter with the outside world confronted it, it now chose without qualification the first: isolationism.

However, the significance of that reversal of choices transcends by far a mere reversal of foreign policies. It bears profoundly and in a negative sense upon the purpose of America. The choice of isolationism carries with it a denial of the American purpose abroad. Isolationism proclaims that America could live and ought to live apart from the outside world, while under the conditions of the twentieth century the outside world inescapably intrudes upon America as America intrudes upon the outside world. Thus, by choosing isolationism, it did not solve the dilemma that was implicit in the confrontation between its purpose and the outside world. It simply exchanged one horn of the dilemma for the other, the one that seemed to be least pointed and, hence, least painful. It acted as though this change of horns did away with the dilemma itself and as though America's confrontation with the world was but the fortuitous effect of Wilson's caprice and not the inescapable result of the objective conditions of American existence. America could act as though nothing had changed since 1890 in its relations with the outside world, but since something had changed, its thinking, attitudes, and actions were profoundly irrelevant to its interests and power in relation to the outside world. Futile gestures, such as the Briand-Kellogg Pact and the Stimson doctrine, took the place of purposeful policies. The America of the twenties and thirties did not return to isolationism as the prodigal son returns to his father's house; this was not a happy home-coming. Rather it returned a frustrated, uncertain, purposeless nation, a nation that had found the easy way out, but darkly aware that it was not the right way, the way worthy of its purpose.

Wilson, and through him America, had been rejected when he endeavored to save the world through the American purpose. Was it, then, not fair for America to reject the world? Yet by rejecting the world America rejected its own better self, its purpose. For, as we have seen, the American purpose was conceived from the very beginning in relation to the world. Since, in view of its domestic crisis, it could no longer serve as a model to be emulated, since, in view of Wilson's rejection, it could no longer serve as a formula to save the world, perhaps the world was right in reacting to it as though it were an illusion, the sham of hypocrites and a figment of the imagination of dreamers. Perhaps the American purpose had failed abroad because it did not deserve to succeed. Perhaps the United States had gone to war not to make the world safe for democracy, but to save the foreign investments of the House of Morgan. Thus, the failure of Wilson brought forth not only a reversal in foreign policy in the form of a return to isolationism but also a crisis of the American purpose abroad in the form of the denial of its validity.

That denial drew strength not only from the debacle of Wilson's foreign policy, but also from the domestic crisis of the American purpose which had been endemic since the 1890's. The oppressiveness of unchecked wealth at the turn of the century, the materialism of the prosperity and the social disintegration of the Prohibition era of the twenties, the economic crisis of the thirties were as potent arguments against the validity of the American purpose as was the failure of Wilson. They all led to one conclusion: the American purpose was at best an illusion and at worst a fraud. America had nothing distinctive to live for and to offer to the world. It was in its virtues and its vices no different from other nations. As a distinguished historian put it in 1933:

> The historical growth of the United States, in short, was not unique; merely in certain particulars and for a brief time, it was different from the European pattern largely because of the processes of settlement. With settlement achieved— . . . class (not sectional!) lines solidified, competitive capitalism converted into monopolistic capitalism under the guidance of the money power, and imperialism the ultimate destiny of the nation—the United States once again was returning to the main stream of European institutional development. Only by a study of the origins and growth of American capitalism and imperialism can we obtain insight into the nature and complexity of the problems confronting us today. And I am prepared to submit that perhaps the chief reason for the absence of this proper understanding was the futile hunt for a unique "American spirit. . . ."[1]

America lost its innocence in relation to itself when society engendered out of its own womb that ubiquitous, crude, and brutal domination of man by man which the Constitution and the American political system were thought to have confined, tamed, and restrained. America lost its innocence in relation to the outside world when power politics proved to be impervious to the American offer of its apolitical purpose. The result of this dual shock was despair at home and abroad.

Only the Second World War would rescue the United

[1] Louis M. Hacker: "Sections—or Classes," in George Rogers Taylor: *The Turner Thesis Concerning the Role of the Frontier in American History* (Boston: D. C. Heath and Co.; 1949), p. 64.

States from this despair. It and its aftermath would answer the question of whether or not the United States had a purpose abroad once and for all in the affirmative. But that answer raised another question: if the United States has a purpose abroad, what is it?

# III

# THE CONTEMPORARY CRISIS ABROAD

## A. *Restoration* (1947-1953)

### 1. *Fascism and the Second World War*

THE SECOND WORLD WAR presented the American purpose with a special challenge and a special triumph. Fascism challenged the American purpose directly, both in what it was and what it sought. It was not only an autocratic form of government, but—in contrast to the Spain of 1898 and the Germany of 1917—it derived its rule from the source that America had thought to be peculiarly its own: the consent of the governed. Fascism laid claim to the democratic title as did America, and even claimed an exclusive title as America once had done; for, pointing to the crisis of the American purpose, it proclaimed the superiority of its own true democracy over the sham democracies of the West. It—and not American democracy—was the "wave of the future," the principle of political and social organization appropriate to the conditions of the twentieth century, as democracy might have been appropriate to the conditions of the nineteenth. As the article on Fascism which appeared over the signature of Mussolini in the *Enciclopedia Italiana* put it:

> Given that the nineteenth century was the century of Socialism, of Liberalism, and of Democracy, it does not necessarily follow that the twentieth century must also be a century of Socialism, Liberalism, and Democracy: political doctrines pass, but humanity remains; and it may rather be expected that this will be a century of authority, a century of the Left, a century of Fascism. For if the nineteenth century was a century of individualism (Liberalism always signifying individualism) it may be expected that this will be the century of collectivism, and hence the century of the State.

That claim could not but disturb America. If it was true, then the American purpose had lost its meaning for America and for the world. And the crisis of the American purpose, coinciding in the thirties with the spectacular successes of Fascism, lent to that claim a measure of plausibility. The self-doubt that the claims and successes of Fascism created in America was counteracted by the popular revulsion against Fascist terror at home and aggression abroad. It was prevented from going very deep by the predominantly pragmatic nature of the Fascist claims; since Fascism derived its claim to superiority primarily from its successes, America had a chance to invalidate these claims by being successful again. Most importantly, the self-doubt engendered by Fascism was neutralized by the—as we shall see—much more profound and plausible challenge with which Marxism confronted America.

Thus, the impact of Fascism upon America's awareness of itself was limited both in depth and in scope. It did not call forth a mass movement or specific domestic and international policies. Rather it added strength to movements and policies that would have come to the fore without its doing. Its impact upon the American scene was supplementary rather than creative. Fascism added another argument to the traditional sympathy of some ethnic minorities for the countries of their origin. It provided some of the native movements of social protest, xenophobia, and bigotry with new arguments, a new impetus, and a model to emulate. It temporarily revived the enfeebled descendants of the Agrarian Revolt and of Populism, which were joined by resentful and bewildered segments of the aristocracy of wealth and of the lower middle class. These groups were opposed to the New Deal; they tended toward authoritarianism in domestic politics and were isolationist in foreign affairs. Yet while Fascism added something of significance, however fleeting, to the domestic scene, its direct contribution to the isolationist movement was negligible; it only provided the foil against which isolationism could reveal its nature. For the isolationism of the thirties was not, as was American Fascism, a superficial growth evoked from marginal social groups by the impact of foreign events. The isolationism of the thirties was rather, as was the McCarthyism of the fifties, a typically American response to a typically American dilemma. That dilemma raised again in a new setting the old question: what is the purpose of America?

From the beginning to 1898, that question in so far as foreign affairs were concerned was answered in terms of isolationism within the limits, at the very most, of the Western Hemisphere. Pinckney and Hamilton agreed on that answer, however much they differed on the means of realizing it. The isolationists of the twenties and thirties found that answer still valid. For them, American intervention in the First World War was at best an isolated foray into the outer world, undertaken for an extraordinary and isolated purpose, one of those abnormalities that fade from the national tradition of thought and action once their purpose has been achieved. At worst, the isolationists regarded that intervention and the attempt to institutionalize it through the League of Nations as Wilson's personal idiosyncrasy used by sectional interests for their selfish purposes, a perversion of the permanent purpose and interests of America. And Franklin D. Roosevelt's intervention in the Second World War, if more openly belligerent until Pearl Harbor settled the issue, was likewise considered to be rooted in the President's whim and in sectional interests rather than in the purpose and the interests of the nation. America, then, appeared to be threatened not by an external enemy, such as Fascism, or by radically changed conditions that had weakened the protection of the oceans, but by the perversity of American rulers who endeavored to drag the people into foreign wars for purposes not their own. Isolationists appeared to themselves as the champions of the purpose of America against its American despoilers.

However, the isolationist claim was false in terms not of philosophy and history, but of contemporary experience. To deny that Fascist imperialism constituted a threat to the American purpose at home and abroad was to deny the evidence of one's senses. Abroad, the Fascist threat to America was not in essence but only in magnitude different from the threat that Imperial Germany had constituted in 1912. It was the threat to the European balance of power, upon which the United States had relied for its safety from the very beginning. The United States has opposed consistently—the War of 1812 is the sole major exception—the European nation—be it Great Britain, France, Germany, or Russia—that appeared to threaten the European balance of power and, through it, the hemispheric predominance and eventually the very independence of the United States. Conversely, the United States has supported whatever European power appeared capable of restoring the balance of power by resisting and defeating the would-be conqueror. In this respect, there is no difference between Hamilton and Jefferson, Wilson and the two Roosevelts.

What was new in the situation that confronted the United States in the late thirties was the combination of a foreign and a domestic threat, the two-pronged attack, emanating from a single source, against the external and internal integrity of the United States. That threat rendered the isolationist response inadequate and potentially self-defeating, and also sharpened through this response the crisis of the American purpose, giving it, as it were, a new twist. It posed the problem of the American purpose in a doubly paradoxical form. The doubt that had beclouded the American purpose abroad since the nineties of the last century now became doubly complex.

The Spanish-American War and its aftermath, like the First World War and its aftermath, confronted America with a simple alternative between two different courses of action. The United States could annex the Philippines, intervene in the First World War, and join the League of Nations, or it could refrain from doing so. The decision was exclusively a matter of its choice on the merits of the case. If the choice was rational, it would be made after the pros and cons had been carefully weighed. If it was not, then the stronger emotions would carry the day. In either event, the decision was rendered in view of one or the other interpretation of the American purpose as the makers of the decision conceived it.

In the late thirties the objective conditions of American existence made it impossible for the decision to be rendered in such simple terms. In 1898, 1917, and 1920 the isolationist interpretation of the American purpose was not only in accord with the literal meaning of that purpose as traditionally conceived, but was also supported by a measure of rational plausibility. In the face of the German and Japanese imperialism of the late thirties, isolationism was an escape from reality but not a rational response to an external threat. Yet the words with which isolationism justified itself and the attitudes it advocated were the words and attitudes through which the American purpose had expressed itself throughout American history. Its authenticity could not plausibly be denied by opposing its interpretation with another one at least equally rooted in the American tradition. That denial could be achieved not by means of the interpretation and resurrection of the past but only through the creation of something that was new in appearance and traditional only in intent.

To the traditional conception of the American purpose, the acquisition of territory beyond the limits of the Western Hemisphere was as alien as military commitments beyond those limits. Yet what in the conditions of the turn of the century could be justly called "the great aberration" and what in the conditions of the First World War and its aftermath could remain an incident without consequences required in the conditions of the late thirties a radical and creative effort at transformation. The isolationist charge of the betrayal of the American purpose, plausible if the American purpose was conceived in terms of its literal tradition, had to be answered by sacrificing the letter for the spirit. America, conscious of its purpose to achieve equality in freedom within its borders as a model for other nations to emulate, had to ask itself whether that purpose, denied and attacked at home and abroad by Fascism, could still be realized with the traditional methods circumscribed by the limits of the Western Hemisphere. The isolationists answered that question in the affirmative, the interventionists in the negative. The European struggle, said William Allen White,

> is not a contest of imperialist nations, struggling for place and power. It is a clash of ideologies. In Germany and in Russia, the state is the master of the citizen. In the democracies of Europe—France and England, Holland and the Scandinavian countries, the citizens control the state. The struggle of two thousand years for human liberty has been wiped out east of the Rhine. . . . These European democracies are carrying our banner, fighting the American battle. These democracies west of the Rhine and north of the Baltic are digging our first-line trenches. . . .[1]

> More than half the world is ruled by men who despise the American idea and have sworn to destroy it. . . . It is not hysterical to insist that democracy and liberty are threatened. . . .[2]

> There was something in the speech [President Roosevelt's of December 29, 1940] more than the mere promise to be the arsenal of democracy. It was also to be the great dynamic power house of the moral purpose of a democracy. We Americans take leadership in a world that is menaced by the counter-revolution of Fascism in its various forms—Naziism, Bolshevism —all one breed of hell cats that gnaw the heart out and take the self-respect and spirit out of the human body and make it a machine that is the servant of a ruthless state.[3]

[1] Quoted after Walter Johnson: *The Battle against Isolation* (Chicago: University of Chicago Press; 1944), pp. 47, 48.

[2] Ibid., p. 101.

[3] Ibid., p. 192.

President Roosevelt, in his annual message to Congress of January 6, 1941, presented a new version of the American purpose in the form of the "four freedoms"—freedom to worship God, freedom of speech, freedom from fear, and freedom from want—combining in a rather vague and abstract formulation the traditional tenet of equality in freedom with the economic aspiration of the New Deal. "If America had no other mission in the world," commented William Allen White, "than to send forth those glowing winged words that carried the new faith for a new world, our country would have justified all the sacrifices its founders have given, all the hope that they have consecrated with their blood and toil."[4]

The Fight for Freedom Committee gave in its programatic statement of April 19, 1941, what appears to be the clearest reformulation of the American purpose in terms both of its tradition and of the novel threat facing it in the Fascist attack at home and abroad.

We must not only meet force with force wherever we can effectively bring our physical power to bear, but we must meet the enemy upon his own chosen battleground, the battleground of mind and spirit.

We must not merely defend today's democracy against the murderous attempt of foreign tyrants to destroy it, but we must make democracy tomorrow far stronger than it is today.

We cannot do this with mere words. We can do it by action.

As a united people we must arise not only to bear arms against the enemy without, but to develop here at home a way of life so just, a brotherhood of man so real, as to give the lie to those who say that democracy is dead—destroyed by the machine age—who say that

[4] Ibid., p. 204.

we must accept the way of the machine and discard the way of free human beings.

We can win this supreme test of democracy at home even as we fight the foreign enemy abroad. We can win on both fronts, if we remember in every waking moment of our lives that we are one people, and that we have one common purpose. Whether we are white or black—Catholic, Protestant or Jew—rich or poor— from the North or South or East or West—we are one. If we waste our strength in internal dissension, we shall surely be conquered, as other nations were conquered who were unable to achieve internal solidarity. But if we stand united, if we consider only our common purpose, we shall conquer, and we shall live as free men in a world released at last from the scourge of slavery.

We must be militantly on guard to protect the right of free workers to organize and bargain collectively; we must protect this right against infringement by government or private enterprise. We must protect the nation as a whole against irresponsible or selfish interests of whatever nature. This is not a matter of legislation but of aroused public opinion.

We must jealously guard our Bill of Rights and militantly oppose all forms of racial or religious discrimination—wherever and in whatever guise they may crop up under the strain of the times and the stimulus of Nazi propaganda.[5]

The paradox that the restoration of the American purpose had to give the appearance of its denial is duplicated by the other paradox that made its denial appear as its defense. Isolationism, by perpetuating the traditional pattern and the literal meaning of the American purpose, de-

[5] Ibid., pp. 224-5.

nied its deeper meaning and stood in the way of its achievement. Worse than that, the logic of circumstances made isolationism the unwitting helpmate of Fascism, the sworn enemy of the American purpose. The Fascist aim of isolating the United States from the designated objects of Fascist conquests in Europe and Asia coincided with the American purpose as conceived by isolationism. Both wanted the United States isolated, Fascism because its success depended upon American isolation, isolationism because it misunderstood the contingent nature of the isolationist tradition. While for the Founding Fathers American isolation had been a goal to be realized by active policies exploiting favorable circumstances, isolationism mistook it, as it were, for a natural attribute of America, one whose beneficial effects depended solely upon American abstention from involvement in the affairs of the world.

European Fascism and American isolationism thus arrived from different points of departure at the same conclusion. The American purpose, as conceived by isolationism, was identical with the foreign policies that Fascism wanted the United States to follow. Considering the existence of a native tradition receptive at least to some of the Fascist arguments, it is little wonder that American isolationism tended to look at the domestic opposition and at the domestic scene in general through glasses that, if not made in Germany and Italy, had been tinted there. Thus, the crisis of the American purpose abroad did more than split the American people into two camps, each denouncing the soundness of the policies advocated by the other as well as denying the authenticity of the national purpose from which the other's policies derived. It also raised a doubt about the American purpose at home.

Here again, it became clear how precarious the American purpose is as the main instrument with which an amorphous society must integrate itself. A controversy about American foreign policy was almost automatically identified with a fundamental disagreement over the American purpose abroad. And that disagreement was easily and almost imperceptibly transformed into a conflict over the American purpose at home, not because of any necessity inherent in the American scene itself but by virtue of the influence that an alien philosophy, hostile to the American purpose, could exert upon the terms in which the American debate was to be waged.

This debate was stilled by the attack upon Pearl Harbor. There is little doubt that even if that attack had not raised the issue of American survival with stark simplicity, the logic of events set in motion by the ever deeper involvement of the United States in the European war would have defeated isolationism. However, the attack upon the main Pacific outpost of the United States, which virtually destroyed its Pacific fleet, and the subsequent attack upon the Philippines left the United States no choice but to wage war far beyond the limits of the Western Hemisphere. In 1917 and from 1939 to 1941 with regard to Europe, the United States had made its own choice by intervening. When Japan attacked Pearl Harbor, it relieved the United States of choosing, and the diehards were reduced to arguing after the event, and without stimulating much more than an academic debate, that the American government, resolved to go to war, had tricked Japan into firing the first shot.

Engaged in a "war for survival," to use Franklin D. Roosevelt's telling phrase, the United States was too deeply involved in the business of survival to have a mind for detecting the nature of its purpose or for weighing the possibility that it might have failed to achieve it. Fascism threatened America at home and abroad, and the outrage of Pearl Harbor appeared to make that threat manifest in an unmistakable fashion. It matters little that the actual connection between the Fascist threat and Pearl Harbor was considerably more tenuous than the man in the street imagined it to be. What is important for our discussion is the fact that popular imagination established this connection and maintained it from the attack on Pearl Harbor to the victory of 1945.

Thus, the war and the victory that ended it were experienced not as strictly military operations and events issuing in a political settlement that would assure to the defeated nations an independent place, however diminished. Rather the war was experienced as a contest between two purposes, a contest whose outcome, in view of the moral superiority of one purpose over the other, was never in doubt. The significance of the outcome could only be found in the extirpation of the evil, of which unconditional surrender was the symbolic expression. Victory was the triumph of the American purpose over its enemies abroad, its reassertion in its most primitive and persuasive form: the annihilation of its enemies. The American purpose had proved its vitality. It had been charged with failure, doubt had been cast upon its very validity, and finally Fascism had challenged it at home and abroad and had made war upon it. Fascism had been wiped off the face of the earth, and the political world lay, as it were, at the feet of America to be remade in the image of its purpose.

## 2. *"The Deadly Hiatus"*

"We can now see," wrote Sir Winston Churchill, "the deadly hiatus which existed between the fading of President Roosevelt's strength and the growth of President Truman's grip of the vast world problem. In this melancholy void one President could not act and the other could not know. Neither the military chiefs nor the State Department received the guidance they required. The former confined themselves to their professional sphere; the latter did not comprehend the issues involved. The indispensible political direction was lacking at the moment when it was most needed. The United States stood on the scene of victory, master of world fortunes, but without a true and coherent design."[1]

The United States took upon itself the task of reconstruction by reviving the Wilsonian conception. Emerging from the war as the most powerful nation on earth, without whose global involvement the political world could not be reconstructed nor its national interests be safeguarded, the United States now faced the Wilsonian dilemma without the benefit of the isolationist escape. On the one hand, it was committed by its tradition to limiting its continuous involvement in international affairs to the Western Hemisphere, whose peaceful and harmonious state in the shadow of American hegemony was contrasted with the rivalries and wars—in short, the power politics— of the rest of the world. On the other hand, with only two power centers left in the world, of which the other happened to be the Soviet Union, the choice of 1920 was no longer open to the United States; that choice would now have meant anarchy in Europe and Asia to be followed by the establishment of order under the auspices of Communism. How, then, could the United States combine its tradition of steering clear of power politics outside the Western Hemisphere with its inevitable involvement in the affairs of the world?

If the United States could no longer isolate itself from a world infected with what it chose to call power politics,

[1] Winston S. Churchill: *The Second World War: Triumph and Tragedy* (Boston: Houghton Mifflin Co.; 1953), pp. 455-6.

it had to decontaminate the world from that infection in order that it might be safe for the United States to become permanently involved with it. Our leaders therefore anticipated and prepared for a post-war world where, in the words of Secretary of State Cordell Hull, "there will no longer be need for spheres of influence, for alliances, for balance of power, or any other of the special arrangements through which, in the unhappy past, the nations strove to safeguard their security or promote their interests."[2] These expectations, voiced in 1943 after Great Britain, the Soviet Union, and the United States had agreed upon the establishment of the United Nations, at a much later date moved President Roosevelt, when on March 1, 1945, in his report to Congress on the Yalta Conference, he declared:

> The Crimean Conference . . . spells the end of the system of unilateral action and exclusive alliances and spheres of influence and balances of power and all the other expedients which have been tried for centuries—and have failed.
>
> We propose to substitute for all these a universal organization in which all peace-loving nations will finally have a chance to join.[3]

When Wilson prepared for the post-war world with similar expectations, his contemporaries could still try to restore the traditional hemispheric limitations of the American purpose by returning to isolationism. They

[2] Report to Congress on Moscow Conference, *The New York Times,* November 19, 1943, p. 4.

[3] *Nothing to Fear: The Selected Addresses of Franklin Delano Roosevelt 1932-1945* (Cambridge: Houghton Mifflin Co.; 1946), p. 453.

simply disavowed him by turning their backs on America's involvement in the affairs of the world. No such disavowal of Roosevelt's and Hull's expectations was necessary, and no such return to isolationism was possible at the end of the Second World War. There was a moment in its immediate aftermath when the United States appeared to yield to the temptation of doing what it had done after the First World War: dismantle the power with which it had won the war and act as though the potential for that power did not exist. This was the moment when it disbanded its armed forces and abruptly canceled Lend-Lease. Yet at the very moment it was thus tempted, the threat of Russian power destroyed the attractiveness of the temptation.

The Soviet Union's interpretation of the Yalta agreements in terms of the expansion of Russian power and not of international co-operation revealed the utopian character of Roosevelt's and Hull's expectations and threatened the European balance of power and, through it, the vital interests of the United States. This made it obvious that for the United States the fruit of victory was to be neither a minimal normalcy without power politics nor the safety of hemispheric isolation. The expansion of Russian power, threatening the security of the United States, ushered in the most formidable of all the crises of the American purpose abroad.

That crisis proceeded in two distinct stages. The first was a period of adaptation, of restoration, of re-creation culminating in the "fifteen weeks" of 1947 during which a whole new system of American foreign policy was devised, derived from a radically new conception of the American purpose abroad. That first stage came to an end with the conclusion of the armistice in the Korean War in 1953. The end was already foreshadowed, as we shall see, in the way the Korean War was conducted. The second stage of the post-war crisis of the American purpose abroad, in which we find ourselves at the moment of this writing, differs sharply both from the first stage and from the preceding crises. It is not a crisis of failure, as was the first stage of the preceding crisis at the turn of the century, nor is it a crisis of doubt, as was the second stage of that crisis in the inter-war period; and it is most certainly not a crisis of restoration and of achievement, as was the first stage of the post-war crisis. Rather it is a crisis of perplexity, of seeming inability to continue the process of adaptation, restoration, and re-creation so auspiciously begun. The novel problems of the post-war world were at first successfully met in one great creative effort, and now the nation, fatigued and almost bored, settles down to meeting the novel problems of today with the remedies of yesterday, transforming yesterday's creative effort into today's routines.

When toward the close of the Second World War the emerging post-war world refused to respond to the Wilsonian expectations of the American leaders, the United States, morally outraged and intellectually stunned, was for some fateful months incapable of translating the shock of disappointment into coherent understanding and consistent action. The political world had again caught up with the American fugitives from politics. They had again stepped beyond the continental limits in order to rid the world of a source of trouble, expecting after the performance of the task to return to the normal peace of the hemisphere. Yet before that task was fully completed the United States found itself already in the throes of new troubles, less tractable than any it had ever faced before and less likely to yield to the drastic remedy of total war. The traditional purpose was now clearly beyond attainment, and no new purpose had yet emerged to take its place. An aimless and inconsistent foreign policy reflected that lack of purpose.

That lack was most clearly revealed and had the most grievous consequences for the United States in Central Europe and in China. In Central Europe the lack of design consisted in the divorcement of military operations from political objectives. Or, to put it more precisely, military operations remained tied to political assumptions that by the spring of 1945 had become obsolete. These assumptions were the Wilsonian expectations of the American leaders. It was on the basis of these assumptions that the West agreed to have its armies stop at a certain line in Central Europe and to pull them back to that line if they should have gone beyond it. And it was on the basis of the same assumptions that the American generals refused to march straight east and take Berlin and followed instead a course of action which was perhaps sounder from a strictly military point of view but proved to be unrewarding politically.

Yet if these assumptions were wrong—as they obviously were—and if the post-war world was still a world of power politics, the balance of power, alliances, and spheres of influence, then these military measures were politically pernicious and laid the ground for the political and military predicament with which we have had to struggle ever since. Had the United States been aware of the nature of the political world that it was to enter at the end of the Second World War, it would have bent every effort, consistent with the overriding goal of winning the war, to keep the Red Army as far east as possible. Had it done this, West Berlin would not have become an island in a red sea, Czechoslovakia would not be a Russian satellite, and the Red Army would not stand a hundred miles east of the Rhine. The United States did not do this because it was so anxious to continue to live in an apolitical environment of security and reasonable harmony—although that environment was now no longer hemispheric but had become world-wide—that it took the expectation for the fact and understood the political world in terms not of its intrinsic political nature but of its own apolitical expectations. In brief, the United States attempted to continue to achieve its traditional purpose abroad by assuming that the world was as conducive to this achievement as the Western Hemisphere had been. The assumption was erroneous; the attempt was bound to fail.

## 3. Restoration

It is a tribute to the pragmatic genius of America, which is capable of meeting a practical problem on its own merits in a matter-of-fact way and without the hindrance of traditional yet obsolete patterns of thought and action, that the "deadly hiatus," filled with such erroneous thinking, inarticulate action, and untoward results, was relatively brief and was followed by a radically new departure in thought and action. By 1947 the new pattern of American purpose and of the foreign policy serving it was set. It manifested itself in three political innovations: containment; the Truman doctrine; the Marshall Plan. They have in common the permanent assumption by the United States of responsibilities beyond the limits of the Western Hemisphere. We have learned to take these responsibilities for granted and have thus tended to forget how complete and unprecedented a departure from the American tradition their permanent assumption constitutes.

The great reversal of 1947 extended the permanent military commitment of the United States immediately beyond the Rhine and potentially to any region anywhere threatened by Communist aggression or subversion. It further committed the economic resources of the United States immediately to the support of the nations of Western Europe, of Greece and Turkey, and potentially of any nation anywhere which needed help to preserve its freedom. It had become the policy of the United States, in the words of the Truman doctrine, "to support free peoples who are resisting attempted subjugation by armed minorities, or by outside pressures." Since peoples throughout the world, in Europe, Africa, Asia, and Latin America, are resisting such subjugation, the commitments of the United States, by virtue of the Truman doctrine, have become world-wide, unlimited geographically and limited only by the lack of need for support or unwillingness to accept it.

Of the traditional purpose of America abroad, this revolution in America's relations to the outside world seems to have made short shrift. Nothing seems to be left of it but a memory and, in some, a vain desire to return to an age when the United States was committed to defend only its own territory and not the nations of Western Europe, Berlin, Pakistan, Thailand, Australia, New Zealand, South Vietnam, Korea, Japan, and Taiwan, and when the United States endeavored to transform the world simply by its own example. The great transformation of 1947 would then constitute a radical break with the past not only on the level of policy ,as it undoubtedly does, but also on the level of the innermost purpose of America. The positive purpose of achieving equality in freedom at home and offering it by way of example to the world would then have been swallowed up by the negative purpose of defending the United States and the other non-Communist nations against Communist subversion and aggression. Even the Wilsonian variant of that positive purpose, of bringing the American achievement of equality in freedom to the world on the wings of victory in war, seems to have disappeared. In the endeavor to fulfill an indispensable precondition for the achievement of the positive purpose—that is, to protect the United States and the non-Communist world from foreign domination—the positive purpose itself seems to have been lost.

That seeming loss is real, but its reality is not encompassed in the world "failure." It is more complex than that. It is not that the United States, after its quick and adequate response to the threat of Russian power, either gave up the game or else tried to play it and lost. Rather the United States, unprepared for the issues of unprecedented complexity and magnitude which suddenly confronted it, found in its armory of political ideas and institutions nothing with which to meet them. To it has fallen the historic task of fashioning the instruments to which the great issues of the contemporary world will yield. It has not yet succeeded in doing this. It has been stunned by the disproportion between what is asked of it and what its tradition has prepared it for. It gropes and stumbles, but it has not given up. This is a crisis not of failure nor of doubt, but of perplexity.

The three great issues of the age with which America has as yet been unable to come to terms are Communism, atomic power, and a viable order for the non-Communist world. Why has America, which in 1947 found within itself the resources to cope so confidently with the threat of Russian power, thus far failed to master these issues? The threat of Russian power is different in magnitude but not in kind from the threats with which America dealt successfully at its western and southern frontiers in the eighteenth and nineteenth centuries and in the two world wars in Europe. The redskins, it is true, threatened the United States more directly than did the Red Army. Yet the threat to the European balance of power, of which the Red Army is the instrument as were the German armies of the two world wars, is but a more insidious and more deadly threat to American security than were the Indian forays, and it was so understood by America. After an initial period of intellectual doubt and vacillation in action, the United States reacted to the successive threats to the balance of power in Europe as it had reacted to the threats to its territorial integrity in America: by appropriate acts of self-defense. The threat of Russian power, then, fits into the American experience of external threats, and the answer to it could be found among the traditional weapons of American self-defense, adapted to the exigencies of a novel situation.

More particularly, the kind of answer required was traditional in two respects. The quality of the answer depended upon American decision alone, and the answer was consummated in one unequivocal action. The United States could take the place of Great Britain as the champion of Greece and Turkey or it could refrain from doing so. The implementation of the decision to take Britain's place through economic and military assistance followed with virtual inevitability from the decision itself. This was the kind of decision and these were the policies to which the United States was conditioned by the experience of its history. As the threat of Russian power was not in essence different from the threats America had faced throughout its history, so the decisions and policies designed to meet that threat did not differ essentially in their unilateral and unambiguous nature from the policies through which the United States had defended and promoted its interests in the past. In brief, the pragmatic bent of the American mind enabled America to make an adequate response to the threat of Russian military power; indeed, it rose magnificently to the challenge. It was inadequate to the other great challenges of the age, however, and foundered in the face of them.

## 4. *The Korean and Chinese Dilemmas*

That inadequacy became obvious in the two encounters with Russian power in which Russian military might was not directly involved, but in which America had to deal with Russian power through the intermediary of Chinese Communism or the North Korean and Chinese armies. The problem of China, as it presented itself to the United States after 1945, and the Korean War tested the ability of the United States to meet with purposeful action a foreign threat that was not of a clear-cut military nature. The United States did not pass these tests.

The Korean War exemplifies with stark simplicity both the nature and the limits of American ability in this respect. The Korean War started as outright military aggression that confronted the United States with the traditional choice of opposing or not opposing it with military means. The American response, in its swiftness, purposeful determination, and effectiveness, was in the best tradition of American responses to military threats. Yet it lost its traditional qualities as soon as the threat lost its purely military character and transformed itself into a complex political issue in which the war appeared as a mere manifestation of Russian and Chinese power and Communist expansionism.

From the outset the Korean War was interpreted, and in all likelihood misinterpreted, as the opening shot, which the Soviet Union had fired by proxy, in a military campaign to conquer the world. The Korean War was seen in the context of Communist world conquest, as an initial limited and probing operation. There is no empirical evidence to support this interpretation of the Korean War, and what empirical evidence there is points to a different interpretation. It is much more likely that in 1950 the

North Korean government was as eager to unite the country by marching south as the South Korean government was eager to unite it by marching north. While the United States was willing and able to restrain the South Koreans, the Soviet Union seems to have given the North Koreans a free hand, after having been assured that there was no risk of American intervention. When events proved this assurance to be false, the general who had been the Russian pro-consul in North Korea was dismissed and only in the late fifties did he emerge from oblivion. Within the over-all context of Soviet foreign policy, the Korean War is likely to have been an accident, the unintended result of an isolated miscalculation rather than part of a grand design for world conquest.

While the Korean War was thus falsely connected with Russian power and Communist expansionism, it was mistakenly divorced from the national interest of China. For because of its proximity to China, Korea has for most of its long history existed as an autonomous state by virtue of the control or intervention of its powerful neighbor. Whenever the power of China was not sufficient to protect the autonomy of Korea, another nation, generally Japan, would try to gain a foothold on the Korean peninsula. Since the first century B.C. the international status of Korea has by and large been determined either by the supremacy of Chinese power or by the rivalry between China and Japan.

From these two fallacious assumptions the United States attempted to develop the purpose of the Korean War. In view of what it thought was Russian involvement, the United States was anxious to limit the war to the Korean peninsula. In view of what it thought was Chinese detachment, the United States did not hesitate to advance to the Yalu River. And Chinese intervention only strengthened American anxiety to limit the Korean War. While the

United States started to fight the war with the purpose of resisting the North Korean aggression, it expanded this strictly military purpose to the political one of uniting Korea by force of arms, to be limited—in view of Russian, and regardless of Chinese, power—to the peninsula. Yet the intervention of Chinese power compelled the United States to limit its purpose to the restoration of the status quo at the thirty-eighth Parallel. Thus, the intrusion of the political factor into what first seemed a strictly military emergency to be met by military means called for political calculations of a much higher order of subtlety and complexity. The United States, unprepared by its historic experience for such a task, was not equal to it.

The subtlety and complexity of the mental processes required to deal with the Chinese civil war with even a chance for success were of a still higher order, and the American failure has been here correspondingly more drastic than it was in Korea; in China it has been total. The issue that the United States had to face in China was from the outset genuine revolution and civil war, inextricably intertwined with Russian power and Communist expansion. Such an issue provided very limited opportunities for successful outside intervention. The Chinese themselves would settle it one way or the other, and outside intervention might at best facilitate and accelerate, but could not determine, the nature of that settlement. A foreign power faced with so essentially intractable an issue would have been well advised not to commit itself too deeply on either side, to keep an avenue of retreat open in case things should go wrong, and to safeguard in advance its freedom of movement in a situation both uncertain and uncontrolable.

The Soviet Union by and large followed this course of action, giving moderate and provisional support to the Nationalists as long as they had the upper hand and switching that support gradually to the Communists as their chances improved. The United States, on the other hand, viewed—and hence misjudged—the issue of China from the perspective of its historic experience. The issue appeared in the light of that perspective primarily as a military problem, as manageable as its predecessors had been, provided the United States put its resources to work with the proper determination. An allied army was attacked by another army that was also hostile to the United States and was supported by the latter's enemy. Give the allied army sufficient military support, and it will prevail against the common enemy, as the allies did in the First World War, as Great Britain did in the Second, and as the Greek government did against the guerrillas within the Greek borders. What the Chinese civil war required of America was conceived to be different only in quantity from what the Greek civil war had required: military support of very large dimensions.

To be fitted into this simple military perspective, the complexities of the real situation in China had to be simplified and in the process distorted, too. The world-shaking event of the Communist revolution in China had to be seen as nothing more than subversion instigated by Communist conspirators subservient to and supported by Russian power. The Nationalist regime, in turn, had to be seen as the legitimate government of China, being undermined by the agents of a foreign power and an alien creed. When it became obvious that this picture of the Chinese scene was at odds with the facts and that the Communists, having large popular support and indigenous military strength, could not be defeated militarily by the Nationalist government supported by the United States—when, in other words, the military perspective, derived from American experience, was found wanting—history provided the United States with a new opportunity to revise its assumptions and bring them into tune with a new experience.

The United States, remaining within the military frame of mind, used that opportunity to substitute temporarily a new misinterpretation of the Chinese situation for the discredited one. The Chinese Communists, who could no longer be disposed of as mere stooges of Russian power and the Communist International, were now deprived of their Communist character altogether and transformed into "agrarian reformers," a party among others, to be dealt with as such. Only on these assumptions was it possible to conceive a coalition government of Nationalists and Communists as the solution of the Chinese problem. Military victory, to be achieved by the Nationalists with American military support, as the purpose of American policy now yielded to a kind of armistice between the warring parties, politically supported by the United States.

Neither purpose could be achieved in view of Nationalist weakness and Communist strength, and the failure of both our purposes was sealed with the Communist victory in 1949. A farsighted government would have made its peace with the inevitable, however distasteful, long before this final debacle; a government of ordinary prudence would at least have begun to do so then. The United States was prevented from taking such a step, dictated by elemental self-interest, by three factors, pointing up in their different ways the American inability to come to terms with a foreign threat that is not predominantly of a clear-cut military nature. These factors were the Russian and Communist element in the Chinese civil war, the challenge of the Communist victory to the assumption of American omnipotence, and the misunderstanding of the nature of the Communist threat.

There can hardly be any doubt that the United States would have reconciled itself without much trouble to the Nationalist defeat had the victor been just another Chinese faction and not a party that was regarded as the spearhead of Russian power and the *avant-garde* of Communist expansion in Asia. That the Soviet Union should add China to its empire and Communism make a convert of her was the more intolerable for America in view of the traditional role America had assumed vis-à-vis China: the disinterested foe of imperialism and the providential friend of China. To be denied that role and to be cast in the role of China's enemy was for America not just a defeat of a sort that nations must take in their stride, but an intolerable outrage.

The communization of China was so experienced not only because of the proprietary interest which the United States had traditionally taken in China and which made China's defection appear as a betrayal, but also and more profoundly because it constituted the first denial, culminating in complete defeat, of what I have called elsewhere the "delusion of American omnipotence."[1] The United States has of course had to acknowledge that the Chinese revolution cannot be undone. But if we cannot undo it in fact, we can at least undo its meaning in our thoughts. We can make it appear, at least to ourselves, that the Communist government is not the legitimate government of China, but that the Nationalist remnant on Taiwan truly represents that nation. This fiction allows us to nourish the illusion that our proprietary friendship for China survives in our relations with the Taiwan regime, that we have been betrayed not by the authentic China but only by usurpers on the mainland who are betraying the Chi-

---

[1] *In Defense of the National Interest* (New York: Alfred A. Knopf; 1951), pp. 129-131; English edition, *The Foreign Policy of the United States* (London: Methuen; 1952). The argument was popularized in this country by Professor Denis W. Brogan in an article, "The Myth of American Omnipotence," published in *Harper's Magazine* in December 1952.

nese people as well, and that, given the possibility of the return of the legitimate government to the mainland, the denial of our omnipotence may be only temporary.

Yet the defection of China, however temporary it may be assumed to be, is an undeniable fact. That fact provided us with two choices. Either we could revise the assumption of American omnipotence in the light of that fact, or we could reconcile the fact and the assumption by explaining the fact in a way compatible with the assumption. We chose the latter course. The myth of collective treason, on which McCarthy rose to power, served the purpose of reconciling the delusion of American omnipotence with the experience of the limits of American power. The theory that we lost China not because we were powerless to hold it or perhaps even because we never had it to begin with, but because we were betrayed by the enemy within, provides two satisfactions at once. It explains the greatest defeat the United States has suffered in its foreign policy, and it cushions the shock of that experience in a way which soothes the wounded self-esteem of the nation and allows it to dispense with the re-examination of the traditional image of itself in the light of the novel experience. While thus sparing it moral grief and intellectual exertion, the theory of collective treason supplies America with an explanation and remedy for the debacle, simple to understand and easy to apply.

# B. *The Crisis of Perplexity*

## 1. *McCarthyism*

The issue that faces the United States from abroad was reduced by McCarthyism to simple terms reminiscent of the familiar military attack. What faces the United States, according to McCarthyism, is not a complex three-pronged challenge—military, political, ideological—which must be met by complex and different but co-ordinated responses and to which there is no simple clear-cut response promising total victory. There is but one threat against which the United States need defend itself: the threat of treason. It is a threat that issues from within, not from without, and it is localized within vaguely defined and, hence, easily identified groups of the population. Whenever an untractable issue needs to be traced to treason, a traitor is available upon whom the guilt can be pinned. The enormously complex, bewildering, and frequently unmanageable problems of foreign policy are thus transformed into the simple police function of detecting treason and ferreting out the traitor. What the nation needs most badly, according to this view, is not a State Department to conduct foreign policy and a Defense Department to provide military protection, but an FBI to discover treason and apprehend traitors.

The historic achievement of McCarthyism is the reduction—and utter falsification—of the great international issues, for which America had not been prepared by its historic experience and political tradition, to dimensions which easily fit into that experience and tradition. Here lies the most obvious attraction McCarthyism has had for the American people: the momentous international tasks, risks, and liabilities of a world power were transformed into a single domestic issue. A nation that had become a world power in spite of itself turned back into itself, and by the very logic of McCarthyism and without the issue of isolationism ever being explicitly raised, isolationism triumphed.

The complexities of the international issues were reduced to the manageable proportions of criminal cases that any competent and reliable detective ought to be able to solve. The availability of criminal cases, by virtue of the vague definition of treason and the equally vague identification of the traitor, was commensurate with the incidence of international problems unmanageable in their own terms. The ritual of detecting an act of treason and bringing the traitor to heel could be repeated indefinitely, and its performance engendered the illusion that the republic was now safer than it had been before and that, with all the issues reduced to the one issue of safety from treason, the international issues facing the nation were closer to solution. McCarthyism not only led the nation back to an implicit isolationism, but, by conjuring up the specter of ubiquitous treason, also gave the nation a sensation of danger— a concession, however counterfeit, to the actuality of danger emanating from abroad—yet of a controllable and controlled danger, thus conveying in the end the satisfaction of being saved in the midst of danger. The nation owed to McCarthyism a triple satisfaction: to return to isolation, to live dangerously, and to be safe in spite of danger.

It hardly needs to be noted that McCarthyism, as an interpretation of reality, was a preposterous fraud and that, as a policy, it was irrelevant at best and at worst a menace to the interests of the United States at home and abroad. Measured by the tasks it pretended to perform—enabling the nation to meet with a sense of purpose and a chance for success the great issues of the contemporary world—McCarthyism was inadequate beyond words. Yet this fraudulent, stupid, and dangerous farce was from 1950 to 1954 the most powerful political influence in the United States. Strong and good men trembled before it. It made the Senate of the United States its captive. The mass media of communication and the administrators of our educational institutions accepted its standards. It drove thousands of innocent men out of public office and private employment and ruined many of them. It did not even spare so noble a figure as General Marshall; and nobody, not even General Eisenhower, dared to come to his defense. According to a Gallup poll of 1954, 50 per cent of the American people approved and 29 per cent disapproved of McCarthyism, with 21 per cent expressing no opinion!

What accounts for this national degradation—intellectual and moral—this obliviousness to the purpose of America, and its denial in action? It will not do to minimize McCarthyism as a temporary aberration that quickly came and quickly passed, as one of those fits of collective absent-mindedness which sometimes befall even the best of nations and for which nobody can really be held responsible; McCarthy was a bad man who managed to deceive the American people, and that is all there is to it. Explanations such as this resemble too much—to be plausible—the German explanation of Nazism as a kind of metaphysical disease or national catastrophe which was suffered by the German people but for which they cannot be held responsible. In truth, the American people were no more victimized by McCarthy than were the German people by Hitler; both followed their tempters with abandon. They were delighted to be seduced, they were proud to play however minor a part in the farce. The very refusal to look the facts in the face even in retrospect, to acknowledge the ignoble part most of us played in different ways, and to stand trial before the bar of history points to an answer to our question more profound and more disquieting than those commonly suggested. The answer must be found in the very nature of American society.

While it is obvious that McCarthyism was thoroughly un-American in its standards of judgment, which were destructive of individual freedom and of the equality relevant to it, it is less obvious how profoundly American it was in its impulse and *modus operandi*. Far from being alien to the essence of America, McCarthyism was, as it were, its illegitimate offspring, a bastard but nonetheless the child of the same mother who had borne and nourished the true purpose of America. McCarthyism was a corruption in the Aristotelian sense, a perversion of what is good.

It sprang from an impulse that, as we have seen, has been endemic in American society: the primordial anxiety about its ability to survive, the fear of losing its reason for being, its identity, itself. Could a society so deprived of the traditional foundations, so deliberately built upon nothing but the consensus to be equal in freedom in a spacious land —could such a society withstand, without losing its identity, a drastic influx of foreign people and alien ideas? Could the new and deliberately chosen loyalty to the American consensus compete successfully with the old-established loyalties—found and not chosen—to foreign governments and alien ideas? Those questions haunted American society from its very beginnings, and whenever the danger of alienation seemed to be particularly acute, a law was passed, the police were called out, a mob was formed, to enforce loyalty to the threatened American consensus. McCarthyism belongs in that tradition of a typically American self-defense against alienation, and it is not by accident that the man who gave the movement his name hailed from a state which in the second half of the nineteenth century was pointed to, on account of its compact foreign settlements, as a prime example of the danger of alienation.[1]

The fear McCarthy exploited was the same fear that made Cotton Mather believe that the devil was conspiring to destroy New England.

> I believe, that never were more Satanical Devices used for the Unsetling of any People under the Sun, than what have been Employ'd for the Extirpation of the Vine which God has here Planted, Casting out the Heathen, and preparing a Room for it, and causing it to take deep Root, and fill the Land, so that it sent its Boughs unto the Atlantic Sea Eastward, and its Branches unto the Connecticut River Westward, and the Hills were covered with the shadow thereof.[2]

It is the same fear which made Timothy Dwight believe in the international conspiracy of the "Illuminati," a masonic society founded in Germany, which threatened America with destruction.

> The means by which this society was enlarged, and its doctrines spread, were of every promising kind. With unremitted ardour and diligence the members insinuated themselves into every place of power and trust, and into every literary, political and friendly society; engrossed as much as possible the education of youth, especially of distinction; became licensers of the press, and directors of every literary journal; waylaid every foolish prince, every unprincipled civil officer, and every abandoned clergyman; entered boldly into the desk, and with unhallowed hands, and satanic lips, polluted the pages of God; enlisted in their serv-

[1] See above, pp. 58, 59.
[2] Cotton Mather: *The Wonders of the Invisible World* (London: John Russell Smith; 1862), p. 13.

147

ice almost all the booksellers, and of course the printers, of Germany; inundated the country with books, replete with infidelity, irreligion, immorality, and obscenity; prohibited the printing, and prevented the sale, of books of the contrary character; decried and ridiculed them when published in spite of their efforts; panegyrized and trumpeted those of themselves and their coadjutors; and in a word made more numerous, more diversified, and more strenuous exertions, than an active imagination would have preconceived.[3]

The defense that McCarthyism put up against alienation was typically American in that it did not promote a particular state of affairs within American society against another, one such as the New Deal *vs.* the *status quo ante* 1933; it was indifferent to all such concrete issues. What it was concerned with was the issue, transcending all others, of the survival of America itself. On behalf of that issue, it appeared to leave behind political partisanship and all the other pluralisms peculiar to America. It appealed not to one particular group against another group, but to all patriotic Americans—that is, to the overwhelming majority of the American people. It was not out to save the proletarians from the capitalists, or vice versa, or the farmers from the city dwellers, or vice versa, or the South from the North, or vice versa; it was out to save America itself. As all of America was the concern of McCarthyism, so were all true Americans its potential supporters. And there was no American who was not its potential victim.

The suspicion of treason attached not to a particular group within American society—ethnically, religiously, or politically defined—but to all members of American society without distinction—that is, to America itself. America had

[3] Timothy Dwight: *The Duty of Americans at the Present Crisis* (New Haven: Thomas and Samuel Green; 1798).

to be saved from itself, from an innate tendency toward self-destruction. The extreme arbitrariness and irrationality of the McCarthyite definition of treason exposed Americans without exception to the suspicion of being traitors. Executive Order 10450, Section 8, which faithfully expresses the spirit of McCarthyism, defines a security risk by enumerating close to one hundred characteristics, any one of which excludes a man from government employment, his employment being not "clearly consistent with the national security." Yet the list of characteristics, according to the preamble of Section 8, is intended not to be exhaustive, but rather to establish general categories to which the security officials may add other related ones.

These characteristics fall into three different categories:

1. Those which make a person unfit for government service on obvious security grounds, such as "commission of any act of sabotage, espionage, treason, or sedition. . . ." [Sec. 8 (A) 2].

2. Characteristics that make a person unfit for government service in general, without any special reference to security, such as "an adjudication of insanity, or treatment for serious mental or neurological disorder without satisfactory evidence of cure." [Sec. 8 (A) 1. IV]

3. Characteristics the absence of which in the composite reveal a picture of the "normal" good American who alone is worthy of government employment, such as "any criminal, infamous, dishonest, immoral, or notoriously disgraceful conduct, habitual use of intoxicants to excess, drug addiction, or sex perversion." [Sec. 8 (A) 1. III]

Here is indeed the crux of the matter. What the security regulations were trying to do in the third category was to localize treason as a surreptitious evil by making it a function of other patent evils. In this philosophy, a man who has deviated drastically in other respects from the moral standards of society is more likely to deviate from those moral standards by committing treason than one who has not so deviated. This assumption is illogical to begin with, and empirical evidence does not support it. Its illogical character stems from the very nature of treason, which is an act of disloyalty committed by a person who, in view of his revealed qualities, appears to be deserving of trust. If it were possible to identify the prospective traitor by some outward quality, the commission of treason would by definition become impossible. That the assumption of a necessary relationship between general immorality and the particular immorality of treason also is untenable on empirical grounds can be shown by putting the following two questions to the empirical test: are people who deviate in a particular respect from the moral standards of society more likely to commit treason than others, and are traitors as a type likely to be immoral in other respects as well?

Executive Order 10450 assumes the existence of two easily discernible types of men, one likely to commit treason, the other not. The visible mark of the former is the refusal to conform. The composite picture of the latter is the ideal type of a Babbitt with strong pseudo-puritanical connotations. He is a person who is "normal" in every respect—that is, who conforms to certain requirements which a "good" American is supposed to meet.

It stands to reason that this ideal of the "good" American is at odds in one or another respect with the actual behavior of most men who are now living or have ever lived. Hardly an American statesman from Franklin and Washington to Dulles and Eisenhower has, or could have, lived up to it, and most of them would fail the test on multiple grounds. That executive order makes virtually everybody a security risk, and for two reasons. First of all, as already pointed out, few men will correspond in every respect to the ideal picture of the "good" American which is implicit in Executive Order 10450 and its application (and it may

be doubted that those who do make desirable public servants). More importantly, few men will be so transparently
good, approaching saintliness, that it can be said that their
employment is "clearly consistent with the interests of the
national security," which is the general standard repeated
again and again by the executive order.

I am myself indifferent honest; but yet I could ac-
cuse me of such things that it were better my mother
had not borne me: I am very proud, revengeful, ambitious, with more offenses at my back than I have
thoughts to put them in, imagination to give them
shape, or time to act them in. What should such fellows as I do crawling between earth and heaven? We
are arrant knaves, all; believe none of us.

These words of Hamlet all men can say of themselves and
of each other. Even the best man's goodness is darkened
at least by the shadow of a doubt, and thus he is a security
risk within the meaning of Executive Order 10450.

By making treason a potential attribute of all Americans, by universalizing treason while at the same time potentially localizing it in whomever it might happen to
single out for defamation and ostracism, McCarthyism remained beholden to the American purpose of equality. In
the eyes of McCarthyism, all men were equally suspect of
treason, Owen Lattimore and Captain Peress, John Paton
Davies and General Marshall, the man who brought your
letters and served your meals, your father, brother, and
son. Yet the equality of McCarthyism was not the equality
in freedom and of opportunity of the American tradition.
Rather it was equality in fearful silence, in the enslave-
ment of the mind, and the equal opportunity it offered was
not the opportunity to rise in the social scale according
to merit and luck, but the opportunity to sink into oblivion
and ostracism through misfortune and regardless of merit.

What the Great Depression, as we have seen, had achieved twenty years earlier on the economic plane, McCarthyism now achieved in the moral sphere.

Much has been made of the failure of McCarthyism to develop a positive program, and its sudden demise has been attributed to that failure. Actually, that failure was a source of strength and the very precondition of success. By a stroke of primitive and probably instinctive political genius, McCarthyism hit upon and exploited to the hilt the one issue which was the American issue *par excellence:* the survival of America endemically threatened by alienation. He rose to the defense of all Americans without distinction; he asked for the support of all Americans without distinction; and he suspected all Americans without distinction. The amorphousness of the issue, as defined by McCarthyism, corresponds to the amorphousness of American society, and its amorphous equalitarianism remains within the American tradition. Similarly, the McCarthyite remedy, acquiescence induced by fear and empty of content, is but a replica of the traditional American consensus: conformity to the social norm regardless of its content.

Had McCarthyism identified itself with a particular group, a particular interest, and a particular goal within American society rather than with American society itself, it would have cut itself off from that element of the American tradition which gave it its strength. It improved upon that tradition and, by doing so, reduced it to an absurdity; for the nineteenth-century "alienator" *par excellence,* the immigrant, it substituted the nonconformist, whom it identified as a traitor. The nineteenth-century threat to America was still limited to a certain group, however large, within American society, while the McCarthyite threat had become all-pervasive and ubiquitous. In consequence, while the nineteenth-century remedy, xenophobia, required an ever renewed supply of concentrated masses of immigrants (as the Nazi remedy required the existence of Jews), the McCarthyite remedy was self-generating and capable of infinite repetition; for as long as there were Americans, there was the likelihood, if not the actuality, of treason. As America was continuously threatened, so it could be continuously saved. McCarthyism, by its own inner logic, had to become a continuous popular purge of potentially unlimited proportions, insatiable in its search for victims, an ubiquitous Thermidor in perpetuity. This patent absurdity proved to be the undoing of McCarthyism, as it proved the undoing of Stalinism.

McCarthyism, both in its conception of the American task and in its *modus operandi,* was congenial to the American tradition. Yet while that tradition—a number of deviations notwithstanding—was subordinated to, and disciplined by, the American purpose of equality in freedom, McCarthyism was not only philosophically indifferent to that purpose, but also hostile to and destructive of it in actual performance. The American tradition enforces conformity for the sake of survival, and it seeks survival for the sake of the American purpose; it finds no meaning in the survival of America without that purpose. McCarthyism, on the other hand, sought survival as an end in itself. It did not care about what America stood for as long as it survived, and the means it chose to assure that survival were a corruption and, as such, the denial of the American purpose. McCarthyism was nihilistic in a dual sense. Its choice of means was destructive of the very values for the sake of which America had been created and by which it lived, and its misunderstanding of the threat to American survival and the inadequacy of the means chosen to meet the real threat actually put the survival of America in jeopardy.

It was this dual denial of the American purpose which put an end to McCarthyism as a political force. Yet it is revealing of the nature of the contemporary crisis of the American purpose that it was the second rather than the first denial which proved decisive, and that the decision was rendered not through a positive affirmation of the American purpose against its despoiler using its name in vain, but rather through the negative reaction of bored lassitude and of lack of confidence in the savior's ability to save. A nation conscious of its purpose would have asked the would-be savior the question that had been the constant theme of American history and had even preceded it: salvation for what? And the void that question encountered would have disposed of the savior's claim. America was primarily concerned with protection from an undefined and seemingly unmanageable threat, which raised the question: salvation from what? And when McCarthyism proved finally incapable of giving a good practical answer to that practical question, it was relegated into the ashcan of history by the nonchalant sweep of a tired hand.

The McCarthyite claim that it could save America from a mortal threat appeared plausible in the short run, especially since its seeming achievement brought America the triple satisfaction of understanding a formerly unfathomable threat in simple terms, of seeing that threat reduced to manageable dimensions, and of living with it while continuously experiencing mastery over it. In the long run, however, the mechanical sequence of the detection of treason and the exposure and ostracism of traitors became not only tiresome but also incongruous. How much more treason was there to be detected and how many more traitors to be exposed and ostracized before America became really safe? And while McCarthyism was able to convince large masses of the people that Communist-inspired treason was indeed a real threat, it was impossible to dismiss as completely irrelevant the fact of Russian power. But if the military threat emanating from the Soviet Union was to be reckoned with, then the United States had to look for protection from that threat not to McCarthyism but to the armed forces. McCarthyism might appear good enough at hunting down the enemy from within; it had no protection to offer against the enemy from without. This was the proper province of the armed forces.

By accusing the Army of being incapable, because of treason in its midst, to perform that vital function which no other agency could perform, McCarthyism raised doubts about American security without supplying a remedy. To raise doubts and, while raising them, to put them to rest was the secret of McCarthyism's success. To raise them with regard to the Army and let it go at that was the ultimate source of its downfall. For if McCarthyism was right in this respect, America was without defense against a mortal danger. This was intolerable and could not be taken for the truth. On this point McCarthy could not be believed. McCarthy had established himself as the defender of America in the domestic sector; here was the source of his power. He could not, in the nature of things, establish himself as the defender of America in the military sector; yet by attacking the trustworthiness of the military without being able to substitute for them, he destroyed his own acceptability and credibility.

Thus, by an ironic twist of fate reminiscent of classic tragedy, the source of his power—fear—became the source of his impotence. His power stemmed from fear relieved; his impotence, from fear sustained. Had he been less unrestrainedly ambitious, he would have stopped at the limits of his weapon's power. As it was, the weapon with which he had slain the innocent at random and held a nation at bay slew in the end its wielder.

The end of McCarthyism was in its way as ignominious as its ascendency. It disappeared as quickly as it had risen, and as thoroughly as it had swayed the nation in its heyday. In retrospect, one is tempted to dismiss it as an episode without antecedents and consequences, a nightmare that came and went, leaving a vague discomfort in the memory. This is indeed the popular interpretation of McCarthyism. It is a convenient and reassuring interpretation, and that is why it is popular. But, in the perspective of the American past, the interpretation is wrong; and, in the perspective of the American future, it is fraught with peril. McCarthyism is in truth an act—and an essential one—in the contemporary drama of America struggling to rediscover its purpose in a novel world, and that drama is part of a trilogy—the achievement of the American purpose and its crises—whose beginnings reach back into history to the Charter of James I. America reacted with splendid determination and appropriateness to the threat of Russian power; McCarthyism constitutes its utter and ignominious failure when it was faced with Russian power, Chinese power, and Communism in combination. That failure was both intellectual and moral.

The intellectual failure is comprised in the complete misunderstanding of the actual nature of the threat and in the complete inappropriateness and the self-defeating results of the measures taken to meet it. The moral failure consists in the corruption of the American purpose, a corruption so thorough as to amount to its destruction. Called to the task of rediscovering the purpose of America in a novel world and of restoring it according to the tasks posed by that world, America responded with McCarthyism, a response irrelevant, self-defeating, and self-destructive. Called upon to renew the American revolution, to perceive again what it was living for, and to live accordingly, McCarthyite America could think of nothing better than to meet an imaginary threat to its survival with the inept and self-defeating weapons of an amateur police state, destructive of its purpose. Far from trying to rise to the challenge and failing, it was not even aware of what the challenge was and acted as though the challenge did not exist.

If this analysis of McCarthyism and its relation to the American purpose is correct, then it becomes clear that the distance which separates McCarthyism from the period that follows it is less wide than it is commonly assumed to be. The active manifestations of McCarthyism have disappeared, the passive and negative attitude toward the American purpose remains. Today's tranquillity and yesterday's frenzy grew from the same soil: the inability to relate the novel issues of the contemporary world to a national purpose and to understand and cope with them in the light of that purpose. Fear and complacency, misdirected action and passivity are but different symptoms of the same disease: the crisis of perplexity of the American purpose.

When the nation feels itself acutely threatened, as in the case of war or the communization of a friendly nation, that inability may drive it into blind frenzy or purposeless action, and it will entrust its safety to a McCarthy. When the threat is subtle and indirect rather than drastic and unmistakable and neither intelligible nor manageable in terms of the traditional categories drawn from the American experience, the same inability tempts the nation into another kind of blindness—to wit, the refusal to take that threat seriously and act upon it, since it does not fit into the categories within which the nation is accustomed to think and act. It is in this fashion that America has failed to meet the great challenge from abroad which came to the fore after the challenge of Russian power had been successfully met: Communism, not as an ally of Russian power, but a competitor of America in the pursuits of peace.

## 2. *Communism*

What baffles the American mind and paralyzes American action in dealing with Communism is the similarity between the American and Communist purposes. Communism has stolen America's thunder. It claims to be able to achieve, and to be in the process of achieving, what America has merely proclaimed and has failed to achieve. The purpose of America, so the argument runs, has remained a pretense and its failure has made it into a sham. As far back as 1935, Alexander Meiklejohn could write:

> And yet the plain and simple fact remains that Russia, whether she be right or wrong, is in the place which we had thought to be ours. She is taking chances while we are playing safe. While we are holding back she is plunging forward. It is to Russia rather than to us that the wretched and oppressed of the earth are now turning as they dream of escape from age-long tyrannies and despairs.[1]

On the occasion of the Fourth of July, 1956, a Russian writer, replying in *The New Times* to the accusation that the Soviet Union was exporting its revolution, paid the United States the compliment of saying that it was the United States itself which had started the export of revolution in 1776. "All the peoples of the world, each in their own way, were affected at the time by the Fourth of July and felt its consequences." In the reactionary Russian press of the nineteenth century, he added, the word "American" was synonymous with "revolutionary."[2]

---

[1] Alexander Meiklejohn: *What Does America Mean?* (New York: W. W. Norton; 1935), p. 79.

[2] *The New York Times,* July 3, 1956.

## Communism

The American and Communist revolutions have five elements in common: the claim to uniqueness, the claim to universality, the claim to liberation, the claim to the creation of a new type of man, and the actuality of a more abundant material life.

"The revolutions which formerly took place in the world, had nothing in them that interested the bulk of mankind," said Thomas Paine with reference to the American revolution. "They extended only to a change of persons and measures, but not of principles and rose or fell among the common transactions of the moment."[3] It is by a similar distinction that Communism sets the Communist revolution apart from all preceding revolutions. The latter "were movements of minorities, or in the interest of minorities." They replaced one exploiting minority with another exploiting minority. In contrast, "the proletarian movement is the self-conscious, independent movement of the immense majority, in the interest of the immense majority." Hence, the proletarian revolution will make an end to exploitation itself. It, too, is concerned with "principles" rather than a mere "change of persons and measures."

Both revolutions, exactly because they were concerned with new principles of government and of social organization, claimed universal significance. "The American Revolution," Jefferson said at the end of his life, "was intended for all mankind." America, to quote Thomas Paine again, "made a stand not for herself only, but for the world, and looked beyond the advantages which herself could receive. Even the Hessian, though hired to fight against her, may live to bless his defeat; and England, condemning the viciousness of its government, rejoice in its miscarriage."[4]

[3] Thomas Paine: *The Rights of Man* (New York: E. P. Dutton and Co.; 1951), p. 154.

[4] Loc. cit., p. 151.

As we have seen, these words have been echoed throughout the length of American history and the breadth of the world. They have been taken up by Communism, substituting the Soviet Union for the United States. The Soviet Union is the "fatherland of socialism," the model nation that guides the members of the socialist camp on their different roads to socialism. The welfare of humanity being identical with the interests of the Soviet Union, loyalty to the Soviet Union meets the Marxist postulate of an international loyalty transcending the nation state.[5] What Thomas Paine said of America, the Soviet Union has said time and again of itself: its cause "is in great measure the cause of all mankind."

The political purpose of both revolutions is the liberation of man. Both claim to make an end not just to the political domination of one group over another, but to political domination itself. Both are apolitical in their objectives, America claiming to have escaped the evils of politics by erecting a new commonwealth in isolation from Europe on the foundations of equality in freedom, the Soviet Union expecting the same consummation from the classless society in which the state will have withered away. Both aim to deprive, in the words of *The Communist Manifesto,* "the public power" of "its political character" and to create a new society "in which the free development of each is the condition for the free development of all." Equality in freedom is the goal of Communism as it has been the purpose and achievement of America.

This radically new society gives birth to a new man, either Crèvecoeur's "new man, who acts upon new prin-

[5] Cf. the testimony of British and Canadian members of the Grouzenko spy ring in *Canada: Royal Commission to Investigate Disclosures of Secret and Confidential Information to Unauthorized Persons, 1946.*

ciples,"[6] or the "new Soviet man," who, liberated from exploitation, works not in order to keep barely alive but to fulfill his human potentialities. While Crèvecoeur's American claims to have made an end to what Marxism calls "self-alienation," Communism claims that only the classless society can restore man's dignity and the fullness of his creative powers. Both America and Communism point to material productivity as the tangible test of their respective claims, and both accept that productivity either as reward for the puritanical virtues of industry and frugality or as the empirical demonstration of the correctness of their understanding of history and society. Nowhere has the competitive character of the American and Communist purposes revealed itself more clearly than here, and it is on material productivity that Communism has in our time staked its claim to superiority.

[It] cannot exist without constantly revolutionizing the instruments of production, and thereby the relations of production, and with them the whole relations of society. Conservation of the old modes of production in unaltered form, was, on the contrary, the first condition of existence for all earlier industrial classes. Constant revolutionizing of production, uninterrupted disturbance of all social conditions, everlasting uncertainty and agitation distinguish its epoch from all earlier ones. All fixed, fast-frozen relations, with their train of ancient and venerable prejudices and opinions, are swept away, all new-formed ones become antiquated before they can ossify. . . .

[It] has through its exploitation of the world-market given a cosmopolitan character to production and consumption in every country. To the great

[6] St. John de Crèvecoeur: *Letters from an American Farmer* (New York: E. P. Dutton and Co.; 1912), p. 44.

chagrin of Reactionists, it has drawn from under the feet of industry the national ground on which it stood. All old-established national industries have been destroyed or are daily being destroyed. They are dislodged by new industries, whose introduction becomes a life and death question for all civilized nations, by industries that no longer work up indigenous raw material, but raw material drawn from the remotest zones; industries whose products are consumed, not only at home, but in every quarter of the globe. In place of the old wants, satisfied by the productions of the country, we find new wants, requiring for their satisfaction the products of distant lands and climes. In place of the old local and national seclusion and self-sufficiency, we have intercourse in every direction, universal inter-dependence of nations. And as in material, so also in intellectual production. The intellectual creations of individual nations become common property. National one-sidedness and narrow-mindedness become more and more impossible, and from the numerous national and local literatures there arises a world-literature.

[It], by the rapid improvement of all instruments of production, by the immensely facilitated means of communication, draws all, even the most barbarian, nations into civilization. The cheap prices of its commodities are the heavy artillery with which it batters down all Chinese walls, with which it forces the barbarians' intensely obstinate hatred of foreigners to capitulate. It compels all nations, on pain of extinction, to adopt its mode of production; it compels them to introduce what it calls civilization into their midst, i.e., to become it themselves. In a word, it creates a world after its own image.

[It] has subjected the country to the rule of the

towns. It has created enormous cities, has greatly increased the urban population as compared with the rural, and has thus rescued a considerable part of the population from the idiocy of rural life. Just as it has made the country dependent on the towns, so it has made barbarian and semi-barbarian countries dependent on the civilized ones, nations of peasants on nations of it, the East on the West.

[It] keeps more and more doing away with the scattered state of the population, of the means of production, and of property. It has agglomerated population, centralized means of production, and has concentrated property in a few hands. The necessary consequence of this was political centralization. Independent, or but loosely connected provinces, with separate interests, laws, governments and systems of taxation, became lumped together in one nation, with one government, one code of laws, one national class-interest, one frontier and one customs-tariff.

[It], during its rule of scarce one hundred years, has created more massive and more colossal productive forces than have all preceding generations together. Subjugation of Nature's forces to man, machinery, application of chemistry to industry and agriculture, steam-navigation, railways, electric telegraphs, clearing of whole continents for cultivation, canalization of rivers, whole populations conjured out of the ground —what earlier century had even a presentiment that such productive forces slumbered in the lap of social labor?

By whom and of what were these statements made? They could have been made of the contemporary Soviet Union by an admirer; they could also have been made of the United States by an admirer any time during the last fifty years or so. They were actually made of the capitalistic system by Marx and Engels in 1848: where I have put "it," the original reads "the bourgeoisie." What the founders of the Communist doctrine admired in the capitalism of the mid-nineteenth century, America—the prototype of a large-scale, dynamic, capitalistic system—has achieved, and the practitioners of Russian Communism are in the process of achieving a century later. As Khrushchev put it in his speech of July 24, 1959, opening the American Exposition in Moscow:

> We consider the U.S. exhibition to be an exhibition of our own achievements in the not-too-distant future, and as testimony to the successes in production and technology our country will achieve when the plans we have outlined are fulfilled.

The fact that the Communist analysis of a modern industrial system applies to capitalism and Communism, the United States and the Soviet Union, reveals strikingly the affinity of the two systems and nations in terms of their economic aspirations and achievements. It is this affinity which has stunned the imagination and paralyzed the will of America.

American productivity had moved ahead of that of all other nations, not through a conscious competitive effort but, as it were, by letting nature take its course. Opportunities for private gain presented themselves, and concrete tasks, especially in war, had to be performed collectively. The qualities of the people and of the land were put to work to meet these opportunities and perform these tasks, and simply by doing what needed to be done we attained our productive eminence among the nations. This greatness was isolationist in that it grew out of indigenous opportunities and resources and without regard to what happened in other nations. America was concerned with itself, and economic pre-eminence was a by-product of this concern, pleasing but unintended.

Yet while America recognizes in theory that this splendid isolation is a thing of the past, its collective actions reflect nothing of the competitive urgency required by the situation. A yawning gap separates action from both facts and consciousness. The psychological mechanism by which this isolation of national effort maintains itself against the evidence of the facts and our awareness of them is similar to that which maintained the isolationism of the twenties and thirties in foreign policy. To act in a way consistent with the knowledge that American isolationism is merely a historic memory requires not only a new pragmatic approach to the concrete tasks at hand but also a radical transformation of our total conception of the political world. The definitive break with isolationism implies a revolution not merely in this or that foreign or domestic policy but in the basic philosophy, emotions, and attitudes of the nation. Such a revolution is like leaving the warmth and certainties of one's father's house for the cold darkness of an unfathomable and hostile world. It demands a moral fortitude, an intellectual creativeness, and a daring in action which are not likely to appear spontaneously within a nation; these qualities are likely to be evoked only by dire and patent necessity.

In foreign policy, only Pearl Harbor eradicated isolationism as a popular attitude—and only for the time being —and it was only the innovations of the spring of 1947 which made the break definitive in the realm of action. However, isolationism as an emotional preference and an intellectual conception has lingered on and has continued to affect political thought and action. Domestically, isolationism has not yet been forced to yield to consistent action against a foreign threat, and the incentives to retain the old ways have thus far proved to be irresistible. Communist competition has not confronted the nation with a challenge so unmistakable and menacing as those presented by Pearl Harbor in 1941 and the military expansionism of the Soviet Union in the aftermath of the Second World War. Its threat is insidious, slow-moving, and piecemeal. The nation, not confronted with the stark choice of resisting or giving up, thinks that it can afford to temporize and meet all-out competition with half-hearted effort.

More importantly, a national effort commensurate with Communist competition would require re-examination and redirection of the fundamentals of our economic, educational, and governmental systems. That redirection would at least have to be a compromise between the traditional ways of thought and action and the new ways demanded by a novel situation. However, considering the ends sought by Communist competition and the human and material resources and the social organization supporting it, there can be little doubt that if we were to treat that competition with the seriousness it deserves, we would have to reshape our economic, educational, and governmental systems on radically new lines.

These systems have their origin in the early formulation of the American purpose, which conceived of equality in terms of equality of competition and freedom from government control. Although this original formulation has been modified, as we have seen, especially in the theory and practice of the relations between government and the economic sphere, it has retained its force as a tenet of the political theology of America, limiting the opportunities for concerted national effort in times of peace. Yet unless such effort is made on an unprecedented scale and with an unprecedented intensity, the United States has no chance of competing successfully with an enemy whose every activity is directed toward its destruction. Were the United

States to face this issue seriously, it would have to tackle the painful, hazardous, and difficult task of reconciling its traditions with its present needs, of separating within its traditions what is essential from what is ephemeral, of giving its purpose of equality in freedom a new meaning. America has thus far spared itself this task by not taking the challenge of Communist competition seriously enough. It has averted its gaze from that challenge because it has shrunk from the burden of reconsidering its purpose.

### 3. *Atomic Power*

Atomic power presents America with two issues that affect its purpose indirectly by posing the question of its very survival. Before the advent of the atomic age, America could take for granted its ability to survive a challenge from without and was anxious only about its ability to survive disintegration from within. Today atomic power threatens the survival of America in a dual way: by raising a fundamental issue of military strategy and by calling into question the viability of the very foundation of America as a nation: the sovereign nation state.

The utter irrationality of all-out violence as a means to the ends of foreign policy poses for the United States, as it does for all major powers, an awful dilemma. If resort to all-out violence is tantamount to suicide, how can a nation defend its interests in an anarchic world in which violence remains the last resort? Must it not then choose between two alternatives, both unacceptable because they put an end to its existence: death by suicide in an atomic holocaust and death by the slow strangulation of piecemeal surrender? The way out of this dilemma is the development of a military capability for all-out nuclear war, tactical atomic war, and conventional pre-atomic war. The capability for all-out nuclear war would be a mere instrument of deterrence which all nations would be ready to use in retaliation or in anticipation of an imminent all-out attack. The capability for limited war, atomic or conventional, might actually be used in support of the national interest, as the circumstances would require. The military establishment of the Soviet Union comes close to meeting the requirements of this triple military capability. That of the United States is far from meeting them.

The American concentration upon the nuclear deterrent and neglect of a capability for limited war is generally justified by financial considerations. Yet on a more profound level of analysis we encounter the pattern we have encountered before: a simple, clear-cut, and definitive response to an external threat is preferred to a complicated one whose results are uncertain. There is no need to dwell upon the incongruity of such responses to a threat that is nuclear in nature. A posture that was rational and eminently successful in the Western Hemisphere in the nineteenth century and in the two world wars has become an implausible anachronism in the second half of the twentieth century. The threat of "massive retaliation"—that is, of a nuclear response to a conventional threat—is obviously plausible only on the condition that the other state is not capable of counter-retaliation in kind.

The doctrine of "massive retaliation," when it was proclaimed in 1954, was an implausible bluff but not a serious declaration of policy, and it has never been acted upon. Yet it evoked that feeling of certainty, of definiteness, of security, which historic experience has taught the nation to expect from its military policies. This feeling could not be anything more than an illusion. But it was a comfortable illusion; it saved the nation intellectual effort and spared it personal sacrifices by reducing a complex and dangerous problem to a simple formula capable of virtually automatic application. That formula covered up the nation's refusal to bring the traditional pattern of its thought and action into harmony with a military situation pregnant with extreme danger to national survival. Its seeming success has strengthened its persuasiveness: for it is true that this formula, however implausible on rational grounds, has made—at least thus far—our prospective enemies cautious because the possibility of irrational action, even with suicidal consequences and even on the part of the highest officials, can never be completely ruled out.

Yet while the policy of "massive retaliation" has had for the time being this beneficial result, it has paralyzed the foreign policy of the United States. Incapable of fighting a limited war of more than very small dimensions, the United States had to stop short of that dreadful alternative between nuclear suicide and retreat which its military policy was bound to open up at every turn. In order not to be forced to retreat it has had to refuse to advance, except when there was no military opposition, as in Lebanon in 1958, or inferior military opposition, as for the time being in China. But when the revolts in East Germany and Poland and the Hungarian revolution of 1956 opened up opportunities for an active foreign policy, the United States felt that it had to resign itself to a passivity that contributed to the stabilization of the Soviet empire.

Yet even if the United States were to devise a more adequate military strategy, atomic power would still pose a threat to its existence which no strategy operating from the nation as its base could do more than mitigate. For the existential threat atomic power poses to all nations of the world cannot be answered at all from within a state system whose basic unit is the nation state.

The most elementary function of the nation state is the defense of the life of its citizens and of their civilization. A political organization that is no longer able to defend these values and even puts them in jeopardy must yield, either through peaceful transformation or violent destruction, to one capable of that defense. Thus, under the impact of the invention of gunpowder and of the first industrial revolution, the feudal order had to yield to the dynastic and the nation state. Under the technological conditions of the pre-atomic age, the stronger nation states could, as it were, erect walls behind which their citizens could live in security while the weaker states were protected by the operation of the balance of power, which added the resources of the strong to those of the weak; under normal conditions no nation state was able to make more than marginal inroads upon the life and civilization of its neighbors.

The feasibility of all-out atomic war has completely destroyed this protective function of the nation state. No nation state is capable of protecting its citizens and its civilization against an all-out atomic attack. Its safety rests solely in preventing such an attack from taking place. While in the pre-atomic age a nation state could count upon its physical ability to defend itself, in the atomic age it must rely upon its psychological ability to deter those who are physically able to destroy it. The prospective enemy must be induced to refrain from attacking.

This psychological mechanism of deterrence operates only if the prospective atomic aggressor is clearly identified beforehand—that is, if no more than two nations are capable of waging all-out war. Today the Soviet Union knows that if it should attack the United States with atomic weapons, the United States would destroy it, and vice versa; that certainty deters both. Yet the time is close at hand when other nations will have the weapons with which to wage all-out atomic war. Then nations will have lost even the preventive capacity of psychological deterrence, which they still possess today. For the United States, if then attacked with atomic weapons, will no longer be able to identify the aggressor with certainty, and, hence, a prospective aggressor will not be deterred by the certainty of retaliation. When this historic moment comes—as it surely must if the present trend is not reversed—the nation state will connote not life and civilization but anarchy and universal destruction.

It is in the shadow of this grim reality and grimmer prospect that the United States must reflect and act not just upon its purpose as traditionally conceived but upon a novel purpose—compatible with and requisite to the preservation of the old—which will safeguard its existence and that of all humanity. How can atomic power be transferred to the control of supranational institutions that will prevent its use on behalf of a particular national interest without submerging the autonomous life of individual nations in a universal tyranny? Can safety and freedom be made to coexist in the atomic age? Must the United States give up its traditional purpose of equality in freedom in order to survive, or could even that surrender not assure its survival? It is to these momentous questions that history expects America to answer—and the answers are expected to be as creative, inventive, and daring as that given by the Founding Fathers in the creation of the United States. What kind of answer has America been able to give?

The answers it has given thus far are ambiguous in that they partake in a special degree of that perplexity which obscures the perception of the American purpose and stifles its achievement. The United States has twice dealt constructively with the problem of supranational control of atomic power: on the occasions of the Acheson-Baruch-Lilienthal proposals of 1946 and of the negotiations of 1958-60 for the cessation of atomic tests. Both attempts failed, and the evidence suggests that at least the first attempt would have failed regardless of what the United States might have proposed. For supranational control of atomic power, as I have tried to show elsewhere, is incompatible with national sovereignty. A supranational authority controlling atomic power, whatever it might be called, would exercise for all practical purposes the functions of a limited world government. The government of the Soviet Union, whose power at home and abroad derives in good measure from its absolute control and the secrecy of its operations, has been adamant in its insistence upon the integral preservation of its sovereignty. Thus, it has been unalterably opposed to effective supranational controls, and whether the Soviet Union might have withdrawn its opposition for a price must remain a moot question.

We are here concerned not with the assessment of blame for the failure of these attempts but with the state of mind in which the United States approached this momentous issue. And it must be said at once that the United States rose to the occasion with a stronger sense of purpose and greater vigor of mind and appropriateness of action in 1946, when the threat to American survival was not yet acute but only foreseeable, than it did in the late fifties, when that threat was real and was clearly approaching the point of becoming unmanageable. On both occasions, however, American initiative was torn by two contradictory, unresolved purposes: to remove the threat of atomic destruction from the United States and from the world while improving at the same time the relative position of the United States in the struggle for power with the Soviet Union. And on both occasions it was paralyzed by the desire for absolute security.

The Acheson-Baruch-Lilienthal proposals for the international control of atomic energy were based upon three sound and bold assumptions: the enormous potential of atomic energy as a source of power for peaceful and military purposes; the impossibility of separating the knowledge and production of atomic energy for these two purposes; the temporary nature of the atomic monopoly of the United States. The conclusion derived from these assumptions was equally sound and bold: that the competitive development of atomic energy was fraught with incalculable danger for all mankind and therefore ought not to be at the discretion of national governments. International ownership or control of all raw materials that may be the source of atomic energy and of all plants capable of producing atomic weapons, cessation of the manufacture of atomic bombs, and destruction of existing ones was the answer of the American proposals to both the threat and the promise of atomic energy; for these measures would combine security from atomic war with the opportunity to develop atomic power for peaceful purposes. The decisions of the international authority and the imposition of sanctions against violations of agreements and decisions were not to be subject to the veto of the great powers.

Had these proposals been put into practice, the resulting international organization would have constituted an unprecedentedly radical step toward a limited world government, and indeed the authors of the proposals envisaged the international control of atomic energy—which would have been really supranational in nature—only as a beginning, a pattern to be duplicated in other fields. What accounts for the failure of so forward-looking a scheme? The answer must be found in the strength of nationalism with which the American proposals had to compromise and which completely determined the Russian attitude.

The authors of the American proposals, however conscious they were of the need to transcend the traditional limits of national sovereignty, had to take into account the misgivings of influential groups among their countrymen who wanted to rely solely upon the power of the nation—that is, the atomic monopoly of America—and assumed that the atomic bomb was just another weapon and that the atomic superiority of America, if not its monopoly, would last forever. The result was a compromise between the supranational ultimate goal of the proposals and the perpetuation of the national advantage of America during the intermediate stages. During these stages the American monopoly was to be preserved, to be gradually shared with the international authority, and the Soviet Union was to be excluded from both the possession of substantial fissionable material and a separate atomic technology.

Considering the probable composition of the international authority, the Soviet Union could have anticipated that its pursuit of atomic interests, hostile to and competitive with the Western world, would be restrained by the decisions of a hostile majority. Furthermore, the unlimited access of international inspectors to the territory of the member states would have deprived the Soviet Union of one of its greatest military assets, the secrecy of many of its military and industrial installations. Yet while the Soviet Union would thus have been put at a permanent military and economic disadvantage by being deprived of nationally controlled atomic knowledge and capability, it was in 1946 already well on its way toward acquiring atomic knowledge and capability of its own. Thinking in strictly national terms, it had no incentive to accept the American proposals and had potent reasons for rejecting them.

Thus, it was the intrusion—probably inevitable in the circumstances—of considerations of national advantage into a scheme endeavoring to transcend such considerations which led to failure. The United States tried to preserve the atomic *status quo* of 1946 until the consummation of the scheme, and after that it aimed for, in the words of

Mr. Baruch, "a guarantee of safety, not only against the offenders in the atomic area, but against the illegal users of other weapons—bacteriological, biological, gas—perhaps —why not? against war itself." The Soviet Union, on the other hand, was unwilling to accept certain disadvantages in the short run in exchange for speculative advantages in a distant future, and its short-term calculations most certainly proved correct. Thus, concern for the national interest conceived in traditional and, hence, obsolescent terms ruined an initiative whose general conception was informed by the insight that the nation state is too small and weak a mold to contain atomic power.

The same pattern of conflict between the rational recognition of the need for supranational institutions and the concern for national interests and absolute security has thus far stood in the way of an agreement on the cessation of atomic tests. In contrast to the international control of atomic energy, the issue here is simple. It is the question of what constitutes an effective inspection system. The United States has insisted upon foolproof, truly supranational inspection; the Soviet Union has countered with proposals that preserve a great measure of national control.

The American insistence upon an inspection system so comprehensive as to be hardly acceptable to the Soviet Union conceals an unresolved conflict of policy between two groups within the American government: those who seek somewhere a beginning of supranational control of atomic energy and those who, like the Soviet Union, prefer the traditional reliance upon national armaments and are opposed to the cessation of atomic tests because they fear that the cessation of atomic tests would weaken the United States vis-à-vis the Soviet Union. The former favor the cessation because they realize that the security gained by uncontrolled competitive armaments is bound to prove illusory in the long run. Yet both are at one in the desire to provide the United States with a security at least approximating that which it enjoyed in the pre-atomic age.

Both the proposals for the international control of atomic energy of 1946 and those for the cessation of atomic tests of the late fifties, then, reveal a common pattern of perplexity. That perplexity derives from an inability to reconcile traditional ways of thinking and acting with the requirements of a novel age. We know that we have moved almost overnight from a condition of complete security from foreign danger into one of utter insecurity, and we also know that the organization of the world into nation states is not only incapable of restoring even a measure of security but is itself responsible for our prevailing insecurity and the greater insecurity we must expect. Never having experienced, except at the beginning of our history, that moderate measure of insecurity lying between the two extremes which has been the common lot of most other nations, we seek to escape from the utter insecurity of the present into the complete security of the past. To this end, we have tried to devise supranational institutions that would also serve the maximum needs of national security. These endeavors have thus far ended in complete failure, and we are at the moment moving knowingly but helplessly into a new period of the atomic age which threatens dispersal of nuclear weapons into the hands of numerous nations, a state of unmanageable insecurity which will put civilization itself in jeopardy.

Whether the Russian commitment to secrecy and national sovereignty could have been overcome is doubtful. This commitment is obviously incompatible with an organization of the world capable of bringing atomic energy under control, and is really an atavism in the atomic age. Yet the American commitment to restoring absolute security by means of supranational institutions is unrealistic in a different way. It connotes a longing for a past that even bold and forward-looking designs cannot retrieve.

The absolute security America enjoyed in the pre-atomic age was due to unique conditions that cannot be artificially duplicated in the atomic age. The futile search for an unattainable absolute security has led, as it was bound to lead, to the perpetuation of utter insecurity. The United States must choose not between absolute security and utter insecurity, but between utter insecurity and a measure of insecurity which, in view of the alternative, is tolerable. It can no longer expect to avoid the risks to which other nations have been continuously exposed and which atomic power has enormously magnified and brought to its very heart. It must weigh the risks of an uncontrolled atomic-armaments race, engaged in by most nations, against the risks that no feasible system of supra-national controls can completely eliminate. Yet by weighing the inescapable risks of the atomic age against a risk-less past and futilely trying to restore it, America has posed itself midway between the past and the future. With its mind's eye, it beholds the needs of the future; yet it wishes for the return of a past that is forever lost. Thus, its purpose to provide for its survival in a surviving world is blurred, and its designs, bold and forward-looking in themselves, are in execution chained to a past that is dead.

## 4. *Free-World Order*

The supranational ordering of atomic power is the indispensable precondition for survival, but it tells us nothing about the purpose for which we want to survive. And while this problem has been the object of protracted negotiations, the United States, as the leading nation of the non-Communist world, was called upon to act as though that problem were on the way to solution, as though mankind and, more particularly, Western civilization would survive, and to fashion out of its power and leadership a common purpose for the whole non-Communist world. The United States was expected to use its predominant power on behalf of a purpose that would be not only its own but also one in which the non-Communist world could recognize its distinct character and in whose achievement it could experience a common destiny. What would America do with its power? What purpose would it make that power serve? More particularly, would America be able to connect organically its traditional purpose with that power and, if need be, to reformulate that purpose so that the power could serve it? The answer to those questions is determined by the nature of American power, on the one hand, and the nature of the American purpose, on the other.

America became a world power, as it had become the most productive and technologically most advanced nation on earth, by putting its human and material resources to the tasks at hand rather than by design. These two achievements are of course closely interrelated; for American productivity and technological proficiency provide the material foundation for American political and military power. America marshaled its human and material resources for the purpose of winning the Second World War by destroying the power of Germany and Japan. And when the war was won, it found itself in lonely pre-eminence among impotent enemies and enfeebled allies. It had not sought the power with which it emerged from the Second World War; it had sought merely to win the war quickly, cheaply, and completely. As a result of its effort and of the distribution of power at the war's end, the United States awoke one morning to find itself the most powerful nation on earth. Thus, when America was at the pinnacle of its power, purpose and power were divorced; its power had far outstripped its purpose, and it had no purpose commensurate with its power. This disproportion made the purpose uncertain and diminished the effectiveness of the power.

America as a world power, once it had met successfully the Russian military threat to its and the non-Communist world's survival, had to achieve certain basic tasks. First of all, out of the makeshift arrangements aimed at meeting the Russian military threat America had to create a viable international order that would translate common interests into a common purpose, fuse the power of individual nations, and assign to them responsibilities commensurate with their interests and power. Second, it had to create a relationship with the uncommitted new nations of Africa and Asia which would further a new domestic and international stability of peace and freedom in the image of the stability achieved by the United States. Third, it had to establish a relationship conducive both to peace and to freedom with nations which were unwilling objects of Communist domination, such as those of Eastern Europe.

These three tasks were not a matter of choice for America. It could reject them only by being unfaithful to its purpose and oblivious of its power. Its purpose— equality in freedom to be preserved at home and expanded and emulated abroad—requires for its achievement at home an international environment that at the very least, does not threaten the existence of the United States. From the beginning of American history to the Second World War, natural isolation and foreign policies maximizing these advantages of nature provided such an environment. With these advantages irretrievably lost, the United States had to create an international environment as a political and social artifact within which it could securely pursue its domestic purpose.

The other two tasks are less vitally tied to the purpose of America, even though without them that purpose would be substantially diminished. For without them the American purpose would lose its dynamic expansionist quality, and its realization at home could not serve as a model for other nations. The United States, with its territorial expansion at an end, had now for the second time to find a substitute for its subsidiary purpose of expanding the area of equality in freedom. When it was first faced with that necessity, it tended under the guidance of Woodrow Wilson, as we have seen, to find that new purpose in the transformation of the world through the establishment of democratic institutions. The United States could then afford to indulge in the experiment of making the world safe for democracy, for the whole world then appeared to present itself as a kind of gigantic experimental stage on which the universal validity of democratic institutions could be demonstrated.

The aftermath of the Second World War precluded a repetition of this experiment. For the failure of the Wilsonian experiment destroyed the simple faith in the universal validity of democratic institutions which had inspired that experiment, and called forth more sophisticated approaches and more cautious expectations. Furthermore, most of the nations in search of a political identity are manifestly unsuited for a democratic system after the American model. And, most importantly, the international environment in which the search takes place offers in Communism an alternative to democracy and, hence, puts strict limits on democratic experimentation.

How has America pursued its purpose under these novel conditions? How has it endeavored to achieve the three tasks which the conjunction of purpose and environment set before it? What kind of viable international order did it try to create as a precondition for its own survival? What kind of relationship did it try to establish with the new nations of Africa and Asia and with the unwilling objects of Communist domination? The answer to these questions is simple, and the very simplicity of the answer is the measure of America's failure. The United States conceived of these tasks primarily in military terms—that is, in terms of actual or potential alliances to defend the territorial *status quo*. By doing so, it identified its survival with its purpose. It came to think that what was necessary and sufficient to assure its survival was also sufficient to achieve its purpose. In the process it lost the vision of its purpose and contributed nothing to its military security and that very survival to which it had sacrificed its purpose.

The relationships within an alliance are determined by the interests and the power of its members. The interests that tie the United States to its European allies are more profound, more comprehensive, and more stable than the interests upon which alliances have traditionally been based. Far from concerning nothing more than a limited territorial advantage against a temporary enemy, these interests enclose the national identities of all its members within a common civilization threatened by an alien and oppressive social system. Thus, this alliance was not formed, as alliances typically are, through a process of haggling and horse-trading among suspicious temporary associates looking already for more advantageous associations elsewhere. Rather this alliance sprang naturally and almost inevitably from a common concern with a common heritage whose only chance of survival lay in common support. The members of the alliance had to choose between the alliance and the loss of their national identities and cultural heritage; that is to say, they had no choice at all.

The cement that kept the alliance together was the paramount power of the United States. In the past there had been alliances in which power was unequally distributed and one ally was predominant; but rarely had there been such a concentration of paramount power in one ally, with all the other allies, even collectively, being in a subordinate position. And rarely had so paramount a power been at the same time commensurate with the all-persuasiveness of the concerns of the alliance. For the United States was paramount not only in the military and economic fields, but also in the intangible spheres of the values of Western civilization.

Had the institutions and operations of the alliance been commensurate with the comprehensiveness and intensity of the interests underlying it and had the influence exerted by the United States been commensurate with its power, the alliance would have fallen very little short of, if it had not amounted to, a confederation of states merging their most vital activities in the fields of foreign policy, defense, finance, and economics. Nothing of the kind evolved. For the United States, again faced with a conflict between the historic manifestations of its purpose and the demands of novel tasks, could not break out of the fetters with which those manifestations confined its freedom of thought and action. It proved incapable of playing the role it should have played as the paramount member of the Western alliance. Three inherited patterns of thought and action prevented it from adapting the traditional conception of its purpose to the new needs and opportunities: the limitation of the direct exercise of American power to the Western Hemisphere, the principle of equality in freedom, and the military approach to foreign policy.

The two previous occasions that carried American power beyond the limits of the Western Hemisphere were peculiar in that they allowed American power to retreat into its traditional limits after it had failed to establish itself firmly beyond them. The liquidation of the conquests of the Spanish-American War, in view of their accidental and peripheral connection with the American purpose, could begin virtually as soon as the conquests had been made. The failure of Wilson's attempt to make the world safe for democracy rendered pointless the presence of American power in Europe. The nature of the Russian threat after the Second World War left the United States no rational choice but to establish its power in permanence at the circumference of the Russian empire. But in what terms was that power to be established? Should it be the supremacy of American power, which in its consistent application would reduce America's allies to the status of satellites, or was it to be the freedom in equality of all members of the alliance, which, in its ideal realization, would issue in the harmonious co-operation of like-minded nations? These alternatives confronted the United States with a dilemma that could not be solved through the consistent realization of either alternative without denying one or another essential of the American purpose.

American power had to operate not in conquered territory where the conqueror could rule as he saw fit, but in the territory of friendly nations whose consent, if not desire, provided the sole title for the American presence. The purpose of that presence was the defense of the freedom and territorial integrity of the allies. The United States, in reducing its allies to the status of satellites, would have defeated the very purpose for the sake of which the European nations had become its allies. On the other hand, the establishment of the alliance on the basis of complete equality was feasible only on the assumption that the identity of interests among the allies and their awareness of it was so complete that they would be capable of pursuing common ends with common measures through free and equal co-operation. In the degree that this co-operation would fall short of the ideal expectation, the purpose of the alliance as a co-operative effort on behalf of the common interests would be defeated.

Of these two alternatives, the United States chose the latter. It refused to bring its superior power to bear on the alliance on behalf of common interests that were naturally inchoate and were competing with divergent ones. Thus it forewent the creation of a common framework of permanent and organic co-operation among allies who would relinquish their equal status in return for the alliance's protection of their essential freedoms. When the United States left the Western Hemisphere, it carried with it its military and economic power, but not its creative imagination or its constructive will. Significantly enough, this imagination and will were applied—and rather abortively at that—in the one sphere which is closest to the American tradition in foreign affairs: that is, in the military sphere, and NATO is presently its rather forlorn and brittle monument.

The United States emerged from the Second World War as the most powerful nation on earth by chance, and it assumed the leadership of the coalition of free nations by virtue of necessity. In consequence, its will and mind were not equal to its power, responsibility, and opportunity. Had these attributes of America been the result of conscious choice and deliberate aspiration, America would have been intellectually and morally prepared when what it had chosen and aspired to came to pass. Since it was not so prepared, it approached the tasks incumbent upon the paramount power of the Western alliance with unbecoming humility and unwarranted self-restraint.

America continued to see itself and its relations with the world very much as it had, say, fifty years earlier: a great nation that had accomplished great things in the material sphere and had achieved a unique political and social order, bringing happiness to itself and offering it to the world. It had achieved great things—military and political—outside the Western Hemisphere not by deliberate purpose but by force of circumstance. Had it not been for these circumstances, it would have been content to be left alone, and it would have left others alone. And only the intractability of the Soviet Union, so the United States thought, prevented the world from corresponding to this state of mind. America's image of itself and of its relations to the world, while taking account of the obvious facts of material power, superimposed the pattern of the past upon the contemporary world. As America has thus far been incapable of the Athenian pride in culture, so has it shunned the imperial attitude of Rome in political relations with the outside world. The political predominance required by its power was incompatible with its anti-imperialist tradition, which is the manifestation abroad of the principle of equality. Confronted with the choice between assuming the position of leadership commensurate with its power and treating its allies as equals, the United States chose the latter alternative. Accustomed to expand its rule into politically empty spaces but not to impose it, however gently and beneficially, upon existing political entities, it endeavored to establish within the Western alliance the same kind of consensus, by the same methods of rational persuasion and economic inducements, that had created, maintained, and developed the American commonwealth.

Yet the application of the equalitarian principle of the democratic consensus to the relations among allies resulted in disintegration and anarchy. For as the integrating effects of the domestic equalitarian consensus depend upon a pre-established sovereign central government, so whatever equality there can be among allies that differ drastically in power and responsibility must be subordinated to a hierarchical relationship between the paramount power and the rest. This hierarchical relationship has been lacking between the United States and its allies. Two kinds of consequences have flown from this lack. Either the alliance has been incapable of pursuing new, positive policies in common, or else the most determined ally has been able to impose its will upon the United States.

Of the former consequence, NATO is the outstanding example. The principle of equality among its fifteen members, applied to the political operations and over-all military planning of the alliance, put a virtually insurmountable obstacle in the way of new policies to be pursued by the fifteen allies in response to new opportunities or new threats. The principle of equality would have been compatible with new departures in policy only if all members of the alliance had an equal interest in such departures, were equally aware of these interests, and agreed completely on the means to be used in support of these interests. Short of an open threat of military conquest or revolution, such as confronted the members of NATO in the late 1940's, these conditions cannot be expected to be present at the same time. In the absence of one or another of them, the best an alliance thus constituted can achieve is to translate the lowest common denominator of agreed interests into common action. That denominator is likely to tend toward the irreducible minimum of common policies without which the alliance itself would cease to exist as an operating agency. Thus, while the objective conditions under which the fifteen allies live require a degree of unity in purpose and action far transcending that of a traditional alliance and while NATO was designed at its inception to be the instrument of that kind of unity, in actual performance NATO has become less and less distinguishable from a traditional alliance, and a rather loosely knit and stagnating one at that.

The other consequence of the equalitarian approach to alliances has been most marked in the bilateral relations between the United States and its allies. Governments that govern only because the United States maintains them, such as that of Formosa, and governments that have no alternative to American association, such as that of Spain, have been able to play a winning game in which the United States holds all the trumps. The United States has not been disposed to play these trumps for two reasons. On the one hand, its commitment to the principle of equality prevented it from bringing its superior power to bear upon a weak ally on behalf of its interests. On the other hand, these interests were conceived in terms of what I have elsewhere suggested calling the collector's approach to alliances. That is to say, the United States has been primarily interested in the conclusion of alliances *per se,* regardless of the specific and concrete interests these alliances were supposed to serve. An alliance thus conceived is a standing invitation, readily accepted, for a weak ally to make the alliance serve its own specific interests. Thus, the United States has paid for the willingness of weak and even unviable nations to become its allies by underwriting the interests of these nations, regardless of whether their interests coincide with or run counter to its own.

This relationship, unhealthy even by the standards of traditional foreign policy, is a far cry from the new order through which the United States was expected to realize the common purpose of the nations of Western civilization in the atomic age. The factors that brought about this relationship are also responsible for America's failure to project the American purpose into the areas of the world which are either uncommitted or unwillingly committed to Communism. The United States was not able to free itself from the pattern of thought and action established both by its tradition and by its successful reaction to the threat of Russian power in the aftermath of the Second World War—that is, to conceive of its relations to the outside world primarily in military terms. Thus, it saw itself surrounded by allies, by uncommitted nations that thus far had refused to become allies, and by satellites that Russian power prevented from becoming its allies. From this picture of the world, three militarily oriented policies ensued. The allies had to be kept in the American orbit, the uncommitted nations had to be drawn into it, and the satellites had to be liberated so that they could join it. The Baghdad Pact, SEATO, and the Eisenhower Doctrine were open-ended—and largely unsuccessful—invitations to the uncommitted nations of Asia and the Middle East to become allies of the United States or at least to accept military assistance from it.

These policies were by and large unsuccessful because the picture of the world from which they derived was at odds both with the facts of experience and with the interests of the United States. What the United States had to cope with outside Europe was not the threat of Russian military power but the promise of the new order of Communism. A policy of military alliances was irrelevant to the problems raised by that promise. It was also counterproductive; for by strengthening more often than not the forces of the *status quo* and the military establishments in the allied nations, it tended to identify the United States with those forces and with preparations for war and gave Communism in turn the opportunity to identify itself with the forces of progress and peace.

## 5. *Foreign Aid and Liberation*

The policy of foreign aid, considered the main instrument for strengthening the uncommitted nations in their uncommitted position, has similarly suffered from this predominantly military orientation. But it has also suffered from two other handicaps, one peculiar to foreign aid and the other providing yet another example of the misdirected projection of the original American purpose onto the international scene.

The American theory and practice of foreign aid derives by and large from certain unexamined assumptions that are part of the American folklore of politics. The popular mind has established a number of simple and highly doubtful correlations between foreign aid, on the one hand, and, on the other, a rising standard of living, social and political stability, democratic institutions and practices, and a peaceful foreign policy. The simplicity of these correlations is so reassuring and so reminiscent of the Wilsonian correlation between democratic institutions and domestic and international order and peace that the general philosophic proposition is hardly ever questioned in public, however much the contrary empirical evidence in specific cases forces drastic changes in practice.

Such fundamental questions as the following, concerning the technological results of foreign aid, are hardly ever asked explicitly: What are the social, political, and moral effects of foreign aid likely to be in various circumstances? Does successful foreign aid require a particular intellectual, political, and moral climate, or will the injection of economic capital and technological capability from the outside create this climate? To what extent and under what conditions is it possible for one nation to transform through outside intervention the economic and technological life of another nation? More specifically, in terms of the political objective of keeping the uncommitted nations uncommitted, how is one to create in the mind of the recipient the positive relationship between the aid and its beneficial results, on the one hand, and the political philosophy, system, and objectives of the giver, on the other? As long as the recipient disapproves of the politics of the giver, despite the aid he has received, the political effects of the aid are lost. These effects are similarly lost as long as the recipient remains unconvinced that the aid is but a natural, if not inevitable, manifestation of the politics of the giver. Foreign aid, then, remains politically ineffective as long as the recipient says either: "Aid is good, but the politics of the giver is bad," or: "Aid is good, but the politics of the giver—good, bad, or indifferent—has nothing to do with it."

Questions such as these require for answers policies of extraordinary subtlety and intricacy. Policies based on a simple correlation between foreign aid and what the United States desires in the uncommitted nations do not suffice. That correlation is a projection of the domestic experience of America onto the international scene. Capital formation and investment and technological innovation created the wealth and prosperity of America, and, so it was assumed, the export of American capital and technology to the underdeveloped nations would bring forth similar results there. The similarity between this and the Wilsonian expectation is striking. Wilson wanted to bring the peace and order of America to the rest of the world by exporting America's democratic institutions. His contemporary heirs want to bring the wealth and prosperity of America to the rest of the world through the export of American capital and technology. Yet while the failure of the Wilsonian experiment was quickly and drastically revealed, the failure of foreign aid has been less obvious, albeit no less drastic.

However, even if the United States had developed a well-thought-out philosophy of foreign aid, its application in practice would have come up against the same equalitarian principle that has frustrated the alliance policy of the United States. Yet while the application of this principle to our alliance policy was rather unwarranted by the objective situation, foreign aid has confronted the United States with a real dilemma. For if you apply the equalitarian principle, expressed in the slogan "no strings attached," to foreign aid, you put yourself at the mercy of unenlightened or corrupt governments that might misuse foreign aid through incompetence or by design. If, on the other hand, you assume responsibility for the way your aid is used, you feed the nationalistic suspicion of "imperialist" motives. By choosing the former horn of the dilemma, the United States has given the recipient governments at least a potential leverage against itself, similar to that its allies enjoy. This leverage is increased by the competitive participation of the Soviet Union in foreign aid, which allows the recipient governments to play one super-power against the other. Yet while the Soviet Union uses foreign aid as an integral part of its political policy, the United States has been incapable of serving consistently either its own purpose or the purposes of the underdeveloped nations.

The insufficiency of America's endeavors to realize its purpose in its relations with the outside world has come to a head in the failure of its policies toward the satellites of the Soviet Union. The total and obvious character of that failure suggests, as we shall see, the nature of the remedy. The inspiration from which the policies toward the satellites are derived is within the tradition of the American purpose of expanding the area of freedom. As a particular manifestation of that purpose, these policies continue the anti-imperialistic tradition of America, yet with one significant difference. The anti-imperialistic tradition of America has operated on two levels, the general one of revulsion against the normal practices of European power politics and the specific one of revulsion against a particular case of oppression of one nation by another. The political consequences of the first type were the abstention and isolationism of the Farewell Address. The second type had by and large no political consequences at all, but only led to an emotional commitment to what appeared to be the cause of freedom and national self-determination and humanitarian assistance to its suffering supporters. Thus, the American anti-imperialism of the nineteenth century supported the national movements of Europe against their monarchical enemies and opposed certain colonial ventures of European nations, and the American anti-imperialism of the early twentieth century took its stand against Imperial and Nazi Germany and against Tsarist and Soviet Russia.

The new anti-imperialism, aimed at the conquests of the Soviet Union, obviously partakes of these characteristics, but it possesses a quality that its predecessors lacked. It has become an integral and crucial part of the foreign policy of the United States. The traditional anti-imperialism of America was without a political objective, either by virtue of its very nature or else because the radius of an active American foreign policy was limited to the Western Hemisphere. The new anti-imperialism can no longer afford to condemn the suppression of liberty from afar and limit its tribute to freedom to charitable deeds. Committed to the containment of Communism—that is, to the preservation of national freedom threatened by Soviet imperialism throughout the world—the United States can reconcile itself to the loss of national freedom on the other side of the line of containment only if it ceases being anti-imperialistic altogether. If it wants to remain faithful to its anti-imperialist tradition, it must embark upon positive political and military policies on behalf of not only the preservation but also the expansion of national freedom. Yet at this point, when it came to adapting the purpose of America to the opportunities and limitations of the contemporary world, the crisis of perplexity of the American purpose was most strikingly revealed.

The American purpose of expanding the area of freedom encountered in its new connection with the foreign policy of the United States a new opportunity and a new limitation. It did not come to terms with either. Of this failure, the policy of liberation and the explicit inaction on the occasion of the Hungarian revolution of 1956 have been the outward manifestations. The policy of liberation manifested unconcern with the limitations; inaction on the occasion of the Hungarian revolution demonstrated unawareness of the opportunities.

The policy of liberation must be seen both as a logical extension of the policy of containment and as the positive implementation of the American refusal to recognize the legitimacy of the European conquests of the Soviet Union. Both Stalin and his successors attempted to liquidate the Cold War by concluding with the United States an agreement dividing Europe, if not the world, into two spheres of influence and recognizing the European conquests of the Soviet Union as definite and legitimate. The United States has consistently refused to consider even the possibility of such an agreement. The United States could let it go at that, satisfied with containing Russian power within the limits reached in 1945, and that is essentially what it did up to the beginning of 1953. The impulse to go beyond this negative, static policy of containment and non-recognition and to give it a positive, dynamic implementation stems of course from the traditional purpose of America and the national preference for mobility. But once America yielded to that impulse, it had to face the problem of what kind of positive policy it should pursue.

Consistent with its general conception of foreign policy, the United States conceived of liberation essentially in military terms—that is, as the evacuation of Eastern Europe by the Red Army. Such evacuation could be brought about only through military pressure carrying with it the risk of war. As the London *Economist* put it on August 30, 1952, when the policy of liberation was first proclaimed: "Unhappily 'liberation' applied to Eastern Europe—and Asia—means either the risk of war or it means nothing. . . . 'Liberation' entails no risk of war only when it means nothing." Since, according to repeated official statements, liberation was to be achieved without resort to war, it could not, as conceived by American policy, be achieved.

Thus, what pretended to be a new dynamic policy in harmony with the purpose of America turned out to be no policy at all, nothing more than a verbal commitment that could not be implemented by action. However, that commitment was taken as a threat by the Soviet Union and as a promise by the satellites. As such, far from contributing anything to the liberation of the satellites, it served, on the one hand, as a pretext for the Soviet Union to maintain its military rule in Eastern Europe and, on the other, as an incentive for the satellites to entertain illusions about what the United States might do and to be disillusioned with American policy and reconciled to their fate when no action was forthcoming.

The unreality of this policy of liberation encountered the ultimate test in the Hungarian revolution of 1956. For here the United States was faced not with the impossible task of liberating without resort to war but with the opportunity to support a liberation already achieved. If it remained inactive under these most favorable circumstances, it would demonstrate that there was no such thing as a policy of liberation but only verbal pronouncements designed to give the appearance that there was one. This is indeed what happened. The United States declared from the outset through its most authoritative spokesman, the President, that it would abstain from active interference. While it is a moot question as to how much the United States could have done, there can be no doubt—especially in view of the dissension within the Soviet government over the use of force, in the meantime revealed by Khrushchev—that it could have done more than nothing.

The United States failed utterly to relate the American purpose of extending the area of freedom to the political situations with regard to which it was called upon to act. Its words gave the appearance of novelty and daring to policies that were at best routine and at worst out of tune with what the times demanded. But its failure revealed both the nature and the innate strength of its purpose. In spite of what it said and did, the facts of its life, past and present, spoke louder than its purposeful words and deeds. The words and deeds had by and large been ineffectual and even counter-productive. Yet they were overshadowed and in rare moments obliterated by the universal awareness that equality in freedom still had a home in America. As the Hungarian revolution illuminated like a stroke of lightning the nature of man, showing the urge for freedom to be as elemental a human quality as the lust for power or the desire for wealth, so did the awareness of the freedom achieved within the American borders act as a corrective for words and deeds seemingly oblivious of the American purpose.

When the Vice President of the United States visited Poland in the spring of 1959 and when the President in the fall of that year visited India, the major uncommitted nation, they were greeted with a popular enthusiasm that was meant not for themselves but for the nation they represented. They were greeted, as Woodrow Wilson and Franklin D. Roosevelt had been before them, as living symbols of what the nation was thought to stand for, and the enthusiasm that the nation evoked in the persons of its representatives was due, it is safe to assume, not to its wealth and power but to the purpose that sets it apart from all other nations and makes it a model for other nations to emulate. When these living symbols of America ventured abroad they carried with them, as it were, the American purpose of expanding the area of freedom. They came as symbols not only of what America has achieved at home, but also of what it was to achieve abroad.

Thus an ironic twist of historic development made the outside world appear to understand the American purpose better than did America itself, and through a paradoxical reversal of roles the outside world had to recall the American message to an America that was incapable of making clear to the world what it was about. America, in ineffectual perplexity, tried to give the world its message, relating its traditional purpose to the contemporary world. Yet what it could not do for itself through the conscious effort of words and deeds, its very existence did for it. The living presence of its achievements carried the promise of further achievements to the world, and the hope of the world carried that message back to America.

# IV

# THE CONTEMPORARY CRISIS AT HOME

## A. *The Social Crisis: Hedonism of the Status Quo*

### 1. *The Decline of the Public Realm*

As THE FIRST DOMESTIC CRISIS of the American purpose grew from its failure—the impairment of freedom and inequality in wealth and status—so the second domestic crisis results from its success. The intervention of the state on behalf of social and economic reform restored a measure of vertical mobility; a succession of technological revolutions opened up interior frontiers; and the loss of freedom—drastic as it was, as we shall see—either did not affect directly the day-by-day activities of the individual or else was compensated for by economic and social gains. The great issues of the past, so it seemed, were dead; the battles fought for their sake had been won by the proponents of equality in freedom; America seemed to have achieved its purpose at home. The great masses whose freedom and equality had in the past been precarious or denied reached a status of middle-class security which was but ephemerally threatened by mild recessions or a slowdown in the rise of the standard of living.

The inequalities of wealth which had given momentum to the movements of social protest at the turn of the century still persist, but they are accepted almost with complacency by the new members of the middle class. Between the proletariat whose condition in the England of the 1830's Engels described and the other half of the nation which did not live in misery and insecurity and without a chance for improvement there was a difference in kind. The difference between the contemporary middle-class workingman and the millionaire is rather one of degree; it concerns the quality and quantity of the amenities of life available to either. In the kind of amenities of life at their disposal and even, in a measure, in the very style of life they lead, they are equal. The proletarian who does not know where he will get his next meal and the man who does not need to worry about that are separated by a whole world, as Marx and Engels correctly pointed out. The contemporary workingman who has his regular wage, medical and unemployment insurance, a pension plan, a house, a car, paid vacations, and scholarships for his children may envy the millionaire the amount of his income, the number of his houses and cars, and the length of his vacations, and he may deplore the slowness of the process that is supposed to narrow the quantitative gap that separates the two. But both of them live in the same world, and what separates them appears to them trivial, at least in comparison to what they have—actually and potentially—in common.

What must be obvious even to the casual observer is borne out by the income statistics. If one compares the income distribution of 1929 with that of 1958 (adjusted for the change in the value of the dollar) and assumes a

1958 income of $4,000 per household as a minimum in terms of adequacy, one finds that in 1929 almost two thirds of all incomes, counted by households, fell below that level while in 1958 slightly more than one third fell below it. If one assumes the income range between $5,000 and $10,000 as typical middle-class, then in 1958 38 per cent of all incomes fell into that range while in 1929 only 21 per cent did. As concerns the highest income group, exceeding $10,000, the percentage of incomes belonging to it had risen from 8 per cent in 1929 to 13 in 1958.[1]

In consequence, social conflict in our contemporary society is neither revolutionary, trying to replace one social system with another by whatever means are at hand, nor is it reformist, trying to change the social *status quo* according to constitutional rules. Rather it is concerned with piecemeal adjustments within the existing *status quo* through the use of political and economic pressures. Social conflict so-called has really been reduced in our time to the competitive attempts of parochial interest groups to increase slightly their relative share in the social product. Relatively little, and certainly nothing vital, is at stake in this competition, and the political issues in which it is reflected partake of its limited importance and unspectacular character. Nothing in these issues is likely to appeal to the imagination, to conjure up a vision of a brave new world or of a rotten old one, as the case may be, to bring men to the barricades to defend or overthrow the *status quo*.

The very distinction between the opposition and the government tends to become devoid of meaning in terms of issues, the former being incapable of presenting a clear, recognizable alternative to what the government stands for. For both government and opposition are essentially

[1] Selma F. Goldsmith: "Income Distribution by Size—1955-58," in *Survey of Current Business,* Vol. 39, No. 4 (April 1959), p. 9 ff.

identified with the same interests, they hold the same convictions, and they advocate and pursue essentially the same policies. National unity, co-operation between government and opposition, and moderation in all things either the government or the opposition does and advocates become the means and ends of national policy. What is at stake in political conflicts is not so much philosophies, policies, and issues as persons and, through them. control over certain segments of society and its economic product.

Under these conditions of—relatively speaking—universal satisfaction and harmony, politics itself, the struggle for power within and over the state, loses its vital force. The prizes of power still appear worth having to those who run for office. The people at large participate in and follow the political contests from habit, a sense of duty, mild self-interest, and in the spirit of a sporting contest, betting on and identifying themselves with one or the other team. In their consciousness the vital nexus between their individual lives and the ways the commonwealth is being governed has been loosened, if not severed altogether. They would rather see one candidate or one party win than the other, but they do not think that it will really matter much.

This decline of politics is reminiscent of, but not identical with, the Marxist withering-away of the state. The state, the domination of man by man, has certainly not been replaced by the administration of things. But the great, vital, and noble issues for the sake of which in times past men have sought power over other men have been replaced by the humdrum issue of control of the administration. The great issues and heroic struggles of politics have indeed withered away, and so have the great political enthusiasms. Their place has been taken by the competition of political professionals, representing parochial interest groups, for the control of the administrative apparatus. The body politic moves slowly on, the great decisions that made it what it is seemingly behind it, administering and expanding what has been achieved rather than achieving a purpose that still awaits realization. The structure and inner purpose of the colossus are seemingly set once and for all. What movement there is within that colossus may at times carry one segment forward at a faster pace than others, and what controversies still remain are concerned with that relative pace. Political apathy joins social complacency. More of the same, improved and better distributed—this is the formula to which the popular mood seems to have reduced the purpose of America.

It hardly needs pointing out that the objective conditions of American existence do not bear out that mood. Millions of Americans are deprived of the middle-class security and comforts that have become the mode of life in America. Thirty-two million Americans have less than $50 a week to spend for a family of four; one fifth of these are children, and eight million are over sixty-five years of age. In 1959 fourteen percent of American families had annual incomes of less than $2,000. The very survival of America and of the civilization of which it forms a part calls, as we have seen, for a new ordering of its relations with the outside world. The inner workings of its government, the democratic relations between government and people, the relationship between public and private— and, more particularly, public and economic—spheres, the modes of economic production and distribution, education, housing, transportation, the very nature of public purposes and standards of thought and action—all these must be re-examined if America wants to remain a living civilization. For with civilizations it is as it is with men: they cannot stand still without losing their vitality; their task is never done; their purpose achieved is but a steppingstone to achievement of a further purpose; and when they say that their purpose has been achieved, what they are really saying is that their life has lost its meaning and that while they may go on living for a while, there is really no point to it.

What, then, accounts for the contrast between the apathy and complacency of the popular mood and the existence and even urgency of these outstanding issues? Some of these issues transcend in importance, not only for society as a whole but for each individual citizen, most of the issues that in the past have commanded the passionate commitment of the people pro or con. Is the nuclear-armaments race, for instance, more important than a tax on tea or the expansion of slavery to new territories? Objectively, there can of course be no doubt that it is, but it has not aroused the political passions of the American people one way or the other to make it a political issue. Why is this so? Two interrelated answers suggest themselves.

First of all, the great unresolved issues, while intellectually recognized by at least a minority, are not experienced by the mass of the people as being of direct concern to, or manageable by, them. The legal issue of slavery could be settled a century ago by a presidential proclamation emancipating the slaves; it takes more than a decision of the Supreme Court to stop the treatment of their descendants as though they were still slaves. It was easier to free the slaves than it is to ensure that their descendants will be dealt with as equals. And a century ago the issue of slavery presented itself in so clear-cut a fashion that a civil war could be fought about it. On the other hand, the contemporary issue of equality in all its practical ramifications is too complex to allow at least thoughtful and responsible people to take so simple a position pro or con.

## The Decline of the Public Realm

Admitted that the nuclear-armaments race threatens all of us with destruction, that our public education is inadequate, that our economic system is wasteful, I personally, says the man in the street, have nothing to complain about, I am satisfied. And if I were not, what could I do about it? The vital link between the intellectual awareness of unresolved issues and the resolution not to leave them unresolved is missing. The man in the street is no longer convinced that public issues will, or even ought to, yield to concerted popular action. They have become remote, unintelligible, and intractable. If the experts cannot deal with them, how can he?

This abdication of political will on the part of the electorate is duplicated by the abdication of political leadership on the part of the representatives of the people. They justify that abdication by citing the political apathy of the electorate. There is no political mileage, they say, in the H bomb, in housing, education, foreign policy. The failure of isolated attempts, such as Adlai Stevenson's in the campaign of 1956, to identify the electorate with the solution of these issues seems to bear out their reluctance. Whatever the reason, whether apathy from above is responsible for the apathy below, or vice versa, or whether there is perhaps a common cause for both, the result is clear: there is apathy all around, and the great issues that demand solution are debated by the politicians, while the people mind their private businesses as though the great public issues were no business of theirs.

This lack of interest in public issues leads of necessity to the contraction of the public sphere. It results in the cessation of genuine political activity by the citizen, the encroachment of private interests upon the public sphere, and the relative shrinkage of national resources, human and material, committed to public purposes.

The citizen becomes so engrossed with cultivating his

private garden that he remains a citizen only in the formal sense of enjoying political rights that he sporadically and lackadaisically makes use of. In the full sense in which citizenship means making the public business one's own, he ceases to be a citizen. The public business is transacted by technicians and administrators who render many and the most important of their decisions without the participation and frequently even without the knowledge of the citizens. The elected representatives of the people in Congress, too, tend to become impotent bystanders who at best can ratify or protest against decisions after they have been taken.

The citizenry, and its elected representatives as well, are then reduced to looking at the public sphere primarily as a source of trouble or of bounty for the private sphere. The involvement of the citizen in politics (aside from voting and ritualistic performances), his active participation in the public sphere tends to be concentrated in three functions: to keep the public authority away from the private sphere in so far as it seeks to regulate and control it and to collect taxes; to make the public sphere a subsidiary of the private one in so far as it transfers public funds and public power into private hands; and to compete with other citizens in the performance of these functions. In so far as citizens appear still to be actively interested in public issues, they are in truth interested in them not *per se* for their intrinsic merits, but because of their effects upon the private sphere. The very concept of happiness which in the Declaration of Independence and the *Federalist* refers to public happiness in the sense of the general welfare now takes on an exclusively private and predominantly material connotation. Happiness and wealth tend to become synonymous.

We are here in the presence of not only a quantitative but also a qualitative shift from the public to the private realm. While in a totalitarian society what ought to be private is forcibly absorbed into the public sphere, all that is public is here viewed as being affected by a private interest. In a telling reversal of roles, many of the regulatory commissions created by the Federal and state governments to regulate business "affected with a public interest" have become instruments through which private business secures its support from the public powers. Indeed, the Bentleyan ideal of the modern state as a congeries of pressure groups finds here an empirical approximation.[2]

A national purpose that has been narrowed to the enjoyment and improvement of the *status quo,* defined in hedonistic economic terms, is bound to attract to the private sphere much of the talent that previously found sufficient material and intangible rewards in the public one. Businessmen may do a stint of public service only to return to the business world richer in prestige and connections. More importantly and ominously, many public officials use public office as a steppingstone and find in business positions the culmination of their careers. The proportion of West Point graduates who leave the service at the earliest legal opportunity to enter private employment has recently amounted to more than a fourth. The President's choice of social companions, on the one hand, sanctions the preference of society and, on the other, sets a pattern that the nation actually and vicariously imitates. Thus, the private sphere becomes the focus toward which the aspirations and actions even of eminent representatives of the public sphere gravitate. Not only is the popular estimation of the public sphere being lowered in consequence; the public sphere is also gravely impoverished by the loss of outstanding talent.

[2] Cf. Arthur F. Bentley: *The Process of Government: A Study in Social Pressures* (Bloomington: The Principia Press; 1935).

The philosophy that underlies this depreciation of the public sphere is of course an echo of the values of nineteenth-century liberalism. The public sphere is seen as a necessary evil; it is the inevitable result of our vices, while the private sphere is the repository of both our private and public virtues. The private virtues are erected as the sole standard by which the qualities of both private and public action, the qualifications of both private and public persons, are to be judged. This philosophy necessarily destroys the tension between the private and the public spheres, between man *per se* and man as a citizen, which has been a perennial theme of Western political thought. For that philosophy, Aristotle's questions of whether the virtue of a good man is identical with the virtue of a good citizen is meaningless, for here the virtue of a good man and that of a good citizen are by definition identical.

This philosophy is translated into the folklore of American politics as the conviction that the main qualification for a political career is personal honesty. A politician may be wrongheaded in judgment, weak in decision, unsuccessful in action. "But don't you see how sincere he is?" people will say. "He is at least an honest man. He means well." The man in the street transfers the values that he cherishes in his private life to the political stage and judges the actors by the same standards he applies to himself and his fellows in their private spheres.

The values of the Eisenhower administration, both in verbal expression and in the character of its most prominent members, have conformed to these popular standards, and its virtually unshakable popularity owed much to this identity of political standards. Mr. Eisenhower, with characteristic frankness and consistency, has time and again measured his public actions by the yardstick of private values and expressed his conviction that since he did not find these public actions wanting when tested by the values of private life, they had passed the political test as well. He summarized his philosophy in his news conference of August 1957, in these terms:

> I, as you know, never employ threats. I never try to hold up clubs of any kind, I just say, "this is what I believe to be best for the United States" and I try to convince people by the logic of my position. If that is wrong politically, well then I suppose you will just have to say I am wrong, but that is my method, and that is what I try to do.

The public sphere appears here as a mere extension of private life, devoid of conflicts of interest to be settled by contests of power, by employing threats and holding up clubs—methods traditionally associated with politics—and subject to the same rational rules of conduct which are supposed to make the private sphere orderly, peaceful, and harmonious.

When the President was asked at his news conference of July 31, 1957, about the circumstances under which Mr. Gluck was appointed Ambassador to Ceylon, he replied with indignation:

> . . . in the first place, if anybody is ever recommended to me on the basis of any contribution he has ever made to any political party, that man will never be considered. I never heard it mentioned to me as a consideration, and I don't take it very kindly as suggesting I would be influenced by such things.

Here again, the issue was seen in strictly privately terms. The issue for the President hinged exclusively upon his personal knowledge of a campaign contribution, and since he had no such knowledge, there was no issue. In this philosophy there is no room for the recognition of an

objective conflict of interests to which the state of the conscience of any single individual may well be irrelevant.

Not only have the dominant members of the Eisenhower administration expressed themselves and acted in
terms of a philosophy alien to politics, but many of them
have been selected in view of their excellence as private
citizens, on the assumption that the qualities which go
into the making of a good man and, more particularly, a
good businessman go also into the making of a good statesman. Many selections have been excellent within the limits
of the standards applied. But these excellent men have in
all innocence done greater damage to the political life and
the political interests of the nation than many of their
less worthy predecessors; for they have brought to their
public offices nothing but personal excellence—no understanding of political life, let alone ability to cope with the
processes of politics.

A good man who becomes an actor on the political scene
without knowing anything about the rules of politics is
like a good man who goes into business without knowing
anything about it or who drives a car although ignorant
of how to drive. Yet while society recognizes the need to
protect itself against the latter, it feels no need for protection against the former. Indeed, the virtuous political
dilettante has for it a well-nigh irresistible fascination. It is
as though society were anxious to atone for the sacrifices of
private virtue which the political sphere demands and to
take out insurance against the moral risks of political action by identifying itself with political leaders who sacrifice the public good on the altar of their private virtue.

Society has learned to take bad men in its stride and
even to protect itself against those who know the rules of
the political game only too well and use them to the detri-
ment of society. Society will have to learn, if it wants to

survive, that it needs protection also against good men who are too good even to take note of the rules of the political game. And it must reconcile itself to the uncomfortable paradox that bad men who put their knowledge of those rules at the service of society are to be preferred to good men whose ignorance and moral selfishness put the very survival of society in jeopardy. In short, it must learn what Henry Taylor taught more than a century ago when he wrote in *The Statesman:* "It sometimes happens that he who would not hurt a fly will hurt a nation."[3]

Corresponding to its moral depreciation, the role of the public sphere is here conceived as merely subsidiary to the private one; only the functions the latter cannot perform ought to be assumed by the former. And it goes without saying that the extent of the functions which are left to the public sphere is strictly interpreted. It also goes without saying that this conception of the relations between public and private domains is completely at odds with the relations actually existing in the contemporary world.

However, this conception, while it is nothing more than a romantic rationalization of an unfeasible alternative to the actual state of affairs, exerts a powerful influence upon the distribution of social functions and the allocation of material resources between the public and private spheres. The latter, taking precedence over the former in philosophic valuation, has a prior claim on both. Thus, it can indulge in the hedonism of production and distribution, and only the availability of resources and of consumptive capacity limits its expansion. On the other hand, the public sphere is strictly circumscribed by the requirements of a balanced budget. Taking an over-all view of national life and comparing the shares of the national product both

[3] Henry Taylor: *The Statesman* (Cambridge: Heffer and Sons; 1957), p. 34.

sectors actually receive with the shares they ought to receive in view of the tasks they must perform for the nation, there can be no doubt that the relative share of the public sector has shrunk by stagnation. For a static budgetary ceiling has not allowed the relative share of the public sector to keep pace with the increase in the national product and in the functions that are called public, such as national defense and internal development, because only the government can perform them.

The subordination of the functions of government to the requirements of a balanced static budget sheds an illuminating light upon the contemporary crisis of the American purpose. It is yet another symptom of that crisis. American society finds its purpose in its own perpetuation, especially in terms of economic productivity, and the American government supports that purpose with its authority and power. That purpose is static; it is tantamount to the defense of the *status quo*. For a budget that is balanced in terms of a certain *a priori* determined figure is the financial equivalent of the *status quo*.

The issue here is not between a balanced and an unbalanced budget, but between a static and a dynamic budget, both balanced. While a static budget takes income and expenditures as fixed, a dynamic budget anticipates and promotes corresponding changes in both in view of purposes transcending the budget. In other words, a dynamic budget is a means to ends that have nothing to do with the budget; a static budget is an end in itself, the end to which all other ends of government are subordinated. There is, then, a world of difference between a dynamic budget that —answering the question: what needs to be done?—is the elastic indicator of the public purposes of the nation, and a static budget that—answering the question: what can we afford?—does not allow the public purposes to rise above a predetermined ceiling. A national policy whose reach is determined by a static budget is in truth a numbers game of self-mutilation, played by the rigorous rules of the accountant's craft.

The philosophy of the balanced static budget requiring the government "to live within its means" provides still another example of the misapplication to the public sphere of principles with which the private citizen is alleged to comply. The government, so the argument runs, can no more consistently live "beyond its means" without going broke than can the private citizen. Yet, leaving aside the ability of the government to create new money on a massive scale, an ability of which at least the law-abiding citizen is deprived, the analogy between private and public budgets falls to the ground because ever more private budgets are becoming dynamic. To an ever increasing extent, the private citizen does exactly what the philosophy of the balanced budget forbids the government to do: he satisfies present needs through the expenditure of anticipated income. By borrowing, especially in the form of credit buying, the private citizen stimulates economic productivity, which, in turn, enables him to meet his financial obligations. While the government asks: what can we afford? the private citizen asks: what do we want? and answers the question within the rational limits of anticipated income. Yet nobody appears to ask the question: what do we need? and try to answer it by applying some objective standards of evaluation.

The substitution of means for ends, which we have noticed before and shall notice again as a specific social manifestation of the crisis of the American purpose, elevates the philosophy of the balanced static budget to the ultimate principle of government. This is consistent; for a nation that has lost its purpose, or is not aware that it has one in spite of itself, must seek a substitute in a subordinate objective. That objective now becomes ultimate since there is no longer a purpose to which it could be subordinated. Yet the kind of substitute chosen is significant. For a society that is amorphous by nature and can find its integrating principle only in conformity with its purpose, congenitally beset by the risk of alienation and deprived of objective standards of conduct—such a society grasps in the balanced budget something tangible it can hold on to, something that cannot be doubted or denied. The balanced budget gives form to what is formless; it sets limits to the pursuit of a limitless purpose. In the midst of the uncertainty of the age, the balanced budget is *terra firma*, an island of absolute and unquestionable certainty. The two ledgers of the public books in balance—they are almost like the two tablets of the Law harmoniously designed. Let no man say that we don't know what we are about, that we have no principle to abide by, that we have no purpose! High-placed officials of our government have been quoted as saying in private that they would rather see us lose out to the Russians than see the budget unbalanced. Yet that obsession with the balanced budget statically conceived—however irrational in itself—is but a symptom of the deep insecurity and malaise induced by the loss of national purpose.

The contraction of the public sphere and its drainage of political controversy over substantive issues is accompanied by a change in the nature of conformity as the integrating principle of American society. Equality in freedom as the formal principle of the American consensus was qualified in its formalism by the substantive controversies over the objective order it was to serve and over the concrete measures and institutional arrangements required for its implementation in a particular historic situation. What did equality in freedom mean in 1860 or 1904 or 1912 or 1932, and what policies did it require? The great controversies over how to answer these questions were the dynamic instruments through which the American purpose was ever again but never definitely achieved. These achievements, born of ever renewed struggle, constitute that series of typical American revolutions through which, from the Declaration of Independence to the Full Employment Act of 1946, American society has continuously renewed itself.

The parties to these great political controversies were concerned with the meaning and implementation of equality in freedom in a particular historic situation, and they endowed with an absolute validity the particular meaning and implementation with which they were identified. From these contradictory and at times irreconcilable claims to absolute validity, the controversies received their intensity and sometimes their ferocity. Were slavery, the power of the trusts, child labor, mass unemployment compatible with the purpose of America? Could they coexist with equality in freedom? To make one answer to questions such as these prevail over another one was deemed worth fighting for. To the support of such claims, we could indeed pledge "our lives, our fortunes, and our sacred honor."

Of what issue can that much be said today? The question answers itself. There is no such issue today. None of the contemporary issues of domestic politics of which the public at large is aware commands for its alternative solutions those loyalties out of which great political conflicts are made. There are divergent opinions and interests, to be sure; but there is no great issue that men deem worthy of sacrifice and risk. In consequence, the integrating principle of American society has lost both its dynamic and its substantive qualities. The great political controveries of American history sought to renew the American purpose by giving it a meaning appropriate to what the times seemed to require. As long as such a controversy lasted, the American consensus, within the universal commitment to the formal principle of equality in freedom *per se,* was split in two or more ways. A number of schools of thought contended with one another to give substance to the American consensus. Once a new substantive consensus had emerged from this struggle through the victory of one school, it was likely to split and be restored again and again.

This dynamic process of substantive renewal has for the time being come to a halt. The American consensus, which in the past was monistic in form and pluralistic in substance, has become monistic in both respects. In consequence, conformism now extends to the substance of policies and constitutional arrangements. Since no issue is any longer worth fighting over, a position must be "moderate," and what once was a compromise between seemingly irreconcilable positions now transforms itself into the adjustment of positions differing only in degree. Since the purpose of America seems to have been achieved—the need for improvement notwithstanding—the *status quo* tends to become as sacred as the purpose itself, and an attack upon the *status quo* almost as unpalatable as dissent from the purpose. Since there is nothing left to fight for, there is nothing to fight against. Enthusiasm for causes and controversy over them tend to become vices since they raise in some way the question of the legitimacy of the *status quo,* and even those who defend the *status quo* with more than moderate passion imply the possibility that its legitimacy could be in doubt and, hence, in need of a pointed defense. The *status quo,* to be truly secure, must be taken for granted, like the seasons and the stars. Conformity, then, becomes a universal virtue, and the preservation and improvement of the *status quo* emerge as the ultimate substantive purpose of society.

The *status quo* is conceived, following the American

tradition, in terms of the enjoyment of material wealth or what is now called the standard of living. The improvement of the *status quo*, then, is synonymous with the continuous increase of material wealth enjoyed by the great mass of people. An ever greater national product, ever higher personal incomes, ever more extensive social benefits, ever more amenities of life, and ever greater variety of novelties, change for its own sake of the cogs and bolts of a hardly moving social machine—such are the goals in which the purpose of America seems to exhaust itself.

The keyword here is "exhaust." For these goals have been constant in the American tradition, but they have not been exclusive. They have been at the service of the overriding purpose of equality in freedom and of substantive principles of justice which were in turn at the service of that overriding purpose. In other words, these material goals were indeed hedonistic, but they were more than that. Their hedonism—as a collective commitment of American society in contrast to the hedonism pure and simple of individuals—was subordinated to the transcendent and objective principles of justice which both restrained and directed it, as it were, beyond itself.

## 2. A Society of Waste

The unrestrained and self-sufficient hedonism of contemporary society has brought in its wake what must be called a society of waste. For where the productivity of the nation feeds, as it were, upon itself and does not serve as a means to transcendent ends that select and assign the goods to be produced, waste necessarily ensues. Production, engendered by the needs of life and carried forward by the desire to make life easier; more attractive, and more nearly complete, becomes like a cancerous growth, multiplying and creating with elaborate and costly artificiality demands that can be called rational only in view of the goal of producing more and more goods. This system of production is rational because it rejects human needs and genuine human desires as determining factors, replacing them with quantity of production for its own sake. There is no economic virtue—nor any other virtue—in producing more automobiles this year than last and more next year than this. Nor is there any virtue except that of prestige in the ability to buy a new automobile every year. And the element of prestige diminishes as that ability becomes more and more general, so that to drive an old car becomes a mark of distinction for the select few who thereby demonstrate that they have prestige enough to be able to dispense with one of its manifestations.

This system of production is irrational not only because it performs no positive economic or other social function, but also because it is wasteful of the resources of the nation. When Mr. Khrushchev looked at the crowded San Francisco highways, he reportedly exclaimed: "What a waste."[1] This waste is a result of artificially induced competition and obsolescence. Essentially identical products compete with one another for a greater share of the market. They are essentially identical because the needs they serve are identical and must in the nature of things be satisfied by identical products. Competition among products of this kind can be justified in terms of price, but not of quality, since sub-standard products would have no chance in the market because they would not serve the customers' needs.

Yet—to take the example of toothpaste and motor transportation of persons, which, while differing vastly in economic importance, exemplify the two prototypes of wasteful competition—the competition among scores of dif-

[1] *Time*, January 18, 1960, p. 76.

ferent kinds of toothpaste and hundreds of different kinds of passenger car proceeds primarily on the basis not of actual differences in price but of fictitious differences in quality. The requirements that toothpaste must meet in order to perform its cleansing function—aside from appealing to different tastes—are of the same order of simplicity as those of drinking water or electricity. One standard product coming in, say, three different flavors, its quality periodically tested in view of standards required by a commercially neutral agency, would satisfy the need. The requirements to be met by the rational production of automobiles are more complex in view of the customers' needs and technological change. Cars must, obviously, vary according to size, power, and comfort, and they must change from time to time to take account of technological developments. One could imagine that, say, ten models to be changed every five years would give rational satisfaction to actual needs.

The enormous, wasteful proliferation of virtually identical products for competitive purposes, sometimes even within the same company, calls for the artificial creation and ever renewed and increased stimulation of demand. These wants are created, stimulated, and satisfied by artificial or imaginary obsolescence, advertising, and marketing. These efforts, as wasteful as the proliferation of products of which they are the inevitable result, add nothing to the substance of the product but serve exclusively the purpose of selling a maximum quantity of the product to people who would otherwise feel no need for it. Artificially induced obsolescence is the result of making products deliberately less durable in order to force the customer to exchange the prematurely used-up product for a new one. For example, light bulbs are designed to burn out quickly. The inducement of imaginary obsolescence has become standard operating procedure in many industries through the annual replacement of last year's models with new and allegedly superior ones. To persuade the public that last year's perfectly serviceable model will no longer do has become one of the main tasks of advertising, and its psychological success is translated into actual sales by elaborate systems of distribution, which in their proliferation and wastefulness of operations are the counterpart of the elephantiasis of production.

This commitment to ever greater competitive production for its own sake is by no means limited to consumer goods. The construction industry thrives on it, tearing down good buildings to make place for new ones. Even an undertaking so important for national survival as the design and production of missiles has been affected by the competitive multiplication of the productive effort. That this kind of competitive effort is irrational because it serves no legitimate need and, hence, wastes scarce material resources stands to reason. That it is also wasteful of human resources is less obvious. Not only are unnecessary cars and office buildings being made of steel that might more beneficially be employed for the construction of dwellings and schools, but hundreds and thousands of skilled men perform superfluous functions at the service of unnecessary production. The spirit of waste that permeates the economic system is reflected in feather-bedding as a well-nigh universal principle of employment. Increase for its own sake has become here, as in production, a principle whose rightness is being accepted as self-evident dogma. The Federal government, committed by statute to the maintenance of full employment, gives at least implicit support to the principle.

That wastefulness is, indeed, not limited to the industrial and commercial spheres. Nothing surpassing our agricultural system in exorbitant wastefulness can ever have been devised by the mind of man. Our secondary education is an enormously wasteful operation in terms of what students learn in the time spent at school. And so is the public bureaucracy in terms of the persons employed. Carelessness about the national patrimony, human and material, tends to become a national habit, partly in imitation of the example set by industry and commerce, partly for a deeper reason. As a spendthrift throws his money around aimlessly because he has no aim by which he could tell worth-while from useless expenditures, so a nation no longer conscious of its purpose will tend to be wasteful of its resources because it lacks the discriminating discipline that a purpose imparts to thought and action.

So irrational a system, which seems to reduce the American purpose to ever increased production for its own sake, is defended, paradoxically enough, in the name of the original American purpose of equality in freedom. Applied to the economic sphere, we have encountered it as free enterprise and freedom of competition. Here we are in the presence of the contemporary version of the intellectual paradox and the practical perversion that Wilson and the two Roosevelts recognized and grappled with. Freedom of economic enterprise and competition are indeed, as we have seen, among the original American freedoms. Yet only in the near-anarchy of the frontier did they come close to absolute realization. Their invocation by the modern concentrations of economic power has served the purpose of keeping such concentrations free from regulation rather than of safe-guarding or restoring the freedom of enterprise and competition of all, jeopardized by the very existence of these concentrations. The wasteful anarchy of our system of production and distribution is indeed akin to the anarchy of the frontier, superimposed upon the economic life of the nation.

Yet the claim that the present system of production and distribution is the very core of the American purpose and that its change would impair the equality in freedom all of us enjoy must be stripped of the ideological function it performs for the concentrations of economic power, and of the ritualistic uses to which it is put by the mass media of public opinion. Instead, it must be put to the test of empirical verification. What would it mean for the equality and the freedoms, especially the economic ones, of all of us—producer, distributor, and consumer—if our multiple choice of toothpaste were abolished in favor of one standard brand supplied by a monopoly as our water and our electricity are supplied? What would it mean if our choice of automobiles were limited as our choice of air, rail, and water transportation is? And what does it actually mean that some of us have imposed such a limitation upon ourselves by driving our cars regardless of age as long as they run? Obviously it means nothing at all for the equality in freedom we enjoy.

Equality in freedom is a qualitative and not a quantitative concept. It is achieved not through the indiscriminate proliferation of choices but through the preservation and extension of those upon which the development and fulfillment of the human person depend. The ability to choose among an irrational number of commodities is not one of them. The limitation of choices such as these signifies nothing more than the freeing of material and human resources, now wastefully employed, for more rational tasks. There is nothing unusual in such a redirection of resources. The economic system engages in it continuously, adapting itself to technological changes and complying with the law of supply and demand, and the government participates in it on a massive scale through taxation, credit policies, purchases, and contracts. But it does so for a multitude of unrelated special purposes, not in view of an over-all conception of the purposes that the resources of the nation ought to serve.

## A Society of Waste

These anarchic and wasteful conditions of production and distribution have been criticized for a long time primarily on doctrinaire social grounds. In the thirties, in particular, a "planned economy" was widely regarded in America in the same light as was nationalization in Great Britain a decade later: a kind of automatic corrective of the obvious deficiencies of the private economic system. In recent years the Russian successes in the exploration of space have shocked an ever growing number of Americans into re-examining their own institutions and practices. They have been critical of the system of production and distribution primarily in view of our ability to compete successfully with the Soviet Union. While I did not share the faith in a planned economy when it was popular, I do indeed share the contemporary concern for America's competitive position. It does not need to be argued that the very physical survival of the United States depends upon the sufficiency of its retaliatory power to deter the Soviet Union and that nothing can be allowed to stand in the way of that retaliatory power being maintained or, if necessary, quickly restored. It also stands to reason, as I have pointed out before, that in so far as the prestige of the United States in the world and, more particularly, among the uncommitted nations of Asia and Africa derives from its reputation for technological excellence, that reputation must be maintained or, if necessary, restored even at the expense of traditional institutions and practices.

However, the popular mind views the deficiencies of the economic system not only in terms of those specific international interests of the United States which require domestic adjustments and reforms, but also and even primarily in the light of a contest in productivity between the United States and the Soviet Union. The Soviet Union has challenged the United States in the field of over-all productivity, proclaiming for all to hear that it will surpass the United States by 1970. The United States has taken up that challenge as though it were engaged in a sporting contest or else in commercial competition with the Soviet Union. The United States, so it appears, is at present the world champion in productivity and cannot allow the Soviet Union to take that championship away from it. The United States appears to look at its relations with the Soviet Union somewhat as the Chevrolet Division of General Motors looks at Ford: it produces today more than its nearest competitor and must stay on top even if to that end it must change some of its institutions and practices.

It cannot be lost on the reader that this conception of the competition with the Soviet Union is a projection onto the international scene of the domestic commitment to ever greater productivity for its own sake. As America tended to reduce its purpose to that commitment when it thought it was alone in the world, so it remains loyal to it now when the Soviet Union has challenged it on that very ground. The Russian challenge gives America an added incentive to persevere in the pursuit of that purpose, to which its own impulses had led it already, of producing more and more for the sake of producing it. And what formerly was nothing more than a national preference, which the nation was free to yield to or give up as circumstances might require, now appears as a national necessity to be complied with for the sake of the nation's self-esteem and standing in the world.

## 3. *The Decline of Objective Standards of Excellence*

The reduction of the American purpose to a hedonism of production and the disappearance of great issues from the political scene are different sides of the same coin. They are symptoms of the general weakening and partial dissolution of objective standards which must guide purposeful individual and collective thought and action and by which that thought and action are to be judged.

American society, like the great vital societies of the past, was created and maintained by the belief in the universal validity of such objective standards. These standards were deemed to underlie society, this particular one and all others. Society had not created these standards and, hence, could not abolish them. Society could but comply with them to its benefit or depart from them at its peril. The standards themselves were the human formulation of the objective nature of things, and it is irrelevant to this discussion whether theological or secular terms were used to formulate them. The validity of these standards owed nothing to society; like the law of gravity, they were valid even if nobody recognized and abided by them; but society owed whatever it achieved or failed to achieve to its compliance with, or neglect of, these standards. In brief, society was believed to be embedded in, and guided by, self-evident truths, rational and moral, from which society derived whatever truth was to be found in its thought and action.

Regardless of one's view as to the merits of this conception of society, it is emphatically not the conception that prevails in America today. In the prevailing view of social life, nothing precedes and transcends society; whatever exists in the social sphere has been created by society itself, and the standards by which it abides are also its own. This view of social life can have no room for self-evident truths or for objective standards of universal validity. It can hold no truths to be self-evident nor any moral standards to be absolute, but must limit itself to stating empirically that at a particular time and in a particular place certain people appear to believe that certain statements are true and certain moral standards ought to be complied with. Reliance upon a common sense that is the rational and moral manifestation of a common human nature experiencing a common world makes way for an unrestricted relativism that is no longer limited by objective rational and moral standards and, hence, finds itself at the mercy of the preferences of society. From those preferences there is no appeal to a "higher law," rational or moral, aesthetic or economic, political or religious. Man-in-the-mass, the majority of men in a given society at a given time, becomes the measure of all things, and what the majority wants is good because it wants it.

Thus, Frank Sinatra, when he must make a moral choice between employing a screen writer who took the Fifth Amendment as a witness in an investigation of Communist influence, and yielding to public criticism by firing him, complies with what he believes the majority prefers, identifying these preferences with the moral law. As he put it in an advertisement in *The New York Times* of April 12, 1960:

> In view of the reaction of my family, my friends and the American public, I have instructed my attorneys to make a settlement with Albert Maltz and to inform him he will not write the screenplay for "The Execution of Private Slovik."
>
> I had thought the major consideration was whether or not the resulting script would be in the best interests of the United States.
>
> Since my conversations with Mr. Maltz had indicated that he had an affirmative, pro-American approach to the story, and since I felt fully capable as producer of enforcing such standards, I have defended my hiring of Mr. Maltz.
>
> But the American public has indicated it feels the

morality of hiring Albert Maltz is the more crucial matter, and I will accept this majority opinion.

A society conceived so as to find the standards for its thought and action only within itself becomes the sovereign arbiter of all things human. The objective criteria of excellence through which civilized man has learned to distinguish a work of art from trash, craftsmanship from shoddiness, scholarship from pretentious sophistication, a good man from a scoundrel, a statesman from a demagogue, greatness from mediocrity—those vital distinctions are blurred if not obliterated by the self-sufficient preferences of the crowd. Those distinctions tend to become altogether meaningless, and what the crowd desires and tolerates becomes the ultimate standard of what is good, true, beautiful, useful, and wise. What you can get away with, then, is morally permitted; what you can get accepted in the market place, to paraphrase the famous saying of Holmes, becomes the test of truth; art is what people like; what can be sold is useful; and what people will vote for is sound. The honest man and the scoundrel, the scholar and the charlatan, the artist and the hack, the businessman and the racketeer, the statesman and the demagogue live side by side, and it is not always easy to tell which is which.

The blurring of these qualitative differences, accomplished by the reduction of the objective standards of excellence to the test of social acceptability, results in a lowering of the quality of actual performance in all fields of individual and collective endeavor. Even to approach the objective standards of excellence requires a supreme effort. The aspiration to satisfy them strains to the limits the capabilities of men and nations and brings out the best in them. Their greatness is measured by the distance between their aspirations and their achievement, and their reward is pride in an achievement that is a living embodiment of a standard of excellence. Where these objective and immutable standards are replaced by whatever society will still accept, the quality of work declines and the stature of man himself is diminished.

Instead of exhausting the potentialities of his nature in the endeavor to achieve what appears to be important, man applies the law of the conservation of energy to his work by summoning to it the least effort necessary to satisfy the demands of social acceptability. With these demands reigning supreme, slovenly work, the cutting of corners, and cheating, which can achieve nothing of excellence, become prudential techniques through which social approval can be secured. Few are fired for lack of competence and many for lack of social acceptability—in ideas, work, or manners. While for the independent businessman the penalty of incompetence is still bankruptcy, the failure of the individual corporation executive is easily absorbed by the gigantic enterprise flourishing as a whole. Diplomats whose judgment is proved to be consistently wrong are frequently promoted to a different area; that is to say, their failure having proved socially disturbing, they are transferred into another social environment. In scholarship and education, where the standards of excellence are often hard to identify, from the grade-school teacher through the Ph.D. thesis to the positions of highest prestige, there is hardly anything that has no chance to be approved by society as long as the professional style remains in tune with the social environment. The people who were shocked by our consistent failures in the rocket field called for more money to be spent on it but—as far as I can discern—not for the replacement of the persons whose incompetence, well known to the scientific community, was in good measure responsible for the failures.

Not only is the quality of work thus lowered, but the social function of work is altered, and certain activities—

among the highest man is capable of—become altogether impossible. Since work is no longer oriented toward objective and transcendent standards from which it once received its meaning, the dynamic distinctions and controversies that once pushed it forward toward ever new achievements also tend to disappear. It is hard to tell what is worth knowing and doing from what is not, and the rewards of conformity and the penalties of its lack tempt the thinker and doer without a purpose to seek refuge in the irrelevant. Facts and figures and their symbols, in particular, become the socially acceptable substitute for the qualitative distinctions that have lost their meaning. Social activities, such as education, scholarship, administration, propaganda, foreign aid, military strategy, tend to transform themselves into self-sufficient technical undertakings that find their standards within themselves in the form of technical competence and efficiency.

In scholarship, for instance, substantive controversy, the life blood of creative renewal here as it is in politics, becomes not only meaningless but also suspect. Controversy is no longer regarded primarily as a contest about who and what is right, but as an attack upon conformity—that is, upon society itself. Dissent is not to be refuted or confirmed on objective rational grounds inherent in the subject matter of the controversy; rather, as a threat to society, it is to be eliminated through ostracism, absorption, or indifference. The contest over what is right, then, transforms itself into a struggle of society to survive as it is against those who appear to endanger it by their dissent.

The other consequence of the decline of objective standards of excellence makes certain activities impossible altogether. In their genuine manifestations religion, philosophy, tragedy, and humor require an objective position outside society. They require objective standards through which society can be understood, judged, and given meaning. When such standards are lacking or are weakened to the point where they no longer provide plausible guidance for thought and action, those great manifestations of human activity change their function and their very nature. Society, having become the be-all and end-all, draws them into its vortex and either uses them for its own perpetuation or else, in so far as it cannot use them, makes it impossible for them to exist.

Thus, religion loses its concern for truth and sin and joins other social forces in justifying, strengthening, and improving society. In the measure that it presumes to sit in judgment over society in the name of objective, transcendent standards it is suspect as a force alien and potentially hostile to society. Philosophy either retreats into the irrelevancies of methodology and semantics or else provides ideological justifications and rationalizations for the *status quo*. Tragedy, having lost the key to the understanding and resolution of the human predicament, either envelops itself in an unrelieved pessimism, as in the work of Eugene O'Neill, or else dissects morbidity for its own sake, as in Tennessee Williams's work. Social humor as a human attitude and literary form becomes virtually inconceivable. For a society that is continuously concerned with its survival and perpetuation cannot afford to understand itself by laughing at its incongruities. Not to take itself seriously appears not far removed from subversion. Thus, America still awaits its Molière and Daumier, its Cervantes and Swift.

A system of production whose purpose exhausts itself in its own limitless and aimless expansion is wasteful of the material resources of the nation, and a social system whose purpose does not go beyond its own perpetuation is wasteful of the human resources of the nation. Since the ultimate standard of social action is social acceptability —that is, conformity with the *status quo*—individual energies are directed toward tasks sanctioned by that standard. They are so directed by the rewards—prestige, money, power—which await the performance of such tasks, and by the disabilities to be braved by those who seek to comply with standards of excellence regardless of social approval. Society thus cultivates in its members social qualities which are conducive to its own perpetuation without drastic change and much friction and which are only by sheer and rare coincidence the ones that make for excellence and greatness. In the process of stifling its own dynamic impulses and of being engrossed, as it were, with the perfection of what it has already become, society cannot help but cripple its own members, remolding them in its sedentary image.

The sterility of society finds its natural counterpart in the atrophy of the individual capacity for self-fulfillment. The vision of human perfection, of all the excellences man is capable of, which carries man beyond the limits of his nature and makes him do the impossible and unforeseen, is blotted out by the utilitarian picture of a society whose members do not deviate too much from one another. The risks and rewards of excellence yield to the utility of being like everybody else, and men who could be great find satisfaction in being useful without being obtrusive. Thus, society compels its members to live below their capabilities rather than exhausting them. It misdirects their energies and wastes the best of their talents. Since it can use excellence only when excellence conforms, it must discourage and neglect excellence that does not conform. In consequence, the very idea of excellence is discredited, and the individual faculty of aspiring to it and achieving it withers from lack of use.

Education itself, whose mission ought to be to institutionalize, demonstrate, awaken aspiration to excellence and guide toward its achievement, becomes the main instrument of subordinating it to the overriding standard of social acceptability. It teaches not to aspire to what is excellent but to adapt to what is common. Who can forget the spectacle of the best of the country's youth entering the institutions of higher learning, thirsting for knowledge and achievement, and so many leaving them dull-wittedly looking for a safe job! They have been educated—that is to say, they have been cut down to size according to the social specifications. Lord Bryce asked seventy years ago "why great men are not chosen presidents." We are raising here the question: why, in spite of an abundance of human resources, does the nation refuse to produce great men?

By subordinating excellence to social acceptability, American society renounces the achievements through which excellence is revealed and compels itself to live on the accumulated achievements of the past. It exchanges the risks and rewards of creative change for the stability of the *status quo*. A society can carry on in this state of mind some length of time, giving the appearance of life where the source of life has been shut off. But no society can go on like this forever without decay following stagnation; the fate of Spain tells us what is in store for such a nation. American society can afford less than any other to stand still, embroidering and enjoying what it has achieved; for its constant renewal in the light of its purpose, culminating in a succession of revolutions, is the very law of its distinctive being. A static, ingrown, self-satisfied society looking back to what it has achieved rather than forward to the achievements demanded by its purpose is in a profound sense un-American; for American society, by denying its purpose, disavows its past and precludes its future.

And such a society is bound to be at war with itself. That is to say, its self-centeredness and complacency, its conformism and dedication to the *status quo* are at odds with its members' frustrated vitality, aimless industry, and searching without a purpose. The vertical mobility that we recognized earlier as a distinctive quality of American society can find no other purpose than its own perpetuation; it joins in this respect industrial production and social conformity. Thus, American society moves and whirls within itself with restless energy, but it does not know what for and where to. In truth, it stands still while it moves.

American culture is the sum total of a number of isolated flashes of genius, of isolated beginnings and accomplishments rather than a continuum, a living tradition that loses nothing and builds the achievements of the past into the foundations of future achievements. Where other societies have built pyramids and temples for eternity, ours tears down what it has built for tomorrow in order to build for another day. Great things are done or at least begun in architecture, higher education, the performing arts, and then wiped off the slate and forgotten as though they had never existed. Fame itself, instead of being the reputation for a particular kind of excellence earned by 'compliance with the standards of that excellence, becomes a product of public relations, to fade away for lack of promotion when the experts decide that a new product is needed to stimulate the public. Significantly, the famous, whose fame ought to be as perennial as the standards of the excellence they personify, transform themselves into celebrities, ephemeral artifacts of promotion.

## 4. *The Symptoms of Malaise*

Contemporary society feels, as even the most self-centered individual feels, that its purpose cannot exhaust itself in perpetuation for its own sake. No longer capable of comprehending and embodying the objective standards from which a transcendent purpose can be derived, it sought a substitute that would leave the social *status quo* intact while creating the illusion of transcendence. It found that substitute in what passes for the achievement of excellence from abroad, and in novelty and eccentricity at home. American society came to admire as superior what was foreign and what was new and eccentric. Here it seemed to find the standards by which it could judge and improve its own achievements, unaware that it was creating the true standards within itself and only needed to recognize them and bring order into their chaotic manifestations.

The cultural provincialism that equates foreign origin with superior quality may have been justified once, but was rendered absurdly out of date by the vitality, creativeness, and accomplishments of American culture. While Europeans began to notice that the creative forces of Western civilization had moved westward across the ocean, Americans continued to look to Europe and, more particularly, to England for standards of intellectual and aesthetic judgment and creative aspiration. They failed to notice that there was more intellectual vitality, although less formal learning and literary polish, in any one of the five or six best American universities than in any two European universities combined. It did not occur to them that in architecture, literature, music, and the theater America had begun to set the standards and pace for all of Western civilization. Long after Europe had begun to imitate America, America still thought it had to imitate Europe. Its own originality, for instance, in the field of ideas remained hidden from it. Americans would listen with rapt attention when traveling Englishmen would tell them what America was all about, unaware that what they heard were American ideas garbed in English dress and speaking with an English accent. American ideas, in order to be intellectually respectable in America, could do no better than to travel to England and return with an English imprint.

The subservience to foreign imports as a substitute for objective standards of excellence depreciates the achievements of American culture. It diminishes its self-respect and daring and, hence, its creativity. The internal substitutes, novelty and eccentricity, result in more serious damage. Novelty destroys what has been created, and must do so ever again. It thereby dissolves the continuity of culture which builds stone upon stone, preserving what has been left behind, and without which there can be no genuine culture at all. The illuminating and warming glow of genuine culture is here reduced to a series of isolated flashes of genius. For genuine culture is first of all reverence for tradition, for the living achievements of the past as the continuing embodiment of the perennial standards of excellence, as a memento of what men were able to do in the past and as an earnest of what they can do again.

Novelty and eccentricity as standards of cultural evaluation are appropriate to a society which finds its purpose in its own perpetuation, which is committed at most to the improvement of the *status quo,* and moves within rather than beyond itself. A society whose purpose it is to comply with objective standards of excellence can measure progress by the distance that still separates it from those standards. A society that has lost the vital link with those standards must define progress as sheer movement, aimless and self-sufficient. What is novel is superior to what precedes it by dint of its novelty. Much of that novelty is spurious; the newest models of consumer goods, of art, of literature, and of scholarship are more often than not the models of the day before yesterday which nobody remembers. But, spurious or not, novelty creates the illusion that a society which has decided to stand still is actually going somewhere.

Where novelty is genuine and consistently so, it is at its most destructive. It has virtually destroyed American education, the very fountainhead of a continuing culture. What has been taught in a certain way before—from reading, arithmetic, and English to foreign languages and social studies—must be taught differently, not because the old methods have proved ineffective, but solely because the methods are old. In the process of incessant innovation, the original purpose of teaching, which is to transmit knowledge, understanding, and intellectual discipline, tends to be lost altogether. What has never been tried before, probably because it is absurd on the face of it, must be tried in order to see what happens. To cite two examples: nobody has ever thought of teaching high-school freshmen symbolic logic instead of first-year algebra; so let's try it, and never mind that a junior who has never learned first-year algebra, even if he did understand symbolic logic, will not learn second-year algebra either. Nobody has ever tried to teach one half of a class of high-school juniors exclusively by television in order to find out what happens to them in comparison with the other half who are taught by teachers; so this must be tried, too, and the professor of education who made this experiment summarized the results by saying in a public lecture: "I think we got something there, but I don't know what it is." How many teachers have asked me for a new method of teaching international relations and no doubt found odd my question as to what was wrong with the old one!

Like the hedonism of production, the hedonism of novelty, the urge to experiment regardless of the consequences, becomes a cancerous growth, threatening life itself with its aimless proliferation. Its most irrational manifestations blend into eccentricity. The toleration and even cultivation of eccentricity, whose original home is England, performs for American society a substitute function akin to that of novelty. Eccentricity—from outlandish experiments in education, art, literature, and scholarship to the political maverick, the beatnik, and the deviationist in dress and manners—creates for a self-centered and self-sufficient society the illusion of a challenge from within. The eccentric does for such a society what the court jester did for the prince: he defies prevailing values without endangering them.

More particularly, eccentricity as a social institution takes the place of the permanent American revolution, the reality of which society no longer tolerates. Society is incapable of even recognizing the reality of that revolution and treats it nonchalantly as mere eccentricity where it still appears in our midst as radical proposals for reform. The eccentric plays the role of a bogus revolutionary kept by society because he does not need to be feared. The eccentric can defy society, he can thumb his nose at it, but he cannot, and would not even if he could, endanger it. Society is secure, and it is exactly because it is secure that it can tolerate and even subsidize eccentricity in its midst. That spectacle of the irrelevant and, hence, innocuous deviation doubly reassures society: it reassures it of its stability and also, as it were, of its revolutionary soul. Society proves to itself through the toleration and institutionalization of eccentricity that it can still transcend itself, although that transcendence has no purpose except deviation and, hence, means nothing for the purpose of society. But a society content with its conformity and ill at ease with it as well is thus enabled to enjoy both the spectacle of nonconformity and the reality of its opposite.

However, the sense of security which society derives

from the enjoyment of the *status quo* is ambivalent and precarious. It is not the sense of security which comes to a man who puts his capabilities to the test by achieving what he set out to do, who vanquishes his insecurity by proving himself. Rather it is the sense of security experienced by a man who is too insecure to venture far afield and prefers the certainty of what he has achieved to the risks and promises of further achievements. His sense of security grows not from insecurity overcome but from insecurity repressed. He feels secure only because he does not venture beyond what has already been achieved, knowing full well that beyond the frontiers of his achievements there lie new worlds to be conquered by somebody, if not by him. And it takes little, as McCarthyism has shown, to cause that security of the surface to be swallowed up by a tidal wave of insecurity from deep within.

## 5. *The Transformation of Equality in Freedom*

These changes and trends in contemporary society all point to a fundamental change in the nature of the American purpose. Equality and freedom are, as we have seen, formal concepts that receive their meaning from substantive concepts to which they are related. The principle of equality raises the question: equal with regard to what? The principle of freedom raises the question: free from what? And both must answer the question: equal and free for what? Throughout American history the commitment to these two purposes renewed itself through the experience of their denial in practice. It was the periodic experience of its precarious achievement and partial denial which restored the vitality of the American purpose. This experience raised those questions ever anew and demanded that they be answered. They were answered through the invocation and application of substantive principles of justice to the issues of the day, such as slavery, state sovereignty, or social reform. These principles were the terminal concepts from which the American purpose of equality in freedom received its concrete content and its structure.

In our time the experience of possible or actual failure has been replaced by the persuasion that the purpose of America has by and large been achieved, and the substantive principles of justice have been dissolved into the standard of social acceptability. In consequence, equality and freedom have changed their meaning. They now stand, as it were, all by themselves; no concrete issue or transcendent principle gives them structure and significance. They must find their meaning within themselves, and those meaningful questions that we have just mentioned can no longer be answered because they can no longer be asked.

If the question: equal with regard to what? can no longer be asked, it is no longer possible to distinguish between legitimate and illegitimate equality. The principle of equality, then, comes to cover the existential equality of men created equal, equality of political rights, and equality of opportunity, on the one hand, and an indiscriminate egalitarianism that makes everybody equal with everybody else. Different persons and things, then, must be treated as equal even though by objective standards they are not equal. The very distinction between what is excellent and what is not in art, literature, ethics, politics, and scholarship appears to be odious, an aristocratic infringement upon the egalitarian principle. Even the elemental distinctions between adults and children, the wise and the foolish, the learned and the ignorant become suspect.

Equality without distinction also destroys the meaning of freedom; for, as we have seen, absolute equality and absolute freedom are identical and without civilized meaning. He who is absolutely equal is also absolutely free; for any limitation upon freedom implies subordination, which runs counter to equality. Yet meaningful freedom requires a distinction between the spheres and modes of action with regard to which man ought to be free and those which ought to be regulated from above. In other words, meaningful freedom requires a distinction between legitimate and illegitimate freedom. Hence, if the question: freedom from what? can no longer be asked, it is no longer possible to distinguish between freedom and license, order and anarchy. The hierarchical orders within which alone legitimate freedom can flourish, such as those between parents and children, teachers and pupils, the government and the citizens, become themselves suspect of illegitimacy because they impair freedom.

If the question: equal and free for what? can no longer be asked, equality and freedom, however conceived, are deprived of meaning in still another sense. Equality and freedom are indeed good in themselves in that they are proper to the nature of man and correspond to his elemental aspirations. Yet their achievement constitutes but one of the preconditions of man's self-fulfillment. To achieve that self-fulfillment itself equality and freedom must be directed toward a transcendent substantive goal, for the sake of which freedom and equality are sought. It is from such a goal that equality and freedom receive their order, their limits, and their purpose—that is, their meaning. Thus, paradoxically enough, equality and freedom, divorced from such a goal and sought for themselves, evolve into an egalitarianism and a libertarianism which first stunt both individual and social development and then put into jeopardy equality and freedom themselves.

In such an egalitarian and libertarian society, order tends to become a mere matter of fact, the result of the distribution of power existing at any particular moment, and the objective principles from which a legitimate order stems are in the process of losing their plausibility. Society transforms itself in the image of the frontier, and what was once a marginal and ephemeral society is now being drawn into the social center. The individual dynamism of nearly absolute equality and freedom, characteristic of the frontier, finds nothing to work on in a society that has lost its great issues because it thinks it has settled them; thus, mobility is sought for its own sake, as it was at the frontier. Lawlessness, much more prevalent than generally admitted in its juvenile, organized, and general social manifestations, and the fascination with violence and disorder both in art and in life provide substitute satisfactions for a frontier spirit that neither enjoys the opportunities of the open spaces nor is contained within a shared framework of objective standards of conduct.

Against the invasion of the realm of quality by equality, American society cannot protect itself through its own inner resources. For American society, as we have seen, has been created and maintained as an egalitarian society. It has been created and maintained in conscious opposition to those structured societies in which an aristocracy of birth or merit imposes not only its political rule but also its standards of excellence upon the majority. The standards of excellence by which American society, as it were, tamed its egalitarian instincts were its own. They were self-accepted and self-imposed. In so far as America has produced an aristocracy it has been an aristocracy of merit, vaguely defined and ever changing in composition, and, as it were, an inner aristocracy as well. It has been created by the deference that the people paid, however falteringly, to certain persons in whom they saw manifest those standards of excellence which they accepted without being able to achieve them. With those standards lost, there was nothing to take their place. There is no Maecenas or Medicean prince who could maintain those standards, oblivious of what the people would accept. For while the aristocracy of the old world was in society but not of it, American aristocracy has been an integral part of American society, which created it. It has been the personification of the standards with which society freely and spontaneously identified itself.

How dependent American society is for the maintenance of qualitative distinctions not upon particular institutions but upon standards of excellence freely accepted by the people at large is clearly demonstrated by the function the great foundations have performed in this respect. Here are institutions dedicated to the support of those media through which standards of excellence are achieved, and endowed with a legal independence and financial resources equal if not superior to those of the old-world aristocracies. Yet while the foundations are so endowed, they must be responsive to the preferences of society in a way the Medicean prince never needed to be. They can support the manifestations of excellence only in the measure that society supports them. When society is oblivious of these standards, so are they. When society turns its back on these standards altogether, embracing itself in narcissist satisfaction, they can only rally to the support of the *status quo* and of the substitutes of novelty and eccentricity with which society tries to compensate for its loss. At their best, they can be no more than a step ahead of society, and it is generally only in foreign countries that they have shown what courageous and imaginative things they can do when they are not hemmed in by the preferences of society.

This dependence of the standards of excellence not upon a clearly defined and stable group within society but upon unorganized society as a whole points to the crucial importance of mass education for the survival of these standards. A culturally stratified society can afford to leave its standards of excellence in the care of the aristocracy, which has assumed that responsibility and has been trained to meet it. Mass education may be desirable for such a society, but it is not necessarily vital. For a society whose cultural elite derives its authority from nothing but merit, spontaneously and only provisionally recognized in a daily plebiscite by those who happen to be capable of recognizing merit—for such a society mass education is the indispensable instrument for the perpetuation of the standards of excellence. For mass education is intended to serve the purpose—although in actuality it is far from serving it—of imparting the standards of excellence potentially to all the people and of continuously recruiting members for that amorphous elite which must preserve, apply, and transmit the standards. Established merit, then, determines who can claim to be a member of that elite.

It is in view of this vital need of American society that one must consider the central place which mass education has occupied in America from the beginning. The pioneers who settled in America and then went west carried the standards of excellence within themselves and could perpetuate them only by implanting them in their children. Whether civilization was to be built in the wilderness or succumb to the barbarism by which it was surrounded had to be decided, as it were, by each man through his own efforts at educating himself and his children. The proliferation of colleges in the Middle West, dating back to the early days of settlement, shows how widespread and persistent these efforts were. The emergence of many great and able men from this society establishes the continuing success of this system of education. In the emergence from it of so unique and august a figure as Lincoln, personifying both the popular origin and the depth and vitality of those standards, this system of education finds its consummation.

American education has failed not in its popular manifestations both secular and religious, which have remained to a degree wedded to objective standards of excellence, but in its big public and private institutions, which have substituted, as we have seen, conformity, novelty, and eccentricity for those objective standards. The patent inadequacy of these institutions endangers American civilization least when they fail by not teaching. They become a positive threat when they succeed in substituting for what ought to be taught their own perverted standards.

Their inadequacy has called into being two essentially un-American substitutes for mass education which try to preserve the objective standards of excellence neglected and destroyed by mass education. Exclusive private institutions of learning endeavor to preserve for the few the traditions of culture, which in American society can be a vital force only when the masses at least understand and value them. While these institutions of learning provide for the aristocracy of wealth a kind of stationary equivalent of the *"grand tour de l'Europe,"* which taught the English aristocrats of the eighteenth century the standards of what was good, true, and beautiful, the uncritical admiration of European culture is, as it were, the poor man's substitute for the aristocratic substitute of the exclusive private school. The "poor man," untaught in the standards of excellence and, hence, incapable of seeing their native manifestations all around him, yet vaguely aware of their existence and longing for them, looks to Europe as their exclusive abode; for in Europe their manifestations are clearly visible in the great monuments of aristocratic achievement.

Both this aristocratic exclusiveness and this pseudo-aristocratic snobbery are un-American in that they are neglectful and contemptuous of the popular source of American culture and of that culture itself. Yet these two un-American deviations have one advantage over mass education, which, as presently practiced, is oblivious of all culture, in that they are at least aware of the existence of, and the need for, culture and the objective standards by which it lives. Both the islands of aristocratic education and that snobbery which seeks beyond the ocean what it could find at home express a collective aspiration that would respond to genuine education and does respond to its sporadic and isolated manifestations.

# B. *The Political Crisis: The Paradoxes of Democratic Government*

## 1. *The Triumph of the Majority*

The instrument with which egalitarianism gains its ascendancy over the objective standards of excellence and through which it can destroy the qualitative distinctions derived from them is the rule of the majority. The rule of the majority is indeed the egalitarian instrument *par excellence;* for the status of the voting members of society, in spite of their qualitative differences, is indeed equality *par excellence.* Politics is, as we shall see, the proper sphere of majority rule. Egalitarianism extends the rule of the majority far beyond the political sphere and through it establishes the preferences of society as the main source of the standards by which society is supposed to abide. By doing so, it not only reduces the objective standards of excellence to the subjective expression of preferences by the majority, but also introduces into the democratic process itself an alien and destructive element.

Originally, the democratic process had nothing to do with the discovery of objective standards of government. It had its origin in the attempt to check the executive power with a power independent of it which was representative at least of some of the subjects. That is to say, it had its origin in representative government. The power of the king, being at the service of his interests, was to be restrained and limited by an institution, composed of subjects or their representatives, whose consent was required for certain actions of the king. The original purpose of democracy was the protection of the people from excessive and arbitrary executive power, not the exercise of governmental power itself. Democracy in its representative manifestation was originally conceived as an instrument of the struggle against royal interests and power; its purpose was a balance of interests and power between government and people; and the distribution of weights within the balance was foreordained by the prescriptive rights of all concerned.

In contrast to its monarchical origin, the republican development of the representative democratic process—which development was foreshadowed in the political philosophy of the Middle Ages and of seventeenth-century England—establishes the principle of popular sovereignty. That is to say, not only is the executive power to be restrained and limited by popular consent, but the very exercise of power by certain persons derives from the consent of the governed. The power to govern is vested by the people in certain persons, to be renewed or transferred to other persons through orderly constitutional processes. The rulers, in order to continue to rule, must retain the confidence of the majority, if not in their policies, at least in their persons. In conditions of perfect democracy, the electorate votes for alternative policies by voting for alternative candidates, each identified with a different policy. In the presently more common conditions of imperfect democracy, the voters elect candidates rather than vote for alternative policies; through their votes they voice their confidence that their candidate will execute honestly and competently whatever policies he may choose.

This republican type of representative democracy still defends the people's interests by limiting the power of the government. It is more particularly the property and liberties of the people which representative democracy is intended to protect from arbitrary infringement by the government. Nowhere in either the monarchical or the republican type of representative democracy is there the implication that the popular vote reveals a degree of truth about matters political unmatched by that accessible to the government. In other words, this type of democracy does not assume that *vox populi*, in contrast to the government, is *vox dei,* that the judgment of the majority is naturally superior in both wisdom and virtue to that of any minority, let alone that it has a monopoly of both. If it makes any assumption about the distribution of wisdom and virtue, it is that nobody has a monopoly of them, neither the majority nor the government nor any other minority secularly or ecclesiastically defined, and that truth and virtue in matters political are accessible to all.

Representative democracy, whose most eminent philosophic spokesman is Locke and whose political home is England, is sharply distinguished from majoritarian or Jacobin democracy, whose most eloquent philosophic representative is Rousseau. The Jacobin type of democracy inspired the French revolution and put its imprint upon the successive democratic regimes of France. It departs from the philosophy of representative democracy by substituting for government with the consent of the governed the government of the majority. The distinction is subtle but real and crucial.

Representative democracy is indifferent as to who governs, a king, an aristocracy, or a parliament; it is concerned with the restraints that the consent of the governed imposes upon the powers of the government. The function of the majority is to control and restrain, not to rule. Majoritarian democracy, on the other hand, postulates the exclusive right of the majority to rule because the people as a whole, to whom the majority is the closest empirical approximation, is the sole repository of truth and virtue in matters political. While representative democracy requires the representation of popular interests in order to control and restrain the interests of the government, majoritarian democracy requires the representation of popular interests because it assumes that truth and virtue will emerge from the meeting of those interests in the political market place. The requirements of this type of democracy are not satisfied, as are those of the representative type, by the government governing as it sees fit as long as the majority has the constitutional power to change the government and its policies by registering dissent. Majoritarian democracy requires that the government's policies reflect at every turn the preferences of the majority, that the majority actually govern through the government as its instrument. The government of a representative democracy must ask itself two questions: what needs to be done in view of the objective requirements of the case, and how can we obtain the consent of the governed to do it? The government of a majoritarian democracy needs ask itself but one question: what does the majority want?

American democracy was created in the image of the English representative type and has developed in the direction of its Jacobin majoritarian counterpart. The principle of the separation of powers and, more particularly, of a system of checks and balances assumes the existence of conflicts of interests, each of which is to be protected by a balance of power. These relationships in which interest counteracts interest and power restrains power are regulated by, and were actually created by virtue of, objective standards of political conduct, of which the Constitution is the most eminent embodiment and the Supreme Court the most authoritative mouthpiece.

The constitutional and political history of the United States is in good measure the story of a contest between the objective and majoritarian elements of the American system of government, with the latter consistently gaining both in quantity and in quality. The quantitative gain is indicated by the extension of the franchise. And while the original function of that extension was the protection of certain interests through changes in the domestic distribution of power, universal suffrage was soon justified as the unfettered expression of popular wisdom and virtue. To the degree that this Rousseauist conception of the popular will prevailed, the plausibility of objective standards, which originally were to limit and direct the interplay of countervailing forces, declined; of these forces the will of the majority was supposed to be one.

The sanction that the system of checks and balances, of which the consent of the governed was a fundamental element, had originally received from the objective standards was replaced by a sanction immanent in the system itself. A system of checks and balances, especially in the form of pressure groups, was now supposed to be a good in itself in that it safeguards the interests and freedom of its component parts. What kind of balance there was mattered much less, if it mattered at all, than that there was a balance of some kind.

Similarly, the will of the majority, regardless of what its content was, began to carry within itself the assumption of rational and moral superiority. This assumption was of course questioned by interests adversely affected, but it could no longer be subjected to the objective test of a "higher law." In consequence, the pluralistic variety of substantive standards by which each political action ought to be judged according to its merits tends to be replaced by the monistic and formal standard of the majority will. The majority will, operating for its own sake, thus joins conformism for its own sake, production for its own sake, and defense of the *status quo* for its own sake as still another principle that locates the national purpose within society itself. None of these principles connects the national life with a goal that lies beyond what society has already achieved and, hence, can serve as its purpose.

The triumph of the majority principle over the objective standards of government has been neither complete nor direct. It has been kept in check by the constitutional arrangements of the separation of powers, the institution of the Supreme Court, and the presidential veto. Its triumph has been psychological and political rather than institutional. It has done for the political sphere what the spirit of conformity has done for society at large. It has consisted fundamentally in the ascendancy of a popular mood adverse to the recognition, let alone application, of objective standards to the operations of government and inclined toward the belief that the decision of the majority is naturally endowed with virtue and reason and should be accepted as final. From this popular mood three perversions of the democratic process have sprung: the decline of minority rights, the committee system as the main instrument of governance, and the public-opinion poll as the principal mouthpiece of the majority will.

The popular tendency to believe that government with the consent of the governed is identical with government by the majority has vitally affected the popular estimation of minority rights. Respect for minority rights is incompatible with the right of the majority to govern as it sees fit. In the measure, then, that the majority is endowed with that right, the minorities, and most particularly the political ones, are deprived of theirs. Yet, paradoxically enough, democracy can perform its political function of limiting the power of the government only if the power of the majority is limited by a respect for minority rights. While democracy requires that the will of the people limit the freedom of the government, it also requires that the freedom of the popular will be limited. A popular will not so limited becomes the tyranny of the majority which destroys the freedom of political competition and thus uses the powers of the government to prevent a new majority from forming and to entrench itself permanently in the seat of power. There is only a small step from the destruction of the freedom of competition—that is, imperfect democracy—to the destruction of competition itself —that is, totalitarianism.

The freedom of political competition essential to democracy can be impaired in two different ways. The people are being deprived of their freedom to choose among alternative policies by choosing among different candidates for office if the different candidates for office are not identified with different policies but compete for power as an end in itself, not as a means to pursue a particular policy. The people may still be able to choose in terms of the personal qualities of the candidates, such as competence and trustworthiness, but their choice has no meaning for the substance of the policies to be pursued. The people, if they do not vote for the person of a candidate as such, will then vote out of habit or not at all, and in the measure in which this happens democratic elections will have lost their ability to protect the freedom of the people by limiting the freedom of action of the government.

The other—and more insidious—threat to freedom of political competition stems from the tendency of all majorities to act upon the assumption that they are more—at best—than temporary approximations to political truth, that they are the repositories of all the political truth there is. They tend to think and act, as long as they last as majorities, as though their will provided the ultimate standard of thought and action and as though there were no higher law to limit their freedom. The majority, as long as it lasts, tends to become the absolute master, the tyrant, of the body politic, stifling in that body the vital spirit of questioning and initiative, and evoking instead the submissiveness of conformity. Yet since there is no higher standard for thought and action than the will of the majority, in theory at least each successive majority may produce a new tyrant with a political truth of its own. One political orthodoxy may be succeeded by another, calling forth a new conformity, and the very relativism which is the philosophic mainspring of the supremacy of the majority will produce not only the tyranny of the majority but also a succession of tyrannies, all justified by the will of the majority.

While this is possible in theory, it is, however, not likely to occur for any length of time in practice. For the majority, by making itself the supreme arbiter of matters political, must at least implicitly deny to the minority the right to make itself the majority of tomorrow. Since the majority of today tends to claim a monopoly of political truth, it must also tend to claim a monopoly of political power, freezing the existing distribution of power. The majority of today tends to perpetuate itself as a permanent majority and, by the same token, to relegate the minority of today to a permanent minority status.

This development deprives the minority of its democratic reason for existing. That reason is its ability, equal in principle to that of the majority, to have access to political truth and act upon it; hence its claim to compete freely to become the majority tomorrow. The assumption that the majority has a monopoly of political truth destroys the minority's political function and gives the respect for its existence an anachronistic quality. Since its continuing existence implicitly challenges the majority's monopolistic claims, is a living reminder of alternative rulers and policies, and may, by virtue of these attributes, become a political nuisance to the majority, the minority cannot for long survive the destruction of its philosophic justification and political function. With its destruction, democracy itself comes to an end. The unlimited freedom —that is, the tyranny—of the rulers corresponds to the unlimited lack of freedom of the ruled.

Thus, decadent democracy goes through three stages before it transforms itself into its opposite: totalitarian tyranny. It starts out by emptying itself of part of its substance: it destroys the freedom to choose policies by choosing men. Then it substitutes for the spirit of free political competition, which derives from a pluralistic conception of political truth, the monistic assumption that only the majority possesses that truth. Then it subjects the minority to restrictions that put it at a decisive disadvantage in the competition for intellectual influence and political power, thus transforming the majority into a permanent one existing side by side with a permanent minority. The process of degeneration is consummated when the majority becomes the sole legitimate political organization and combines the claim to a monopoly of political truth with a monopoly of political power.

Against these tendencies toward self-destruction, in-herent in the dynamics of democracy, the institutions and the spirit of classical liberalism stand guard. Liberalism has erected two kinds of safeguards: one in the realm of philosophic principle, the other in the sphere of political action.

Liberalism holds certain truths to be self-evident which no majority has the right to abrogate and from which, in turn, the legitimacy of majority rule derives. These truths, however formulated in a particular historic epoch, see in the individual—his integrity, happiness, and self-develop-ment—the ultimate concern of the political order. This concern is thought to be inherent in the nature of things to owe nothing to any secular order or human inspiration.

It is on this absolute and transcendent foundation that the philosophy of genuine democracy rests, and it is within this immutable framework that the processes of genuine democracy take place. The pluralism of these processes is subordinated to, and oriented toward, those absolute and transcendent truths. It is this subordination and this orientation which distinguish the pluralism of the genuine type of democracy from the relativism of its corrupted types. For in the latter the will of the majority is the ulti-mate point of reference of the political order and the ulti-mate test of what is politically true. Whatever group gains the support of the majority for its point of view gains thereby also the attributes of political truth, and the con-tent of political truth changes with every change in the majority. Out of this relativism that makes political truth a function of political power develops, as we have seen, first the tyranny, and then the totalitarianism, of the ma-jority. Thus, the relativism of majority rule, denying the existence of absolute, transcendent truth independent of the majority will, tends toward the immanent absolutism of a tyrannical or totalitarian majority, while the pluralism of genuine democracy assumes as its corollary the existence of such truth limiting the will of the majority.

As a matter of philosophic principle, the political order is oriented toward the individual: the political order is the means to the individual's end. Yet, as a matter of political fact, it is the very earmark of politics that men use other men as means to their ends. That this cannot be otherwise is one of the paradoxes of the politics of liberalism; for political reality disavows, and does so continuously and drastically, the postulates of liberal philosophy. Liberalism believes in the truth of man's freedom, but it finds man everywhere a slave. Thus it adds another paradox—more shocking than the first for being the result of liberalism's own efforts—by creating political institutions that limit the freedom of some in order to preserve the freedom of others. Constitutional guarantees of civil rights and their legislative and judicial implementation are the liberal defenses of freedom of political competition. While the will of the majority decides how these guarantees are to be implemented, the existence of the guarantees themselves is not subject to that will. Quite the contrary: these guarantees set the conditions under which the will of the majority is to be formed and exercised. They establish the framework of democratic legitimacy for the rule of the majority.

Yet the very need for these safeguards points up the dilemma that liberalism faces. If the majority could be trusted with its power, the liberal safeguards would be unnecessary. Since it cannot be so trusted, its freedom must be curtailed for the very sake of freedom. The dilemma manifests itself in our time typically in the concrete terms of the antinomy between individual rights and some collective good, such as general welfare, administrative efficiency, national security. The liberal concern for individual rights may stand in the way of the maximization of such a collective good, and the greater the need for the full realization of a collective good appears to be, the greater is the temptation to sacrifice individual rights for its sake. Is individual freedom more important than national security, without which there will be no freedom at all? What benefits does a man draw from the Bill of Rights if, in the absence of measures of general welfare, it guarantees him the right to sleep under bridges and sell apples in the street?

However, aside from the dilemmas rising from its substantive tasks, contemporary democracy faces also the dilemma posed by the character of certain of its minorities. The Rousseauist philosophy of democracy had to presume as a matter of course that the people, if they were free to do so, would want to rule themselves and that they were prevented from doing so by obsolete monarchical and aristocratic institutions. It could not conceive that a considerable fraction of the people might freely choose not to rule themselves but to surrender their freedom to a tyrannical ruler or elite. Yet what few in the Western democracies thought conceivable actually came to pass.

On the right and left of the political spectrum movements and parties sprang up which sought to use the mechanics of the democratic process to abolish democracy itself. How was democracy to protect itself against these enemies from within? If by upholding its principles it extended its liberal protection to these minorities, it risked committing suicide. If it suppressed these minorities as enemies of the democratic order, it ran the risk that an eager and careless majority might suppress legitimate minorities along with the illegitimate ones and kill democracy in the process of trying to save it. The destruction of the Republic of Weimar by the Nazis' misuse of the liberal safeguards of minority rights exemplifies one horn of that dilemma; the partial, temporary impairment of minority rights by McCarthyism offers an example of the other. That the restoration of these rights was in good measure due to the intervention of the courts points to the organic connection between the judicial function and the preservation of the objective standards essential to genuine democracy.

Besides weakening the rights of minorities, these two dilemmas produced, as it were, by the mechanics of the democratic process itself have robbed the very position of the minority of some of its plausibility and respectability. The intellectual and social embarrassment of being of the minority is of course a by-product of the disappearance of great issues and of the concomitant transformation of conformity which I have discussed before. In the absence of great issues worth fighting for there is little incentive to take a strong stand against what appears to be the view of the overwhelming majority. Where conformity for its own sake has become the integrating principle of society, there is a very strong incentive not to dissent, and that incentive is greatly strengthened by the difficulty of making one's dissent effectively heard. A writer, for instance, who either cannot find an outlet for his dissent at all or can find only an ineffective one is naturally tempted to give up dissenting altogether.

The devaluation of the minority position itself has been most decisively advanced by the centralization of the mass media of communications. Press, radio, and television are the products and the major instruments of conformity. They are its products because they are commercial enterprises whose success is measured by the support they are able to obtain from advertisers and the consuming public. The range of diverse opinions to which they can afford to give hospitality is circumscribed by what these two groups of supporters are thought to be willing to tolerate. Thus, the mass media cannot help but reflect the opinions that the great mass of the population are supposed to hold or at least to deem respectable. Yet by lending these opinions their prestige and their circulation, the mass media strengthen the assumption that these opinions are right simply because most people hold them or that at the very least the range of respectable opinion coincides with the opinions presented. It is difficult for an opinion that does not fall within this range to make itself heard at all; for it to get an effective hearing is virtually impossible without the help of events that either suddenly or through the slow accumulation of empirical evidence give it plausibility and, hence, respectability. At best, such a minority will speak in a sporadic whisper, carried by some esoteric outlet, while the majority can shout its views from the rooftops day after day.

This decline in the ability of a minority to make itself heard—that is, to act as a minority within the dynamics of democracy—is primarily the result of modern technology. In the technologically primitive age, when printing was done by hand, any man of moderate means could reach the public by having a book, pamphlet, or newspaper printed and distributed at his own expense. Any man could reach the public ear by mounting a soapbox or addressing a public meeting, and any man could talk back to him. This age was characterized by an essential equality, or at least by a not radical inequality, of access to the democratic forum where the majority competes with the minority for the support of the public. Modern technology has created a radical inequality in this respect. For it is in the very nature of the technology of mass communications that they require considerable capital for their support and highly organized machinery for their operation. The great mass of citizens are bound to be excluded from both, and the few who exert economic and technological control over the mass media of communications, by selecting the persons to be heard and the issues to be debated, enjoy a great advantage over the many.

The difficulty of taking a minority position as a matter of fact, the depreciation of the minority position as a matter of judgment, and the dilemma of reconciling the protection of minority rights with the protection of democracy have co-operated to diminish the vital function that minorities must fulfill in the democratic process. In consequence, the democratic process itself has been drained of some of its vitality. The democratic process, which in its perfect manifestation gives the people a choice of persons and of policies, has tended to revert to its imperfect type which allows the people a choice of persons but not of policies. The majority view, in so far as it is deprived of a dynamic minority opinion as its counterfoil and potential replacement, tends to be accepted as the only plausible and respectable view. The Rousseauist conception that the majority is right because it is the majority here finds support in the actual operation of the democratic process.

The Rousseauist conception supposes that the democratic process yields through the rule of the majority the closest available approximation to the truth. The majority takes the place of objective standards not only in politics but in all spheres of thought and action. The democratic process becomes the universal instrument through which the truth is to be discovered by ascertaining the views of the majority. The function that monistic conformity performs for unorganized society finds its organized realization in the universalized democratic process. As the majority of the electorate, of the legislature, and of the court reveals the truth in matters political, so the majority within committees makes the truth known in all fields of human endeavor—artistic, scientific, diplomatic, military, and so forth. Even the rediscovery of the purpose of America has been entrusted to a committee.

The universal committee system, operating by majority rule and preferably through unanimity, replaces the decision by one wise and expert man. Such a decision, derived from the standards of excellence appropriate to this particular sphere of action, is denounced as undemocratic because not everyone who has an interest in a decision is allowed a voice in it. The intellectual process of discovering the truth among a welter of diverse opinions is assimilated to the democratic process of protecting divergent interests. In consequence, the very distinction between truth and error is reduced to the distinction between different interests of which none is *a priori,* but of which one may turn out to be, by virtue of the distribution of votes in committee, entitled to particular respect.

## 2. *Government by Committee and by Public Opinion*

The perversion of the democratic process, confounding the consent of the governed with the rule of the majority and endowing the latter with a monopoly of virtue and reason, finds its apogee in the misunderstanding and misuse of the committee system and of public opinion. The committee system has become the prevailing method of reaching decisions in government. Literally thousands of departmental and interdepartmental committees—the State Department alone is reported to be represented on four hundred of them—from the National Security Council dealing with the most momentous matters of state to those dealing with the most mundane chores of housekeeping thrash out decisions. Nor is the committee system limited to the government. It has become a way of life for the whole nation. Businesses, families, and nursery schools are run that way. Authority qualified to find the truth and responsible for it is being replaced everywhere by the collective representation of interests. The extension of democratic procedures to all spheres of social action is being hailed as the triumph of democracy and its ultimate consummation. Thus, the committee system of the National Security Council has been defended as "democracy in action," "government of laws and not of men," "representative" government; and the proposal to substitute for the committee system of the Joint Chiefs of Staff a single command has been condemned as contrary to "democratic process and procedures which are the basis of our government at home" and as "regimentation of opinion."

This point of view is doubly mistaken; for it misunderstands both the nature of democracy and the nature of policy formation and perverts them in practice. Democracy as popular control of public officials is responsible government; that is to say, the people or their representatives can hold the officials of the government to account for their policies. Yet it is the earmark of government by committee that it shifts responsibility from an individual to a faceless collectivity. Who is responsible for the neglect of Latin America or the surprise of the Iraqi revolution of 1958? Who will be responsible when tomorrow a renewed crisis over the islands off the Chinese coast confronts us with a new dilemma and an increased danger? Below the President, one can point to nobody in particular. In a sense, all the committees who had a hand in these policies are responsible, and since, as it were, everybody is responsible, nobody is.

As democracy demands individual responsibility, so does the process of policy formation. The conception of that process as "representation" of different points of view misunderstands the difference between the executive and the legislative decision as well as the relation between the making of a decision, on the one hand, and information and consultation, on the other.

The policy decisions of the executive branch of the government, like the decisions of the business executive or any decision an individual must make in his private affairs, are fundamentally different from the legislative decision. The latter is supposed to represent the compromise of divergent interests wherever one interest has not won out over the others. The executive decision is supposed first of all to be the correct decision, the decision more likely than any other to bring about the desired result. The committee system is appropriate for the legislative process, and it is not by accident that it originated and was institutionalized there. The executive decision requires that one man, after hearing the evidence and taking counsel, should himself decide what action under the circumstances should be taken.

The relation between the making of the decision, on the one hand, and information and consultation, on the other, is hierarchical, not equalitarian. The informant and the consultant are the servants of the decision maker, not participants in the decision-making process. They provide the raw material for the decision, not the decision itself.

This universalized committee system acts as a powerful incentive to evade decisions and replace them with compromises that reshuffle, rather than point beyond, the *status quo*. For the committee system tends not toward sharpening the differences between alternative policies but toward glossing them over and making them disappear. Not the daring initiative or the bold innovation is the natural product of this system, but rather the defense of the *status quo* through the perpetuation of established routines. The committee system naturally shies away from a clear-cut decision in which one side wins and the other loses, and tends as naturally toward a compromise or else conceals the evasion of decision altogether in a vague and frequently exhortative formula that satisfies everybody because it means all things to all committee members.

Consequently, the spirit of compromise permeates the whole executive branch. Before an issue reaches the President, it has already been formulated, generally several times over, on the lower levels of government with a view toward compromise on the highest level. Whatever spirit of innovation may have animated the lower levels cannot survive the process of adaptation to the views of a number of agencies with different outlooks and interests. When the issue reaches the President, its outlines, in terms of both information and judgment, are likely to be blurred, while the alternative solutions have been dissolved in the formula of compromise. The President is thus relieved of the burden of choosing; he approves what is presented to him as the unanimous advice of the agencies concerned.

Then, when the formula has become the policy of the United States, the process of compromise starts all over again. For since the formula has not really resolved the issue but only glossed it over for the sake of agreement, the agencies charged with the execution of policy must now go to work to give the formula operational meaning. In doing this, they again act as representatives of their respective agencies, each interpreting the formula in terms of his agency's preferences. The result again is either compromise or no new policy at all. At the level of policy execution, what connects the several agencies is not coordination and supervision, but a soothing and amorphous something that might be called "departmental courtesy." It follows its own golden rule: mind your own business, and I shall not mind yours; don't criticize me, and I shall not criticize you. Thus, the general tendency of society to turn within itself and administer what it has achieved rather than move forward into the unexplored is powerfully supported by a system of reaching decisions which is really a device for avoiding decisions and continuing safe routines that are incapable of disturbing the *status quo*.

Democratic governments must be responsive to public opinion as the potential source of voters' preferences. A government that is neglectful of public opinion risks being disavowed by the voters and losing its ability to govern. In this sense the concern for public opinion is simply the concern for the consent of the governed, the very fountainhead of democratic legitimacy. This, however, is not the sense in which contemporary democratic practice conceives of public opinion and its relation to the government. It considers public opinion less as the source of democratic legitimacy whose consent for the government's policies must be secured than as the ultimate arbiter of policy with whose wishes the government must comply. It then becomes incumbent upon the government to ascertain the preferences of public opinion in order to be able to comply with them.

The public-opinion poll serves that purpose. It has become the chief instrument through which the will of the people is ascertained. The men and measures the polls find supported by public opinion are found acceptable in democratic terms. These men can govern, and these measures can become policies. The men and measures that fail the test of the polls are excluded from democratic legitimacy. Thus, the polls define the limits within which the government can safely operate. The poll becomes the oracle telling both government and people who can be elected and which policies can be pursued. Democracy is no longer government with the consent of the governed, nor is it government by majority rule expressed in the votes of the people and their representatives. It has become government by public opinion revealing itself through the plebiscite of the polls.

This last type of democracy is a perversion of the democratic process because it perverts the relationship between government and people. That perversion, in turn, derives from a fundamental misunderstanding of the nature of public opinion. This conception of democracy assumes that public opinion, supporting or opposing a certain policy, exists before that policy itself, somewhat in the manner in which a rule of law exists before the action to be judged by it. In truth, public opinion is not a static thing to be ascertained by polls as legal precedents are by the science of law or as the data of nature are by the natural sciences. To the contrary, public opinion is a dynamic thing, created and continuously being changed by the very policies for which its support is sought. Public opinion does not exist before a policy, except perhaps as a vague, inchoate, and inarticulate disposition.

People do not possess opinions on policies as they possess tangible things; rather they arrive at opinions through experiences of which the policy itself is the most important one. What the public-opinion poll taken in advance of a policy tests is not opinion but at best disposition, mood, or taste. Public opinion becomes aware of itself only by being aware of a policy behind which it can rally, or which it can oppose. Of this dynamic relationship between policy and public opinion, the crystallization of French public opinion as a result of De Gaulle's leadership provides a classic example.

Without being able to choose among policies that some authority has put before it, public opinion will remain passive, and its answers to pollsters will accentuate the negative, since it will inevitably prefer what is known and familiar to what is purely speculative and cannot really be known outside a clearly defined political context. The popular mood is certainly against taxation, to cite but one example, and a poll taken in a political vacuum will show this. But that poll can tell us nothing about how public opinion would receive a particular piece of tax legislation that served a particular purpose and was supported by certain persons and interests while being opposed by others. For only after such a measure has been made "public" by having been made a political issue can public opinion crystallize around it.

For the government to postpone action until after public opinion has spoken is tantamount to doing nothing, since public opinion will speak with precision only after the government has committed itself. The democratic process thus degenerates into an Alphonse-and-Gaston routine, the government waiting for public opinion to tell it how far it can go and public opinion waiting for the government to guide it. Having surrendered the initiative to a public opinion that does not exist until the government has taken the initiative, the government can do no more than carry on the day-by-day chores within the established *status quo.*

Worse than that, the government, and with it the nation, continuously runs the risk that the place of leadership vacated by the government will be occupied by someone else, more likely than not a demagogue or a demagogic elite catering to popular emotions and prejudices who will create a public opinion in support of a certain policy more likely than not to be unsound and dangerous. The predicament of the government, originating in its own passivity, is then magnified and complicated by the emergence of a public opinion that, far from being passively contented with the *status quo,* is actively committed to a policy that dangerously disturbs it. The government, unwilling to mold public opinion on behalf of the policies it would like to pursue, then blames an unenlightened public opinion for its difficulties in defending the *status quo* against a demagogic onslaught.

In truth, however, the contest here is not between the government and public opinion, but rather between the government and a counter-elite to which the government has surrendered its initiative by default. It may happen in the end—and it has actually happened—that the opposition, supported by an aroused public opinion, will impose its will upon the government and force it to pursue the policy of the opposition. The government cannot help doing this halfheartedly and ineffectually. Because it knows better than the opposition and, furthermore, bears responsibility for the consequences of its acts, whatever it does in order to satisfy the opposition always falls short of the standards that the opposition has erected and the government has accepted as its own. In consequence, the policy of the government will always stand condemned in the eyes of public opinion for having sought and achieved less than public opinion had a right to expect of it in view of the standards which the government had professed as its own.

Incapable of governing as it would like to and always in danger of losing the support of public opinion to a counter-elite, the government is compelled by its subservience to public opinion to cater to it through concealment and misrepresentation. In a working democratic system, the government, while having an obvious advantage in the contest of opinion, ideally at least cannot afford to conceal and misrepresent nor does it need to do so. A responsible parliament and an alert public force it to lay its cards on the table or at the very least check the government version of the truth against their own. And the assumption of democratic pluralism that neither the government nor anybody else has a monopoly of truth in matters political minimizes the temptation for the government to impose its version upon society by concealment and misrepresentation. Yet a government that has abdicated as the leader and educator of the people and allowed the democratic contest for the consent of the governed to degenerate into a contest for popularity cannot help but put appearance in the place of substance. Thus it is not by accident that the techniques of advertising have so thoroughly replaced the processes of free discussion in the relations between government and people. Inevitably the people are being reduced to the status of an inert object of expert manipulation. Their reactions to competing public-relations techniques are the contemporary version of the consent of the governed, which ideally is supposed to issue from the dialectic interchange of competing philosophic conceptions and political conclusions.

### 3. *The Paradox of the Thwarted Majority*

It is the supreme dual paradox of contemporary democracy that the expansion of its methods goes hand in hand with the recession of actual popular control over the government and that this decline of the power of the people is not compensated for by a corresponding increase in the power of the government. As the power of the people has declined, so has the power of the government. It is not so much that the power of the government has been dislocated, as has been said, by being shifted from the executive to the legislative branch. Rather the power of the government is being dissipated because it is being arrogated by numerous semi-autonomous public and private agencies, business enterprises, and labor unions. In other words, we are in the presence of a new feudalism that resembles the old one in two important respects. On the one hand, the substance of governmental power slips piecemeal into hands in which it does not belong. On the other, the public authorities, such as the President, the Supreme Court, Congress, and the people at large, continue to perform their constitutional functions though these have to a degree been emptied of the substance of power. Four factors are responsible for these two paradoxes: a new distribution of power between the government and the people; the nature of the issues facing society; the rise of autonomous concentrations of power; and the abdication of government before the specter of public opinion.

The ultimate safeguard of popular rights has been in modern democracy, as it has been in all other systems of government, the ability of the people to overthrow the government by force—that is, to make a revolution. This ability provided a double safeguard. On the one hand, the fear of revolution imposed effective restraints upon the government. The popular rights in defense of which the people were willing to take up arms were safe as long as the government calculated the mood of the people correctly. On the other hand, the actual threat or fact of revolution was capable of protecting or restoring the rights of the people if the government should calculate wrongly.

This protection with which the possibility of revolution surrounded the rights of the people is predicated upon an approximately equal distribution of the means of physical violence between the government and the people. Before the beginning of the century, roughly speaking, the government met the people, barring superior organization and training, on a footing of approximate equality. Both sides had virtually the same weapons with which to cut, to thrust, and to shoot. Numbers, morale, and leadership, then, decided the issue.

This approximately equal distribution of military power between government and people has in our age been transformed into the unchallengeable superiority of the government. The government has today a monopoly of the most destructive weapons, and the people can neither defend nor protect themselves against them. Due to their centralization, the government can acquire instantly a monopoly of the most effective means of transportation and communications as well. For the people to revolt against such a monopolistic concentration of superior power is utterly impossible, and the very thought of revolution, still lingering on, transforms itself into either a utopian dream or else a neurotic nightmare.

The same concentration of military power which makes popular revolution impossible has, however, the paradoxical effect of diminishing drastically the effective power of the government vis-à-vis other governments similarly equipped. For modern weapons have become so destructive that their use in support of the traditional goals of foreign policy is suicidal folly. What rational purpose would be served by blowing up the United States and China and probably the Soviet Union as well in a contest over control of the islands off the shore of China? In consequence, governments must tolerate infringements of their rights, impairments of their interests, and personal affronts that in former times would have called for a military response. Since the results of all-out violence are less tolerable than virtually any such disadvantage, governments cannot help but reconcile themselves to the latter. Unprecedented concentration of military power finds them unchallengeable at home and paralyzed abroad.

Thus it is not by accident that for technologically advanced nations this is the age not of popular revolution but of the *coup d'état*. That is to say, what a modern government must guard against is not primarily the disaffection of the people but the disloyalty of the armed forces. A modern government can rule over a thoroughly disaffected people as long as the armed forces support it; but it cannot rule, albeit supported by a loyal people, against the disaffected armed forces. A modern government may be overthrown by the armed forces acting alone, but it can no longer be overthrown by the people acting alone.

A people, in order to make a successful revolution, must gain the support of the armed forces and may do so in the measure that the armed forces partake of the popular mood. The success of the Hungarian revolution of 1956, however temporary, and of the Korean and Turkish revolutions of 1960 was assured when the armed forces made common cause with the people. Thus, in the last analysis, the ultimate contest is no longer between the government and the people, but between the government and the armed forces.

The extent that the fate of modern democracy is in the hands of the armed forces is clearly shown by the fate of the democracies of Germany, Italy, and France. In the rise of Nazism to power in 1933 the support of the armed forces was decisive, and Nazism survived the military revolt of 1944 only because the armed forces were split and that segment which supported the revolt was half-hearted and vacillating. It was the distribution of power within the armed forces that was decisive. Both in the assumption of power by Italian fascism in 1922 and in its dislodgment in 1943 the Italian army played the determining role.

Nowhere, however, has the ascendancy of the armed forces at the expense of the people been more clearly revealed than in the history of France since 1958. Once the army had resolved to make an end to the Fourth Republic, the doom of the regime was sealed. Regardless of the support it enjoyed in Parliament and in the population at large, the last government of the Fourth Republic could only choose between the voluntary surrender of power and being forced by the army to surrender it. Government with the consent of the governed had become government with the consent of the army. And once the Fifth Republic had assumed power with the consent of the army, government with the consent of the army became government by the will of the army.

The army has taken the place of the people and its elected representatives. The refusal of the army to obey certain orders necessary for the execution of a certain policy performs the function that the refusal of parliament to pass a law performed before. That refusal compels the government to refrain from pursuing that policy either altogether or in a certain way. The refusal of the army to obey the government altogether has the same effect that a parliamentary vote of lack of confidence had before. That refusal compels the government to resign. The government, in order to be able to govern, must negotiate its policies with the army as before it had to negotiate them with the parties in Parliament. What the people and their elected representatives want and are willing to support does not matter. The composition and the policies of the government are determined by what the army wants and is willing to support.

In no other of the Western democracies has the shift of power from the people to the armed forces been revealed with such stark simplicity as it has in the Fifth Republic of France; nor have anywhere else the political consequences been drawn from this shift with such radical consistency. Yet the shift has occurred everywhere by virtue of the irresistible superiority of the means of violence which modern technology has put in the hands of the armed forces. The political consequences of that shift have differed from country to country by virtue of different political and social conditions. In the United States it is not so much the armed forces specifically as the executive branch as a whole which that shift has benefited.

With respect to the issues which concern the armed forces most—military strategy, assignment of missions, and appropriations—the armed forces appear on the political stage not as a unit but divided into competing branches. The mechanics of checks and balances, characteristic of the American government as a whole, reappear within the military establishment and exert their limiting and restraining influence.

Furthermore, the principle of civilian control of the armed forces is firmly established not only in the Constitution but also and more particularly in the political mores and practices of America. Heeding the wisdom of the *Federalist*, America has been consistently mindful of the potential threat that a standing army constitutes to the democratic order. America has never brought itself to accepting a truly unified command for fear of the man-on-horseback, and it has compounded the military inefficiency of the committee system—the Pentagon houses more than seven hundred committees—by superimposing upon it a plethora of civilian secretaries, undersecretaries, and assistant secretaries—twenty-five all told—intended to harness the armed forces to the civilian will.

Finally, the armed forces have consistently and eagerly accepted that subordinate role. Even when the civilian direction of the military establishment temporarily lapsed, as it did in Europe in the last months of the Second World War, leaving a vacuum waiting to be filled, the military leaders refused to fill it. When in April 1945—during that "deadly hiatus" in American political leadership to which Sir Winston Churchill referred—the British government suggested in vain to the American government that our army go as far east in Czechoslovakia as possible and in particular occupy Prague, Generals Marshall and Eisenhower refused to take an action both militarily feasible and politically advantageous "unless," in the words of Eisenhower, "I receive specific orders from the combined Chiefs of Staff." The different course of action General MacArthur took under somewhat similar circumstances during the Korean War was an exception to the rule.

This subordination of the armed forces to civilian control and, more particularly, their own commitment to that subordination make the executive branch as a whole rather than the armed forces specifically the beneficiary of the shift of power away from the people. The results of that shift are in normal times intangible and potential and become obvious and acute only when the country approaches a revolutionary crisis. The country may be said to approach such a crisis in view of the resistance of Southern states to the Federal government's attempts to enforce the application of Constitutional guarantees to Negroes. Yet while a century ago such a conflict would have raised the specter of revolution and civil war, as it actually did with regard to a different but related issue, the unchallengeable military superiority of the Federal government precludes the possibility of armed conflict. It is the absence of this possibility, of which both the government and the people are vaguely aware, which removes a restraint from the power of the government and a weapon from the armory of the people.

However, modern technology, which has thus given the government a decisive potential advantage over the people in the over-all distribution of power, has also actually strengthened the hand of the government in its day-by-day operations. The great issues of state in the fields of foreign policy, military organization and strategy, economics, and finance can no longer be understood, as they formerly were, by any knowledgable man of average intelligence.

Their understanding requires a larger degree of expert knowledge, which is much more readily available to the government than to the individual citizen and part of which, because of its classified nature, is available only to the government. Thus, the government can speak in these matters with an authority unmatched by that of any individual or group outside it.

Not only can the government speak with superior authority, but it can also act with finality. The natural advantage of the executive branch in being able to confront the people and their representatives with an accomplished fact is increased by its control over the technological initiation and implementation of policy. Once the executive branch has started building, say, one kind of missile or radar warning system, it becomes impractical for Congress or for the people at large to insist upon a different program; for the complicated technology, costliness, and lead-time of such programs preclude the possibility of changing them in view of—perhaps but temporary—Congressional or popular pressure. The disavowal of the government's policies in the elections, provided their import could be clearly ascertained, could influence policy at best only in the long run and only if there were a reasonable assurance, which of course there is not, that later elections would not reverse the position again. In consequence, the democratic corrective of elections has become at best a tenuous instrument of the popular will.

The preferences of the people and their representatives, in so far as they can be articulated at all, have in these matters hardly any relevance for the substance of the policies of the executive branch. They may, however, influence greatly the manner in which these policies are presented to the public and the amount of information the executive branch is willing to make public to begin with. Thus in these matters of the highest importance,

while the executive branch acts, setting the course of
policy perhaps for years to come, the people and Congress
can but deliberate, investigate, and resolve; they can approve within the limits of the information accessible to
them or, if they have no knowledge to go on, forgo judgment altogether, on the assumption that the executive
branch knows best since it knows more. This advantage of
the executive over the legislative branch and the people at
large derives of course from the nature of the executive
function itself and, hence, is inherent in a system of government which makes the executive independent of the
legislative branch. What is unprecedented is the qualitative shift—paralleling the shift in the control of the means
of violence—of the power of decision from the people to
the government in matters of life and death. It has made
the government the master of the national fate.

### 4. The New Feudalism: The Paradox of Thwarted Government

We have thus far dealt with one of the two paradoxes
of contemporary democracy, the paradox of thwarted majority rule: universal democratization goes hand in hand
with a drastic shift of power from the people to the government. We turn now to the paradox of thwarted
government: that drastic increase in the power of the government in relation to the people goes hand in hand with
a drastic decrease in the over-all power that constitutional
authorities exercise within the state. In other words, universal democratization and the increase of the power of
the government at the expense of the people result in a
net loss of governmental power. While more powerful vis-
à-vis the people than it has been in living memory, the
government governs less than it did when it was weaker.

This paradox is the result of the decomposition of governmental power from within and without: through the feudalism of semi-autonomous executive departments and through the feudalism of the concentrations of private power.

When we refer to the executive branch of the government, we are really making use of a figure of speech in order to designate a multiplicity of varied and more or less autonomous agencies that have but one quality in common: their authority has been delegated to them either by the President or by Congress. But neither the President nor Congress is able to control them. The reason must be sought in the inadequacy of the Presidency and of Congress for the control of the executive branch as it has developed in our time. The executive branch of the American government has become an enormous apparatus of the highest quantitative and qualitative complexity. The functions of the executive branch have been divided and subdivided and parceled out to a plethora of agencies. Most of the functions these agencies perform overlap or are at the very least interconnected to such an extent that an agency needs the support of other agencies in order to perform its functions. There can be but few policies of any importance which an agency is able to pursue without regard for the position of other agencies. In the absence of hierarchical direction and control, one agency can act only with the consent of another agency, and how to secure that consent—through co-operation or competition—becomes a vital issue upon which the usefulness of the agency depends.

This quantitative proliferation of the executive function is accompanied by its qualitative atomization, which is due to the technological complexity of many of the most important executive functions. This complexity gives the agency that masters it an advantage in policy formation which may well amount in some of the most important areas to a virtual monopoly. Such specialized knowledge, which is a unique source of power, is typically guarded by a wall of secrecy, and excluded from it are not only the general public and Congress but also other—and especially rival—agencies.

Upon this sprawling and unwieldy agglomeration of executive agencies, which are legally speaking but an arm of the executive and the legislature, the President and Congress try in vain to impose their will. The President as Chief Executive and Commander in Chief has of course the constitutional power to impose his conception of policy upon the executive departments, with the exception of the independent regulatory commissions, which are supposed to operate according to the statutory standards laid down by Congress. However, reality diverges sharply from the constitutional scheme. Even so strong and astute a President as Franklin D. Roosevelt was incapable of assuming full control even over the State Department, the constitutional executor of his foreign policy. His successors have had to an ever increasing degree to limit themselves to laying down general principles of policy in the hope that they would not suffer too much in the far-flung process of execution. On the other hand, the main weapon at the disposal of Congress, the investigating power, is clumsy; it can at best deal effectively with abuse and violation of the law, but is hardly able to correct an executive policy that is at variance with its own. For the statutory standards by which Congress must judge the executive performance are generally so vague as to leave the executive branch and, more particularly, the regulatory commissions a vast area of discretion.

Thus the constitutional intent to translate the presidential and congressional will into purposeful action, as the movements of the arm reflect the impulses emanating from the brain, has produced instead the anarchy of a war of all against all, fought among as well as within the executive departments. The objective of the war is the determination—either directly or by influencing the decisions of higher authority—of at least that segment of policy which falls within the jurisdiction of the agency. The proliferation of agencies with overlapping functions and the equal status of many of them make the interagency phase of the war almost inevitable. The absence of clear lines of authority and of an organization appropriate to the functions to be performed invites intra-agency war and in certain departments, such as State and Defense, makes it inevitable. To win these wars, the belligerents enter into alliances with other belligerents, with factions in Congress and in the White House, with business enterprises, and with the mass media of communications. The deliberate leak to a journalist or member of Congress becomes a standard weapon with which one agency tries to embarrass another, or force the hand of higher authority, or establish an accomplished fact.

This process of policy formation and execution resembles the feudal system of government in that the public authority is parceled out among a considerable number of agencies which, while legally subordinated to a higher authority, are in fact autonomous to a greater or lesser degree. The executive agency, competing for the determination of policy with other agencies, more and more resembles a feudal fief that owes its existence to the delegation of powers by higher authority but becomes in active operation an autonomous center of power, defending itself against other centers of power and trying to increase its power at the expense of others. This system of government resembles the feudal system also in that the fragmentation of public power carries within itself a diminution of the sum total of public power. Fragmented power is weak power, and the sum total of the fragments, each following its own impulse, is of necessity inferior to what the public power would have been had it remained in one piece, harnessed to a single purpose. The government, instead of speaking with one strong and purposeful voice, speaks in many voices, each trying to outshout the others, but all really weak as well as contradictory.

It is worthy of note that this fragmentation and consequent diminution of the public power, which characterizes the executive branch of the government, was erected by the Constitution into a fundamental principle of the American system of government in the form of the separation of powers. The separation of the public power into three separate departments, in good measure independent of one another, seeks to prevent one branch from imposing its will upon the whole and thereby becoming too strong for the liberty of the citizens. It seeks to weaken the government by dividing it. What the Constitution sought to achieve for the whole government by intent, the executive branch has achieved for itself through haphazard, fissiparous growth.

The debilitating effect which the separation of powers was intended to exert upon the government was innocuous as long as the functions which the government had to perform were limited and exercised in normal circumstances. However, when a crisis required strong action by the government and, more particularly, by the executive, which alone is capable of direct action in the true sense of the word, it was the President who, through the authority of his office, the strength of his will, and the persuasiveness of his vision, gave the government that unity of purposeful action commensurate with the task to be performed. And the Constitution designed the Presidency to be equal to such a crisis situation by investing the President with the powers of an "uncrowned king."

## The New Feudalism: The Paradox of Thwarted Government

What the philosophy of the Constitution could conceive only as the extreme and exceptional conditions of crisis have become the normal conditions of American existence. The revolutions of the Civil War, the Square Deal, the New Deal, and the Cold War have established in permanence the dominant role of the government in the affairs of the nation. The quantitative proliferation of executive agencies implements that role. Yet the organization of the Presidency is adequate only to lead and control the weak and but sporadically active Federal government of bygone times, but not a Federal government which has become in permanence the determining factor in the vital concerns of the nation. No President can perform at the same time the functions of Head of State, Chief Executive, Commander in Chief, and head of his party. He can not even plan, formulate, co-ordinate, and supervise the execution of policy at the same time. The President has the constitutional authority to do all these things: but he has not necessarily the extraordinary combination of knowledge, judgment, and character required for such a task; and most certainly he does not have the time. In the absence of an effective Cabinet system, the President is separated from the day-by-day operations of the executive branch by a gap which he can but occasionally bridge. Normally, he presides over the executive branch, but he does not govern it.

Congress, on the other hand, is kept from effective control of the executive branch by the constitutional separation of powers, especially as interpreted by the executive branch itself. This impotence, bred in good measure by ignorance of what the executive branch is doing, has engendered in Congress an endemic mood of frustration and irritation which seeks relief in the harassment and persecution of persons rather than in the formulation, supervision, and enforcement of policies. Lack of party discipline and archaic rules of procedure make it difficult for Congress to discover a will of its own and impose it upon the executive branch. The disintegration of the executive branch and the debilitation of the public power resulting from it must be cured by infusing the executive branch, on the one hand, with a purpose transcending the feudal interests and loyalties that rent it assunder and, on the other, by superimposing upon it a power capable of neutralizing, subduing, and fusing the fragments of feudal power which tend to be a law unto themselves. Both purpose and power can come only from the President's office. For only here do we find the visible authority and the fullness of implied powers necessary to make the national purpose prevail over the parochialism of feudal fiefdoms. As in sixteenth- and seventeenth-century Europe the monarchical authority and power had to be called into being in order to create a nation out of the fragments of a territorial feudalism, so in our age must the presidential power and authority come forward to save the unity of the national purpose from functional fragmentation.

The debility of the executive power, caused by its inner fragmentation, invites attack from the concentrations of private power, especially in the economic sphere. Throughout history, factions within the state have frequently made common cause with a foreign enemy in order to improve their position in the domestic struggle for power and have thereby delivered the state itself into the hands of its enemies. So the feudal lords within the executive branch ally themselves with the princes of private power, each ally pursuing his particular goal. The former seek to expand their fiefdoms within the executive branch and thereby increase their share in the power of the government. The latter seek to turn the instruments of government control to their own advantage and expand their own power without regard for, and at the expense of, the public power.

Thus, the public power is diminished through concerted action from within and without. The economic sphere has lost whatever autonomy it has had in the past: it is subject to political control as it, in turn, tries to control political decisions. We are in the presence of the revival of a truly political economy, and the major economic problems are political in nature.

The interconnectedness of the political and economic spheres is not peculiar to our age. Even in the heyday of nineteenth-century liberalism, the strict separation of the two spheres was in the nature of a political ideal rather than the reflection of observable reality. The monetary, tax, and tariff policies of the government had then, as they have now, a direct bearing upon the economic life—and so had the outlawry of associations of workingmen as criminal conspiracies. Yet the ideal of strict separation served the political purpose of protecting the economic forces from political control without impeding their influence in the political sphere.

What is peculiar to our age is not the interconnectedness of politics and economics but its positive philosophic justification and its all-persuasiveness. The state is no longer looked upon solely as the umpire who sees to it that the rules of the game are observed and intervenes actively only if, as in the case of the railroads, the rules favor one player to excess and thereby threaten to disrupt the game itself. In our age, aside from still being the umpire, the state has also become the most powerful player, who, in order to make sure of the outcome, rewrites the rules of the game as he goes along. No longer does the government or society at large rely exclusively upon the mechanisms of the market to ensure that the game keeps going. Both deem it the continuing duty of the government to see to it that it does.

In the United States the state pursues three main purposes in the economic sphere: observance of the rules of the game, maintenance of economic stability, and national defense.

The rules of the game are oriented toward the pluralistic objectives of American society. Thus they seek to prevent any sector of the economy from gaining absolute power vis-à-vis other sectors of the economy, competitors, or the individuals as such, by controlling and limiting its power. Regulatory commissions, legislation controlling and limiting the strong and supporting the weak, tariff and monetary policies serve this purpose.

While the state started to assume responsibility for the rules of the game in the last decades of the nineteenth century, it made itself responsible for economic stability in the 1930's. Economic stability, in this context, signifies the mitigation, if not the elimination in certain sectors, of the business cycle. Its main positive characteristics, as conceived by the government of the United States, are stability of employment, stability of the value of the dollar, and stability of agricultural prices. A plethora of legislative and administrative devices serve this purpose.

Since the end of the Second World War, technological research and industrial production have become to an ever increasing extent the backbone of military defense. The regular annual expenditure by the government of more than forty billion dollars on national defense, its decrease or increase from year to year, its shift from one sector of the economy to another, all exert a sometimes drastic influence upon the economic life of the nation. They have made the government the most important single customer for the products of the national economy. In addition, many tax and monetary policies and price and wage policies are determined by considerations of national defense.

With the government thus exerting an enormous controlling, limiting, and stimulating influence upon the economic life, the ability to influence the economic decisions of the government becomes an indispensable element in the competition for economic advantage. Economic competition manifests itself inevitably in competition for political influence. This political influence is exerted through two channels: control of, and pressure upon, government personnel.

The most effective political influence is exerted by the direct control of government personnel. The economic organization which has its representatives elected to the legislature or appointed to the relevant administrative and executive positions exerts its political influence as far as the political influence of its representatives reaches. In so far as the representatives of these economic organizations cannot decide the issue by themselves, the competition for political influence and, through it, economic advantage will be fought out within the collective bodies of the government by the representatives of different economic interests. While this relationship of direct control is typical in Europe, it is by no means unknown in the United States. State legislatures have been controlled by mining companies, public utilities, and railroads, and many individual members of Congress represent specific economic interests. Independent administrative agencies have come under the sway of the economic forces they were intended to control. The large-scale interchange of top personnel between business and the executive branch of the government cannot help but influence, however subtly and intangibly, decisions of the government relevant to the economic sphere.

However, in the United States the most important political influence is exerted through the influence of pressure groups. The decision of the government agent—legislator, independent administrator, member of the executive branch—is here not a foregone conclusion by virtue of the economic control to which he is subject. His decision is in doubt, for he is still open to different economic pressures. The competition for the determination of the decisions of the government takes place not among the government agents themselves but between the government agent, on the one hand, and several economic pressure groups, on the other. Only after this competition has been settled will the government agents, provided the issue is still in doubt, compete with one another.

The political struggle, ostensibly fought for victory in periodical elections by political parties, reveals itself in good measure as a contest of economic forces for the control of government action. In consequence, the decision of the government, and more particularly of legislatures, ostensibly rendered "on the merits of the case," tends to reflect the weight of economic influence and, at worst, to give political sanction to decisions that have been taken somewhere else. Legislators and administrators tend to transform themselves into ambassadors of economic forces, defending and promoting the interests of their mandatories in dealing with each other on behalf of them. The result is again a new feudalism which, like that of the Middle Ages, diminishes the authority of the civil government and threatens it with extinction by parceling out its several functions among economic organizations to be appropriated and used as private property. And just like the feudalism of the Middle Ages, these new concentrations of private power tend to command the primary loyalties of the individual citizens who owe them their livelihood and security. In the end, the constitutionally established government tends to become, in the words of Chief Justice Marshall, a "solemn mockery," glossing over the loss of political vitality with the performance of political rites.

If giant concentrations of economic power, in the form of business enterprises and labor unions, were thus to become laws unto themselves, deciding with finality the matters vital to them and using the government only for the purpose of ratifying these decisions, they would not only have drained the life blood from the body politic but also have destroyed the vital energies of the economic system. For the vitality of the American economic system has resided in its ability to renew itself from new technological opportunities unfettered by the interests identified with an obsolescent technology. Seen from the vantage point of individual enterprise, this is what we call freedom of competition. This freedom of competition has been a function of the rules of the economic game, as formulated and enforced by the state.

Yet the new feudalism, if it is not controlled and retrained, must inevitably tend to abrogate these rules in order to assure the survival of the economic giants which, in turn, tend to take over the functions of the state. The consummation of this development, possible but not inevitable, would be a state of affairs in which for those giants the rule of life would not be freedom of competition, which might jeopardize their survival, but freedom from competition in order to secure their survival. The dynamics of the capitalistic system, especially in the United States, as continually destructive and creative as life itself, would then give way to a gigantic system of vested interests in which the established giants would use the state to make themselves secure from competitive displacement, only to die a slow death from attrition.

It is the measure of the quandary which modern society faces in this problem that the most obvious cure raises issues as grave as the disease. That cure is a state strong enough to hold its own against the concentrations of private power. Yet such a state, by being strong enough for this task, cannot fail to be also strong enough to control, restrain, and redirect the economic activities of everybody. In other words, as the liberal tradition correctly assumes, a strong government, whatever else it may be able to accomplish, threatens the liberties of the individual, especially in the economic sphere. Thus, modern society is faced with a real dilemma: a government which is too weak to threaten the freedom of the individual is also too weak to hold its own against the new feudalism; and a government which is strong enough to keep the new feudalism in check in order to protect the freedom of the many is also strong enough to destroy the freedom of all.

There can be no doubt as to which horn of the dilemma the government has chosen. It is in full retreat before the onslaught of private power and a passive onlooker at its unbridled exercise. It can no more see to it that the natural monopolies in the fields of transportation, utilities, and mass communications be used in the public interest than it can protect the public interest in its dealings with the suppliers of manufactured goods. The government has become the biggest customer of private industry, but it has also become one of its most hapless customers because it is among the most impecunious ones. In the field of military supplies in particular, the government is at the mercy of its suppliers. Only within very narrow limits can it do what customers in a market are supposed to be capable of doing if they do not like the terms of trade and the quality of the product: take its business elsewhere.

This dependence of the government upon the suppliers of its military matériel evokes still another similarity with the feudal system. As the king had to buy military support from the feudal lords with parcels of his land and fragments of his power, so is the government within the terms of a commercial relationship at the mercy of its suppliers who control not only the quality of the product and the terms of trade but in good measure also the very identity of the product.

## The New Feudalism: The Paradox of Thwarted Government

While the government is thus a weak contractual partner of the concentrations of private power, it is a virtually impotent bystander when it comes to the control over the exercise of private power. The government is incapable of enforcing the laws against a corrupt and tyrannical union. It cannot enforce the criminal laws against its officials, nor can it protect the members of the union against the abuse of power on the part of the union officials. The government of the union has become in good measure an autonomous private government, making and enforcing its own laws and pursuing its own policies, regardless of the public laws, the public policy, and the public interest.

What holds true of unions applies to the legitimate business enterprise, and it applies likewise to the illegitimate business enterprise, the racket. The racket is in our society the most highly developed type of private government in that it operates not within the letter of the public law, as do the private governments of legitimate business, but, by definition, outside it. Its distinctive characteristics are the institution of private criminal justice and methods of commercial competition resembling feudal warfare.

The retreat of the public power before the expansion of private governments has been particularly patent when it has failed to perform its most elemental function: to defend the public interest—and more particularly the public peace—against the war, industrial or physical, of private governments. Both Truman and Eisenhower were unable to prevent or settle industrial warfare between the giants of industry and labor. After Truman's seizure of the steel industry during the strike of 1952 had been invalidated on constitutional grounds, Eisenhower did not even attempt to intervene in the steel strike of 1959.

The issue in industrial wars of this kind is but ostensibly economic; in truth, it concerns the distribution of power between either management and labor or different labor unions or both. The economic settlement by which such a war is finally terminated amounts essentially to a conspiracy between management and labor to shift the economic burden of the settlement to the consumer. Whether or not such a settlement is actually supported and sanctioned by the government and whether or not its effects upon consumer prices are postponed for tactical reasons, as was done in the settlement of the steel strike of 1959, does not affect the intrinsic nature of the settlement and the government's impotence in the face of it.

The impotence of the government to assert its authority against the private governments comes nowhere more strikingly to the fore than in its dealings with the rackets. A racket is actually not only a private government but also a counter-government, complete with all the characteristics of a public government, such as police and military forces, executive organs, courts, taxation, and its similarity with a feudal fiefdom in its organization, functions, and relations to the public power, other rackets, and its outside tributaries is indeed most impressive. The racket as an institution has proven invulnerable to the authority of the public power. The best the latter has been able to accomplish has been sporadic harassment of the institution and the elimination of some of its members through criminal, contempt-of-court, and deportation proceedings. The very fact that the public power has found its most effective weapon in the income-tax laws, whose evasion constitutes neither the most serious of the misdeeds of the rackets nor one peculiar to them, demonstrates the weakness of the public power's position.

Harassment by the public power, more or less good-naturedly submitted to by private government, has become the essentially ritualistic method by which the public power asserts, and the private government submits to, its authority, similar in its symbolic function to the feudal obeisance. The arrest of known hoodlums, the indictment of labor racketeers, and the anti-trust proceedings against business enterprises perform that function. The general futility of such public measures in terms of the institutional relationship—in contrast to their effects upon certain individuals—only serves to underline the weakness of the public power and the semi-autonomy of private government. Were it not for the public power's ability to tax the private governments—which has remained effective albeit impaired—and for the public power's control over the most potent means of physical violence, the autonomy of the private governments would be complete. And it must be said in passing that the public power is weak in meting out justice even to individual wrong-doers; of 2,340,000 persons arrested in 1958 for major crimes only 88,780—that is less than four per cent—were sent to state and Federal prisons.

The decline of the public power, revealed by disintegration from within and usurpation from without, can be traced to a paralysis of will within the public power itself. That paralysis, in turn, has been brought on by that perversion of the democratic process which reduces the government to an agent of what is thought to be public opinion. Such a government, as we have seen, cannot be but a weak government. A government which considers itself the agent rather than the molder of public opinion cannot help setting in motion that fatal mechanism through which influence over public opinion is being surrendered by default to the counter-elite of the private governments. Public opinion, which in view of its interests ought to be the ally of the public power, then becomes the instrument with which the private governments disarm the public power.

That so enfeebled a government still gives the appearance of governing and actually governs with a modicum of coherence is due to the discipline of the budget, the leadership of the President, and the immanent force of the national purpose.

The budget of the Federal government is, as it were, the master plan that assigns missions to all the branches of the government and determines the material resources to be expended for their achievement. However much the quality of the achievement and its faithfulness to the budgetary policy may depend upon individual performance, the budget constitutes a detailed charter of policy which ties all agents of the government to its choice of ends and means. It operates as the great centrifugal force that tends to neutralize the feudalism from within. It delineates, as it were, the outer limits which that feudalism cannot overstep without forsaking the sanction of the law.

The degree of firmness of these budgetary ties depends not only upon the strict interpretation of the letter of the law but also and most importantly upon the will and skill of the President and, to a much lesser extent, of Congress. The members of the executive branch are, legally speaking, merely agents of the President as Chief Executive, from whom they have received by way of delegation whatever authority they possess. The unity and purposefulness of action the Federal government is capable of is largely determined by the degree to which the President is capable of making his conception of policy prevail throughout the executive branch and of imbuing with his will the myriad separate steps of which the execution of policy is composed. That task of the President as the initiator, executor, and supervisor of policy is served by the administrative and political measures through which the Presidential presence makes itself felt at all levels of the execution of policy. It is also served more intangibly and perhaps more importantly by the President as the articulator and living symbol of the national purpose.

## The New Feudalism: The Paradox of Thwarted Government

The public power is weakened and threatened with disintegration from within and without by a new distribution of power, by new private interests, and by the universalism of the democratic processes misunderstanding the nature both of democracy and of executive decision. These threats are of a material and, to a greater or lesser degree, of a tangible nature; they are social facts that are subject to direct empirical observation. Yet the public power is being protected and in a certain measure immunized against disintegration by a factor which is intangible in that its existence can be ascertained only by indirection from certain words, deeds, and conditions pointing to its existence. That factor is the all-persuasiveness of the national purpose. Both the defenders and the opponents of the public power—like the partisans of the other great political controversies of the past—are parties to the purposeful consensus which sets America apart from other nations. They are Americans before they are partisans. The vitality of that consensus stands in inverse relation to the strength of the disintegrating factors threatening the purposeful unity of the nation itself. The disintegration of the public power remains relative so long as the national consensus outweighs in the thoughts and deeds of the people the commitment to parochial interests. That disintegration becomes absolute and, hence, disastrous for the public power when this commitment takes precedence over the consensus. Either the public power will then survive only as a shadow to which autonomous feudal fiefdoms will pay ritual tribute, or else it will be destroyed in one cataclysmic act through revolution and civil war, perhaps to be resurrected by one feudal power prevailing over the others.

In this confrontation between national consensus and parochial commitments what matters first of all is the vitality of the consensus, however defined. Even the purpose of equality in freedom at the service of a hedonism of the *status quo* can provide the element of integration which will keep in check the disintegrating tendencies—at least as long as the *status quo* remains intact. Could equality in freedom, severed as it is from a generally recognized objective order, and the public power committed to it survive the jeopardy of the *status quo?* The volatility of a hedonistic commitment and the precariousness of the American consensus, to which I have referred before, as well as the historic experience of other societies preclude a confidently affirmative answer. Thus while the consensus, albeit serving nothing more than a hedonism of the *status quo*, strengthens the public power, the decline of objective standards adds to the weakness of the public power, which must find in the maintenance and improvement of the material *status quo* its foremost purpose and justification.

# V

# WHAT IS TO BE DONE?

### 1. *What Is Not to Be Done*

CONTEMPORARY AMERICA'S CONCERN with the national purpose testifies to the vitality of that purpose; for if people did not feel that there is something essentially amiss in American life and if they did not point to the crisis of the American purpose as a source of failure, one could indeed conclude that the purpose of America had died, to quote John Adams' phrase again, "in the minds of the people." The urge to renew the national purpose is strong, yet the most spectacular attempts to renew it are misguided, and the inadequacy of these attempts is itself a symptom of the crisis of the national purpose.

The most common and most irrelevant of these attempts has been the ritualization of the historic manifestations of the national purpose. History offers a respectable and virtually invulnerable escape from the duties and risks with which the tasks of the present disturb our thoughts and our actions. Thus we commemorate the great men and deeds of the past, we enshrine the Founding Fathers and sanctify Lincoln, not as a spur to new thoughts and actions, but as an assurance that greatness is vouchsafed us because we are the heirs of those great men and the beneficiaries of their deeds. We worship the past and use the great historic pronouncements that put the living experience of the national purpose into words as so many magic formulas which seem to protect us from the contemporary world and at the same time create the illusion that we have come to terms with it.

The other misguided attempt at renewing the national purpose results from what might be called the "intellectual fallacy." It is represented by a presidential commission that is charged with telling us what our national purposes are, and by a symposium, organized by a mass-circulation magazine, in which a number of eminent men tell us what their conception of the national purpose is. What is fallacious in these endeavors is the assumption that facts will yield to the power of abstract thought. In truth, facts will yield only to facts that prove to be stronger, and old experiences will yield only to new ones that prove to be more persuasive. "American democracy," to quote Frederick Jackson Turner, "was born of no theorist's dream; it was not carried in the *Susan Constant* to Virginia nor in the *Mayflower* to Plymouth. It came out of the American forest, and it gained strength each time it touched a new frontier."[1] Similarly, the purpose of America was not created, and it will not be renewed, in an editorial office or a committee room—nor, for that matter, in a professor's study. It was created and achieved in the encounter of purposeful action with a natural and social environment conducive to that action, and so it will be renewed. Crèvecoeur, Thomas Paine, Benjamin Franklin, Charles Pinckney, John Adams did not speculate about the American purpose, they did not figure out what it was or what it ought to be. Rather they saw that purpose in action and reported what they saw.

What holds true of the achievement of the American

[1] Frederick Jackson Turner: *The Frontier in American History* (New York: Henry Holt; 1920), p. 293.

purpose also applies to its crises. In those crises the great revitalizers of the American purpose—Lincoln, Wilson, the two Roosevelts—had no doubt about what that purpose was and what actions it required. Wilson did not ask in the speech with which he began the campaign of 1912: what is the purpose of America? Rather, taking that purpose for granted, he asked: have we failed to achieve it? And, answering that question in the positive, he inquired: what do we need to do to restore it?

Our awareness of the national purpose, then, has always been inseparable from experience and action. The deliberate attempts to revive it by invoking the past or to reformulate it in abstract terms, divorced from the concrete issues of the day, have produced literature, most of it bad, and all of it irrelevant to those issues; the intellectual worthlessness and practical futility of the literature of "Manifest Destiny" should warn us against substituting a literature of the national purpose for action on behalf of it. The purpose of America was created and renewed by men who had a purpose in mind and sought to achieve it. They cannot teach us *what* we must think and do today, but they can teach us something that is more difficult to learn and more worth learning: *how* to think and *how* to act and *how* to bring our thinking to bear upon the issues of the day. They teach us, not by examples to be mechanically repeated, but through the intellectual and moral qualities that have gone into their work.

These considerations point also to the limitations of conservatism in American politics. Conservatism concerns either the philosophy and method of politics or its purpose. These two applications of the conservative approach to politics have been confused in contemporary American thought, yet they were sharply separated in the American political tradition. Conservatism of philosophy and method is indeed part and parcel of that tradition. *The*

*Federalist* is its greatest literary monument, Alexander Hamilton is its greatest theoretician, John Quincy Adams and Abraham Lincoln are in different ways its greatest practitioners. That conservatism holds that the world, imperfect as it is from the rational point of view, is the result of forces inherent in human nature. To improve the world, one must work with those forces, not against them. This being inherently a world of opposing interests and of conflict among them, abstract principles can never be fully realized, but must at best be approximated through the ever temporary balancing of interests and the ever precarious settlement of conflicts. Conservatism, then, sees in a system of checks and balances a universal principle for all pluralist societies. It appeals to historic precedent rather than abstract principles and aims at the realization of the lesser evil rather than of the absolute good.

On the other hand, the conservative view of the purposes of politics endows the *status quo* with a special dignity and seeks to maintain and improve it. This conservatism has its natural political environment in Europe; it has no place in the American tradition of politics. Europe, in contrast to America, has known classes, determined by heredity or otherwise sharply and permanently defined in composition and social status, which have had a legitimate stake in defending the present *status quo* or restoring an actual or fictitious *status quo* of the past. But for the defense or restoration of what *status quo* could the American conservative fight? The great majority of Americans, in contrast to the states of the Confederacy and other special interests, such as the contemporary concentrations of private power, have never known a *status quo* to whose preservation they could have been committed. For America has been committed to a purpose in the eyes of which each *status quo* has been but a steppingstone to a new achievement, a new *status quo* to be left behind by another new achievement. To ask America to defend a particular *status quo*, then, is tantamount to asking it to forswear its purpose.

The great issues of American politics concern neither the preservation of the present nor the restoration of the past but the creation, without reference to either, of the future. American politics does not defend the past and present against the future; rather, it defends one kind of future against another kind of future. While in philosophy and method conservatism is the most potent single influence in American politics, the purposes of our politics from the very beginning were unique and revolutionary, not only in the narrow political sense, but also in the more general terms of being oblivious to tradition. They have so remained, only temporarily disfigured by periods that were dominated by a conservatism of purpose and, hence, in the context of American politics spelled stagnation. In other words, the point of reference of American politics has never been the present, and only in a historically inconsequential way has it been in the past. Thus, the political program of both parties favors domestic changes in the *status quo;* for it is only with such a program that they can hope to appeal to the voters. We have no conservative political party because the number of conservative voters is not sufficient to support one on the national scale. We have only conservative minorities, which must try through obstruction and subterfuge to prevent change or at least to slow it up.

Conservative in philosophy and method, revolutionary in purpose—such has been our political tradition from the beginning of colonization. It has been so by dint of its own inner dynamics, of the peculiarly American way in which human purpose transformed the natural and social environment into an experience confirming and expanding the purpose. Yet we have tended to view the restoration of that purpose primarily as a means to the end of keeping up with the Russians. We have been doing so in a dual sense. Since the Russians have a simple and intelligible purpose, we have been arguing, so must we, and what the Russians are trying to achieve we must achieve, only in a bigger and better way. Yet even if we can compete successfully with the Russians in this fashion we shall in the process defeat our true purpose. The very essence of the American purpose, as we have seen, is that it is uniform in procedure and pluralist in substance; as a national purpose, it exists only as a particular mode of procedure. Give it a uniform substance as well, in imitation of the Soviet Union, and you have destroyed its very essence, its very vitality, its very uniqueness. Thus, it is heartening to note and testifies to the innate strength of the American purpose, truly understood, that the attempts to invent a slogan which would tell us and the world what we are about in substantive terms have remained utterly futile.

Even if we were still living in the isolation of the western hemisphere, we would owe it to ourselves to restore the national purpose that gives meaning to our existence as a nation and is our original contribution to the patrimony of mankind. It is primarily in order to be able to compete not with the Russians but with ourselves, to stay ahead of ourselves rather than of the Russians, that we must restore that purpose. That we are driven to the re-examination of the national purpose by fear of Russian superiority rather than by the awareness of our failings, in view of what our own past demands of us, illuminates from still another angle the depth of the contemporary crisis.

The distinction between these two attitudes toward the restoration of the national purpose is crucial. If to stay ahead of the Russians is what we primarily seek, then we shall really accept the Russian standards as our own. What they do we must do, only better; what they achieve we must achieve, only more of it. Even if we are successful in this competition, as we might well be, we shall have transformed ourselves into a soulless giant, armed to the teeth and producing abundantly, but for no other end than to stay ahead of the Russians. We shall have lost our purpose in the process of trying to restore it.

Our national purpose is not to stay ahead of the Russians quantitatively—even though this is obviously required by considerations of foreign policy—but to be different from, and superior to, them in those qualities which are peculiarly our own. We must make clear to ourselves and to the world—by deeds rather than by proclamations—that equality in freedom still has a home in America and is still worthy of emulation. Let us, then, compete with the Russians on our terms—since compete we must—as they compete with us on theirs, and let no one say that in such a contest we cannot win. For if this were true and if the world were to look to the Soviet Union rather than to America for a model to emulate, America would be the loser even though it continued to outproduce the Soviet Union. If the world were to assume that America had nothing to offer it, or nothing but material gains, it would have destroyed the very assumption of universal significance on which the American experiment has been built. Were this to come to pass, America would have gained a world of production and lost its soul.

An intimate and necessary relationship links America's alienation from its purpose to the alienation of the world from America. The world has been conscious of America's purpose in the measure that America was determined to achieve it. This has always been so. However, there is now added to this permanent and necessary relationship a new one which links the achievement of the American purpose to the very survival of America. In times past, America's failure to achieve its purpose was a matter between itself

and its sense of mission; it deprived its existence of meaning commensurate with its past. Today such a failure is
also a matter between ourselves and our will to survive; for
if we fail, the nations of the world will look elsewhere for
models of social organization and political institutions to
emulate, and we will be alone in a hostile world. Alone in
a hostile world, we would no longer be able to renew our
sense of purpose through the experience of territorial expansion and universal emulation. At best, equality in freedom would still have a home in America. Yet, thus mutilated, could the national purpose survive in America
itself? And if it should not survive, could America survive
without its purpose?

Thus, the restoration of the national purpose in our
time takes on a novel urgency. That restoration is no
longer, as it was in the crises of the past, a matter of social
justice, economic order, and the limits of territorial expansion. Rather the survival of America and of the civilized world depends upon it. We must, then, ask again the
question that Americans have asked whenever the national
purpose has met with a crisis: how can equality in freedom
be achieved in America? How can the area of equality in
freedom be expanded beyond the territorial limits of the
United States? How can equality in freedom be offered to
the world as a model to emulate? The answer must evolve,
as it has in the past, from the character of the natural and
social environment within which the purpose of America
is to be achieved. This environment has today six main
characteristics: a vertical mobility that still functions and
promises to expand, by virtue of the rapid succession of
technological revolutions, into new and unknown areas,
but that is threatened by the concentrations of private
power; the opening of a new cultural frontier that needs the
support of organized society to bring forth a great American culture; the need for a new horizontal mobility of

world-wide dimensions because of the obsolescence of the nation state as principle of political organization; the new significance of America as a model of equality for the nations emerging from colonial or semi-colonial status, and as a model of freedom for the nations living under autocratic rule; the nuclear threat to survival; the need to restore democratic government and defend freedom against it.

## 2. *The New Mobility and the New Frontiers*

Of the three American frontiers—the territorial, the natural, and the frontier as social artifact—the territorial one no longer performs a function for the purpose of America, but has become the rampart that protects the existence of America. The natural frontier of resources to be exploited and tasks to be performed has changed its character but not its importance for the achievement of the American purpose. New resources wait to be exploited, such as nuclear energy and space, and major tasks wait to be performed, such as the rebuilding of our cities and the reform of education.

The frontier as social artifact—that is, social contrivances facilitating vertical mobility—has remained open to an impressive degree. Yet we must be on guard against the potential threat that the concentrations of private power constitute to its continuing effectiveness. They do so as potential agencies not only of economic but also of social and political stratification and as impediments to competition. The combination of functional stratification with personal mobility, which we found to assure a considerable measure of vertical mobility within the concentrations of private power, is threatened by tendencies inherent in these concentrations. For they tend to develop into stratified structures of power on the basis not only of wealth but also of social and political distinctions. While stratification on the basis of wealth is naturally most pronounced in the big corporations, the tendency toward the other type of stratification is clearly revealed in the structure of the big labor unions. Equal access to the positions of power, not only at the top but also in the middle layers, is here sharply limited by the formation of closed ruling groups impervious to control and displacement by the rank and file. The degree of this stratification and the corresponding decline of democratic competition for office is indicated by the fact that hardly any of the leaders of the big unions or their lieutenants have ever been replaced or compelled to change their policies by a vote of the union members. The government must protect and restore vertical mobility in such conditions either by controlling directly the procedures of such private organizations or, more effectively, by promoting outside competition that provides those whose mobility is impaired with an alternative chance for advancement.

Vertical mobility is further threatened by the concentrations of private power because they are able to retard technological changes that would affect their interests adversely. Corporations and labor unions have under certain conditions a vested interest in the preservation of the technological *status quo,* and they have preserved the *status quo* at least for the time being when technological change requires large and risky investments that private sources will not provide. They have thus retarded the peaceful uses of atomic energy, they are artificially preserving uneconomic enterprises, and have made us pay through systematic featherbedding an unnecessary price for automation. The government must, because it alone has the ability, see to it that the technological frontiers of America remain open by using its economic and political resources to advance technological change.

## The New Mobility and the New Frontiers

The vitality and creativity of American society imposes upon the government still another and entirely novel task: that of guarding and caring for the cultural frontier. It may be deemed paradoxical that the government should be called upon to be the guardian of culture when society is superior to government, not, as nineteenth-century liberals thought, in virtue but in accomplishment. This is as it must be; for bureaucratic organization, however efficient, and political decision, however wise, can at best facilitate and make more effective, but can provide no substitute for, the creativity of the individual. Yet it is extraordinary and intolerable that the vitality and creativity of American society in all its various manifestations should be so inadequately reflected in the collective image the nation presents to itself and to the world. The nation does not recognize nor does it reward excellence in its midst through the instrument of its collective will, the government. The American landscape is dotted with innumerable islands of excellence, which are surrounded by an ocean of mediocrity and threatened with being swallowed up by the tidal waves of incompetence. Societies that are not only economically stratified, as is ours, but, in contrast to ours, culturally as well, have created autonomous institutions and devices by which excellence is recognized, encouraged, promoted, and held up as a standard for judgment. Academies, competitions, honors, and prizes create a commonwealth of excellence, composed of the federated republics of letters, scholarship, and so forth, which bring the isolated and dispersed excellences of individuals to bear upon the life of the nation as a whole.

The cultural institutions, such as those of a higher learning, and the professional organizations, such as those of scholars, which America has developed in great proliferation have not been able to institutionalize consistently standards of excellence. For these organizations have fashioned themselves after American society as a whole and have allowed themselves to be guided by the standards of conformity rather than excellence. Thus, the standards of excellence are supported only by isolated individuals or small nuclei of them, and not by a coherent identifiable group, endowed with the prestige of tradition and achievement, bestowing or withholding rewards according to objective standards, and looked up to by society as the guardian and embodiment of these standards. When standards of excellence are in conflict with those of conformity, these organizations have frequently been responsive to the pressures of conformity. For these anonymous pressures of unorganized society present real and—for the individual—well-nigh irresistible social power, to which only organized society in the form of its government is able to furnish an effective counterweight.

Governments have indeed provided such a counterweight throughout the civilized world in all periods of history. They have recognized, encouraged, and promoted the standards of excellence in art, literature, scholarship, and education by supporting them materially and lending them their prestige. This has been so in ancient Greece and Rome, in the Italy of the Renaissance, in Elizabethan England, in seventeenth-century France, and wherever else a great culture has flowered. The anarchy of American culture was tolerable as long as there was little of it and most of it was only the concern of a few. But no nation is rich enough in cultural endowments to be able to afford squandering its cultural resources in a period of great creative vitality and of mass participation in it. More particularly, it cannot allow a majority of its children to be cut off from contact with its cultural heritage and contemporary achievement by being either miseducated or not educated at all. No nation can afford such neglect under any circumstances; for through such neglect it lowers the level of its creative attainments and renders itself inferior to what it could be. Yet in our time such neglect may well endanger the very existence of civilized society. The central social problem that our society is likely to face is the problem not of work but of leisure; it is not unemployment and exploitation of labor that will plague it, but wasted leisure, hours emptied of content and life shorn of meaning. And the deadly threat against which our society must defend itself is likely to be, not the struggle of classes, but the alienation of the masses which have lost a stake in society because they have lost a stake in life.

Society, when care for the necessities of life is no longer its primary task, must concern itself with the meaning of life—that is, its culture. It can do so effectively only in its organized form, as government. Yet the government of the United States is singularly ill-equipped to perform that task. For it is itself to a large degree a product of the conformity that it is its task to overcome. Whoever has contact with members of our government must be impressed by the excellence of many of them as individuals and by the inferiority of their collective achievements. What a galaxy of eminent men the Senate of the United States can boast of, and how undistinguished are generally its policies! What a wealth of intelligence, knowledge, and good judgment one can find in the middle layers of government— say, the Department of State—and how frequently dismal is the product of their labors in the form of policy! That product is the result not of their individual excellence, but of their collective fear of a public opinion to whose actual or fancied preferences they hasten to conform. Thus, few officials of our government actually believe in the soundness of our Far Eastern policy; but since public opinion seems to approve it, it is not changed. Here, again, conformity tends to win out in the contest with excellence.

If a government so oriented were to intervene actively

in the cultural activities of the nation, it would probably drown individual creativity in a uniform mediocrity, born of conformism. It would encourage the very forces which it is its task to overcome, and stifle those which it ought to promote. Thus, it must free itself first of all from that deadly servitude to conformity, the fear of public opinion, which we saw confine the government's political initiative as well. Supported by all the centers of excellence the nation can muster and supporting them in turn, it must encourage and help develop what is creative in all fields of endeavor. By what society creates and what the government encourages, America will give at least implicit recognition to the existence of objective standards that are the measure of all things. The isolated islands of excellence will then be joined together, so to speak, in a coherent mass of land, a dam before which the ocean of mediocrity will recede and against which the waves of incompetence will break. America will have created the first mass culture in history, which will be a high and creative one. It will have opened yet another interior frontier, one which resembles the other frontiers in its purpose and is new in the territory it opens up. The old frontiers have given Americans equal access in freedom to wealth and power. The new frontier will give them equal access in freedom to the achievements of culture and equal opportunity to share in their creation.

However, when we speak of equality in freedom in America and pride ourselves on its achievement, we cannot ignore what has been a hindrance to its full achievement—that is, the denial of racial equality. This denial is, in the words of Jefferson which we have quoted before, "a moral reproach," a "condition of moral and political reprobation." To remove that reproach from our consciences and that condition from our body politic has been for a century the declared aim of our government and of the great majority of our citizens. The progress we have made, considerable in absolute terms but small in comparison with what still needs to be done, has been in good measure the result not of constitutional and legislative enactments and judicial decisions but of changes in the moral climate and of social pressures that a discriminatory minority cannot resist. That is likely to be true of the progress we must make in the future. For that progress the President, as the moral leader of, and the moral example for, the nation, will bear the major responsibility.

Progress in the achievement of equality in freedom by our racial minorities has become in our time an urgent matter not only because of the sharpening of our moral sensibilities and of changing economic and social conditions but also because of the emergence of the non-white members of the human race into consciousness of their individuality and into political independence. The racial minorities of America are in the process of merging into that vast movement of non-white peoples, comprising four fifths of mankind, who demand equality. These peoples have undertaken to achieve for themselves and in relation to the white man what America has offered to the world as its purpose: equality in freedom. What an irony it would be if the majority of mankind were to achieve the American purpose for itself in opposition to America! And how dangerous it would be for the very survival of America if America were to harbor an irredenta which was to strive for the achievement of the American purpose against its professors!

### 3. *The Global Frontier as the Condition for Survival*

The direct bearing that the achievement of racial equality in America has today upon America's relations to the world is but a particularly obvious example of the radical transformation of the American purpose in our time. That transformation offers new opportunities for horizontal mobility towards the expanding of the area of equality in freedom potentially to the whole globe. It gives a new significance to America as a model for other nations to emulate. And it makes the achievement of the American purpose a precondition for American survival.

We have seen that the territorial frontier has lost its significance for the expansion of equality in freedom, and we have also seen that the moral, political, and technological conditions of the age require a principle of political organization transcending the nation state. The great tasks that our age poses for America in its relations to the world can no longer be performed by America acting in isolation. What it must do for the non-Communist world—its allies and the uncommitted nations—and for and about the Communist world as well, it can do only in associations more intimate than those provided by traditional alliances or *ad hoc* alignments. Yet the modern world has left the sovereign nation state behind as a viable principle of organization for the purpose not only of the new supranational tasks but also of the elemental task of any political organization: to safeguard the biological survival of its members.

It is the great paradox of this task, which arises from the opposition of sovereign states armed with nuclear weapons, that it cannot be accomplished by sovereign states armed with more and better nuclear weapons. To the contrary, if these weapons are left in the hands of sovereign states, their increase and improvement increase the danger. Thus, it becomes the task of all governments to make themselves superfluous as the guardians of their respective territorial frontiers by transferring their nuclear weapons to an agency whose powers are commensurate with the worldwide destructive potentialities of these weapons. There is no need to stress the magnitude of this task in view of the obstacles that technology and politics, domestic and international, put in the way of its accomplishment. But there is perhaps need to point to the paramount and vital importance of its accomplishment. Without it, what we are saying here about the purpose of America may well turn out to be an exercise in futility, like designing a house for the top of a volcano that, barring a miracle, cannot fail to erupt.

America would perhaps not be quite so perplexed in the face of these new and world-wide tasks if it were aware of the connection that ties these tasks to its traditional purpose. That purpose has always sought the expansion of equality in freedom either by pushing the territorial frontiers outward or by offering America as a model for other nations to emulate. These two methods would become indistinguishable were America to become the spearhead of a free association of nations committed to the achievement of equality in freedom. Within that association, the territorial frontier, instead of having to be pushed outward, would lose its significance as a barrier to the expansion of equality in freedom, and America, instead of serving as a model for other nations to emulate, would share its purpose with its associates. The national interest and the national purpose of America would then merge with their interests and purposes.

Beyond such a free-world association lies the task of drawing both the uncommitted and the Communist nations into a viable world order. The uncommitted nations seek first of all equality; the Communist ones, freedom. America, in a more direct and vital fashion than ever before, can offer a model for both. That much is obvious. What has baffled us is the great constructive task of making our purpose and its achievement relevant to the aspirations of these nations. The failures of Wilson, of foreign aid and liberation remind us in different ways of the complex and delicate nature of that task. The failures teach us that neither the export of American institutions nor verbal commitments without deeds will serve our purpose. Yet the successes, persistent and impressive, however largely unintended, also teach us that we have succeeded in being a model to other nations in the measure that we have tried to be ourselves and to perfect the achievement of our purpose for its own sake. This plausibility of the American purpose, established in the eyes of the world by deeds, must again become the foundation upon which, supported by the modern techniques of propaganda and foreign aid, the world-wide influence of America must rest.

That world-wide influence must serve the interests not only of the nation but also of mankind; for it must build the foundations for a supranational order that will take the control of nuclear weapons out of the hands of the nation state. Thus it will be as it was at the beginning: what America does for itself it also does for mankind, and political experimentation on a world-wide scale in order to save mankind will be in direct line of succession to the political experiment as which at its inception America offered itself to the world.

Thus, the traditional relationship between domestic and international issues has been reversed. The paramount issues that put our ability to achieve the national purpose to the decisive test are no longer economic and social but concern the political organization of the world. We find ourselves today in an intermediate stage; the old domestic issues have lost their urgency, and we have yet to become fully aware of the urgency of the new international ones. When we are so aware, the great political debates and decisions of the future will deal with the relations between America and the world.

### 4. *The Restoration of Democratic Government and the Defense of Freedom*

In order to enable it to perform these momentous tasks, we must restore to the government the ability to govern and to the people the ability to control. The subordination of the public to the private realm, which once reflected the actual priorities, has been made obsolete by the nature of the issues facing society, which will not be met if the government does not meet them. While objective social needs thus put into the hands of the government the paramount responsibility for the achievement of the purpose, the welfare, and the very survival of American society, both the quantity and quality of the new public power must threaten the individual's equality in freedom; for the new public power will have to concern itself with matters once thought to belong "by nature" to the private sphere, and the novel dangers that threaten the individual's inalienable rights, such as life, liberty, and the pursuit of happiness, will compel the public power to extend its protective hand more deeply than ever before in order to secure those rights. While the public power thus expands, it must strengthen old, and erect new, safeguards against itself.

Hemmed in as it is by the feudalism of the concentrations of private power and of its own bureaucracy, the government can no longer act as it must. Can it be made able to do so? In dealing with the concentrations of private power, the government has at its disposal four fundamental powers; the power to license, the power to control, the power to tax, and the power to allocate resources. That is to say: the government can determine the conditions under which concentrations of private power shall come into being and how they shall operate, and it can directly interfere with the distribution of private power by controlling the distribution of economic resources. Experience has shown that the latter type of government action is the more promising. The power to license has generally limited competition and thereby at the very least established one of the conditions in which concentrations of private power flourish. If the power to license were used systematically for the prevention of concentrations of private power, the government would determine from the outset who was to compete for economic power and would thereby destroy the very freedom of competition which it is its task to preserve and, if need be, restore.

The history of our anti-trust policy shows that it is impossible to control effectively concentrations of private power which have already been established. These concentrations yield not to legal prohibitions and administrative regulations but only to superior power, private or public. Here lies the government's chance to tame the giants of private power; for it is itself the biggest giant of all. It can do so either as the sovereign power by collecting taxes, controlling the circulation of money, and granting or withholding economic benefits, or as the most potent competitor and customer. In either capacity, the public power attacks directly the economic sources of private power. It has done so systematically and with a fair measure of success during relatively short periods of our history, in the different "Deals" with which the names of Wilson and the two Roosevelts are associated. But while since the Second World War both public and private power have grown by leaps and bounds and, hence, both the need for the defense of the public interest by the government and the latter's ability to defend it have greatly increased, the government has used its vast and superior powers only sporadically and inconsequentially. Thus, as we have seen, the concentrations of private power have either acted without regard for the public interest or have made the public interest serve theirs. It is for the government to reverse these roles by making use of its powers.

The government must free itself from the feudalism of its bureaucracies by restoring to its own procedures a rational order and to its policy-making members, especially to the President, the will to govern. At all levels, yet especially at the highest, government requires one man to act who, for better or for worse, will bear the responsibility for his actions. The government thwarts itself by surrendering the power of decision to committees that debilitate and dissipate the power of decision. The government must limit committees to their proper function, which is to supply information and advice to those who make decisions, and it must restore to the latter the hierarchical order that assigns to each decision its proper place and to each man who decides his proper responsibility.

When we approach in the President the summit of the governmental hierarchy, we come face to face with two additional tasks: to restore the President's ability and will to govern. In 1937 the *Report of the President's Committee on Administrative Management* stated that "The President needs help." The President has received in the intervening years abundant help in the form of the enormous expansion of the executive office and a plethora of advisory and co-ordinating committees and presidential commissions. Yet, paradoxically, he is today more in need of help than ever before. The help the President has received has lightened his workload by institutionalizing and bureaucratizing his office; that is to say, it has dealt with administration. But it has not concerned itself with the substantive functions of the President as initiator and architect of policy. It is here that the President needs help.

As the initiator and architect of policy, the President must be able to perform two vital tasks. On the one hand, he must acquaint himself with the issues that require initiative on his part, and he must weigh the alternative policies designed to meet the issues. On the other hand, once he has rendered his decision, he must make sure that the decision is executed. All modern Presidents have expressed their frustration on this latter count. "He'll sit here," Truman has been quoted, referring to President-elect Eisenhower, "and he'll say 'Do this! Do that!' *And nothing will happen,"* and an aide of Eisenhower is quoted as having remarked in 1958: "The President still feels that when he's decided something, that *ought* to be the end of it . . . and when it bounces back undone or done wrong, he tends to react with shocked surprise."[1] What Jonathan Daniels, a former aide to Franklin D. Roosevelt, has observed applies not only to members of the Cabinet:

> "Half of a President's suggestions, which theoretically carry the weight of orders, can be safely forgotten by a Cabinet member. And if the President asks about a suggestion a second time, he can be told that it is being investigated. If he asks a third time, a wise Cabinet officer will give him at least part of what he suggests. But only occasionally, except about the most important matters, do Presidents ever get around to asking three times."[2]

However, the President, while in the nature of things generally unaware of it, has reason for complaint also on the ground of lack of information. What he knows of the great issues that face the government, and of the relative merits of alternative solutions, he has learned from members of the White House Staff, of the Cabinet, or of the National Security Council. Yet these top officials may well be a number of bureaucratic layers removed from the acute

[1] Richard E. Neustadt: *Presidential Power. The Politics of Leadership* (New York and London: John Wiley and Sons; 1960), p. 9.

[2] Jonathan Daniels: *Frontier on the Potomac* (New York: The Macmillan Company; 1946), pp. 31-2.

focus of the issue, and the issue, when it reaches either them or the President, may already have been resolved and the alternative solution may never come to their or the President's attention. Thus it has been said that when the President chose the Vanguard over the Redstone as the missile for space exploration, he actually confirmed a choice made on lower levels without being aware of the relative merits of the two missiles. This danger—that the President will see through the eyes of his immediate subordinates the great issues he must decide—is always present. It is aggravated if some of these subordinates have strong policy preferences of their own or seek to shield the President from controversy.

This "extraordinary isolation," to which Woodrow Wilson called attention,[1] from the great issues he must decide and from the implementation of his decision is indeed the great ailment of the modern President's office. The President tends to become the top manager of an administrative machine, the co-ordinator of the co-ordinators. He presides over the "Presidency" but governs neither it nor the executive branch as a whole. This diminution of the President's power is in part the result of the help the President has received in the form of an institutionalized and far-flung "Presidency." It has lightened his workload to such a degree as to make his continuous participation in the day-by-day operations of the government virtually superfluous. With regard to these operations, the "Presidency" has for all practical purposes become the President, either collectively or in the person of a powerful assistant to the President, such as was Sherman Adams.

By curing the ailment of overwork we have—paradoxically enough—aggravated the ailment of isolation. The real problem is no longer that the President has too much to

[1] Woodrow Wilson: *The President of the United States* (New York and London: Harper and Brothers, 1916), p. 39.

do, but that he can no longer do what he alone must do—that is, to govern intelligently and decisively. In this he needs help. Where can he get it?

The President has been cut off from direct and full contact with the issues that await his decision by layers upon layers of agencies and inter-agency committees which as a rule present him, not with the issue in all its complexity and controversiality, but with a dehydrated condensation and a solution that satisfies and hurts nobody and, hence, is acceptable to all and susceptible to presidential approval. If the President were to make a rule of what is now but the exception—namely, that no draft of a decision be submitted to him without an alternative where such exists—if he were to hold an individual official responsible for such correct and complete information in a particular field, and if he were to seek out the areas of controversy and expose himself to its pressures, he would be taking the first steps toward the restoration of his power to govern. The President must also draw upon informal sources of information and might well consult with groups of experts, official or private, of differing points of view, which in a sense would duplicate the alternative solutions of the pending issue. If this were to make for a degree of administrative untidiness, let us rejoice in it if this be the price we must pay for presidential leadership.

The help the President needs for the task of making his decisions stick, he must essentially provide himself. He can make his will prevail within the executive branch to the extent that he is willing and able to use the power of his office and of his person. For, as Chief Executive, the President is the politician-in-chief of the nation. In order to see his decision put into action by his subordinates, he can and must promise and threaten, reward and punish. He needs assistance in the exercise of this power, but he cannot delegate its substance to a Vice President or "First Secretary," without risking either its dissipation or its abuse.

There is no remedy outside himself for the heaviest burden the President must bear: his loneliness at the pinnacle of decision and power. But there is a compensation. For from that loneliness, calling forth the ultimate reserves of his mind and soul, springs the President's greatness. Let us beware lest, by hemming him in with still another batch of assistants or managers, we impair the source of that greatness.

The President needs that greatness to restore his will to govern. That will, as we have seen, has been paralyzed by the unfounded fear of, and the misplaced deference to, public opinion. Here the task of the President is both clear and decisive. He must reverse the established pattern of subservience to public opinion and become its molder. The words that I addressed in 1949 to President Truman and in 1956 to President Eisenhower with respect to the conduct of foreign policy apply to their successor in his conduct of all policy:

> It is for the President to reassert his historic role as both the initiator of policy and the awakener of public opinion. It is true that only a strong, wise, and shrewd President can marshal to the support of wise policies the strength and wisdom latent in that slumbering giant—American public opinion. Yet while it is true that great men have rarely been elected President of the United States, it is upon that greatness, which is the greatness of the people personified, that the United States, from Washington to Franklin D. Roosevelt, has had to rely in the conduct of its foreign affairs. It is upon that greatness that Western Civilization must rely for its survival.

Subservience to public opinion has enfeebled the will to govern and has bred deception and secrecy as instruments of policy consistently used by our government; it has thereby impaired the democratic process itself. Conversely, the reassertion of the President's leadership will reopen the dialogue between the government and the people and thereby restore to the democratic process at least a measure of vitality. We have pointed to the paradox of how the universal application of democratic principles, misunderstanding the nature of the democratic process, in the form of government through committees and public opinion has thwarted both government and democratic control. We must now point to the corresponding paradox of how the restoration of the government's leadership and responsibility will assist in the restoration not only of the government's ability to govern the people, but also of the people's ability to control the government.

The contribution of the President's leadership to the renewal of the American purpose is not limited to the restoration of the government's ability to act and of the people's ability to control. The President's most persuasive impact upon the consciousness of the nation stems from the very fact of his leadership, the very example he sets as the head of a government that knows how to govern. For before men want to be governed well, they want to be governed. Before they choose between good and bad policies, they want some policies to choose from. Regardless of the course they want the ship of state to take, they want to be sure that a strong hand is at the helm. The great revolutions of the modern age—from the French Revolution of 1789 through the two Russian revolutions of 1917 and the Fascist revolutions in Italy and Germany to the Communist revolution in China—were carried forward by men who were dismayed, not only at being governed badly, but also and more importantly at not being governed enough. These revolutions owed their success to the determination and ability of their leaders to seize power, to hold it, and to use it to govern, badly perhaps but firmly. The modern masses have risen in despair and fury not against some particular policy but against the weakness of government reflected in spectacular failures. Thus, the very experience of having a President who leads and a government that governs will restore the people's confidence that their fate is still subject to human control and that as their leaders can act to determine it, so can they by choosing and influencing their leaders.

A government that has thus made itself strong enough to accomplish its great new tasks will also have become strong enough to impair the life, the liberty, and the pursuit of happiness of the individual for the sake of whom it was instituted. We encounter here again the dilemma, which we have encountered before in American history, of the government that must be strong enough to protect individual rights and by the same token is strong enough to destroy them. From this dilemma there is no escape. For if the government does not perform the tasks which only it is able to perform and, more particularly, if the government does not keep open the old frontiers, open up new ones, and protect individual rights against the concentrations of private power, nobody else will. Our commitment to the purpose of America does not allow us to choose between a strong and a weak, an active and a passive government, but it compels us to surround a strong and active government with safeguards against the abuse of its power.

These safeguards can be found in the American system of government itself. One of these safeguards is the rule of law. It limits the power of the government by subjecting its actions to review by the courts. That these safeguards have not been more effective in our time has been less the fault of the courts, which in the recent crisis of the

McCarthy period have been the main bulwark of individual liberties, than of the carelessness of legislative enactments and of the neglect of executive agencies.

The other safeguard is suggested by the principles underlying the constitutional devices, institutional arrangements, and political dynamics of the American system of government, by which *The Federalist* successfully tried to combine, in the simple relations between society as a whole and the state, a strong government with a pluralistic society. The same combination, in the complex conditions of the contemporary three-cornered contest among government, the concentration of private power, and society at large, must rest upon the same foundation of the intricate interplay of multiple systems of checks and balances. Thus, to give only one example, our economic system is a system of "countervailing powers" in which autonomous social forces check each other.[1] These systems, if they work perfectly, limit at all levels of social interaction, private and governmental, the freedom of all for the sake of all. They do so in two different respects: through their internal structure and through their relations with each other. The classic analysis of these two functions is found in Number 51 of *The Federalist*. As concerns the function of the internal structure of a particular system:

> This policy of supplying by opposite and rival interest, the defect of better motives, might be traced through the whole system of human affairs, private as well as public. We see it particularly displayed in all the subordinate distributions of power; where the constant aim is, to divide and arrange the several offices in such a manner, as that each may be a check on the other; that the private interest of every individual, may be a sentinel over the public rights.

[1] Cf. John Kenneth Galbraith: *American Capitalism; The Concept of Countervailing Power* (Boston: Houghton Mifflin; 1952).

And for the relations among different systems:

> It is of great importance in a republic, not only to guard the society against the oppression of its rulers; but to guard one part of the society against the injustice of the other part. Different interests necessarily exist in different classes of citizens. If a majority be united by a common interest, the rights of the minority will be insecure. There are but two methods of providing against this evil: the one by creating a will in the community independent of the majority, that is, of the society itself; the other by comprehending in the society so many separate descriptions of citizens, as will render an unjust combination of a majority of the whole very improbable, if not impracticable. . . . The second method will be exemplified in the federal republic of the United States. Whilst all authority in it will be derived from, and dependent of the society, the society itself will be broken into so many parts, interests, and classes of citizens, that the rights of individuals, or of the minority, will be in little danger from interested combinations of the majority. In a free government, the security of civil rights must be the same as that for religious rights. It consists in the one case in the multiplicity of interests, and in the other, in the multiplicity of sects. The degree of security in both cases will depend on the number of interests and sects.

In the end, the freedom of the individual in the modern state is not the result of one specific constitutional device or institutional arrangement, although such a device or arrangement may well make freedom more secure. It is not enough for society to recognize the inalienable right of the individual to life, liberty, and the pursuit of happiness and to have on the statute books laws controlling the activities of public officials and limiting concentrations of private power. The freedom of both the individual and the concentrations of private power will in the end repose upon the social order as a whole, the actual distribution of social power. Since officials and concentrations of private power cannot be allowed the power they would often like to possess, government must intervene by deciding the value it wishes to put upon the capabilities and interests of each and assigning to each a sphere and mode of action. That intervention may take the form of an explicit decision settling the issue once and for all. More likely and more typically, it will result from the interplay of the totality of social forces, opposing, checking, supporting one another, as the case may be, in ever changing configurations, forming an intricate web of horizontal and vertical connections. It is upon that complex and shifting ground that freedom rests in the modern world.

In the achievement of these tasks, the government must indeed take the lead. But there must be a people able to follow. A government hemmed in by the feudalism of its bureaucracy and of the concentrations of private power and paralyzed by its fear of public opinion cannot lead. A people that fears public power more than private power, that values the private interest more highly than the public, and that judges the actions of government by what public opinion wants rather than by objective standards, cannot follow. The restoration of the national purpose, then, requires a reorientation of the national outlook, a change in our national style. We must recognize that while the public power is to be feared, so is the private, and that the possibility of the former's abuse is no argument for submitting to the actual abuse of the latter. We must further recognize that private happiness is a function of public happiness—that is, of the public welfare—and that in terms of both the allocation of resources and the resolution of conflicts the public power must take precedence over private interests. Finally, society at large must help the government to free itself from the tyranny of public opinion by testing its own preferences against the objective standards that once gave meaning to its aspirations for equality and freedom. In brief, society, too, must free itself from the tyranny of public opinion.

These are the tasks that the purpose of America imposes upon our government and people. Shall we achieve them? That question will be answered by what Machiavelli called *virtù* and *fortuna*. The one, the quality of our wills and minds, is in our hands; the other, the benevolence of fate, is beyond our reach. Those who came before us knew their purpose and had the courage and ingenuity to transform their environment in the light of their purpose. The purpose, courage, and ingenuity with which they conquered the wilderness were different only in terms of the demands of the environment, and not in intrinsic quality, from the purpose, courage, and ingenuity with which we are called upon to conquer nuclear power, space, anarchy, and ourselves. Those who came before us made it, as it were, easy for fate to grant them victory. Even so, they were not vouchsafed victory. Yet even if they had been defeated, posterity could have said of them: they deserved to be victorious. Let us comport ourselves in such a fashion that posterity can say at least as much of us!

# THE LAST YEARS OF OUR GREATNESS?[1]

## *Mr. Khrushchev's Challenge to the 86th Congress*

WE ARE IN Mr. Khrushchev's debt for having warned us, and in Mr. Lippmann's for having conveyed the warning, that the United States may be enjoying "the last years of its greatness." The scene is extraordinary and full of meaning, and the meaning is in the best Marxist tradition. Other would-be conquerors have foretold the impending doom of their prospective victims, arguing from their weakness and from the decline of their greatness, reminding them perhaps of a greatness of which nothing remains but the trappings. Such is not Mr. Khrushchev's argument. He recognizes America's present greatness and he denies its future not because it will itself decline but because the Soviet Union will surpass it. One is reminded of the tribute—unmatched both in praise and insight by any defender of capitalism—which Marx and Engels paid the bourgeoisie in *The Communist Manifesto:* "It has been the first to show what man's activity can bring about. It has accomplished wonders far surpassing Egyptian pyramids, Roman

[1] From *The New Republic,* December 29, 1958.

aqueducts, and Gothic cathedrals. . . . The bourgeoisie
. . . has created more massive and more colossal productive forces than have all preceding generations together."
And it is both in spite and by virtue of these achievements
(because it could achieve nothing else, exhausting its historic mission with these achievements) that the founders
of Communism were as confident as is their present heir
of the impending doom of capitalism.

The message which Mr. Khrushchev, echoing Marx and
Engels, sends us through Mr. Lippmann, then, is this: you
are doomed not because you are small and weak, but because your greatness and strength are inextricably tied to a
particular period of history which Communism is in the
process of leaving behind. Your greatness is of necessity of
the past and of a quickly disappearing present, while our
greatness is necessarily of the future.

The threat of that message is twofold. As a general
proposition, the point it makes is well taken. For history
bears indeed witness to the truth that a society which is
unable to adapt itself to new conditions and restore its
vital energies in the successful contest with new problems
is doomed and that all historic societies have sooner or
later been so doomed.

What makes the truth of that general proposition
acutely poignant for us is a general climate of opinion and
a general trend of policy which, if they do not appear to
bear out that truth, do not deny it persuasively. Our Government appears to act upon the assumption, which the
people are pleased to accept as self-evident, that our greatness is a kind of inherited, if not natural quality owing to
certain traditional ways of thought and action and to be
perpetuated through the perpetuation of these ways. This
state of mind derives from what is in essence an isolationist conception of our greatness. Time was indeed when we
could afford to compare our political institutions and so-

cial arrangements with those of other nations and rest assured. Time was when we could be satisfied to compare our present with our past strength and with the prospects for the future. Yet the superiority of our way of life, in terms not of abstract philosophic principles but of political and economic results, is no longer as obvious either to us or to the rest of the world as it used to be. To hundreds of millions of people the Communist way of life appears more attractive than ours. Our strength vis-à-vis other nations can no longer be measured by the degree of our unchallengeable superiority within the Western Hemisphere. It must be measured against a competition which is resolved to leave us behind and is dogmatically certain that it will.

It would of course be preposterous to suggest that we don't know all this. Yet our actions belie our knowledge. We know that we are fighting for our lives, but we act as though it could not be quite as serious as that. This contrast between knowledge and action distinguishes the new isolationism from the old. The old isolationism did not know what the score was and acted as though the score did not exist. The new isolationism knows the score, but in its actions it hankers back to the times when we could afford to ignore it.

The neo-isolationist state of mind causes almost of necessity a perversion of the priorities of national policy. National policy is at all times confronted with demands which exceed, or seem to exceed, the available resources. It is the task of statesmanship to judge correctly both the actual and potential amount of the resources available and the relative importance of the demands upon them in order to support what is important with what is necessary. The Administration has failed in both tasks. Starting with a static, pre-Keynesian conception of economic life and of the creative role of government within it, the Administration has erected the balanced budget to the measure of all policy. The question, can we afford it? has pride of place before all questions of substantive policy. And since the answer is in the negative, the argument in reverse comes easy that there is no emergency and, hence, no need for such expenditures.

This state of mind not only perverts the priorities upon which the Administration acts, it also exerts a subtly corrupting influence upon the public debate on public issues. With the Administration having set the tone, public and, more particularly, Congressional opinion tends to divide not according to the substantive merits of the issues but according to how expensive one kind of policy is compared with another kind. The President having stigmatized the opposition as "spenders," the opposition is tempted to join the issue by either proving that it is at least as budget-conscious as the Administration or else by defying the Administration and providing more than it has asked for.

Yet in truth the controversy over spending is utterly absurd. Since its strictly economic absurdity has been argued with special competence by others, such as the businessmen of the Committee on Economic Development, it only needs to be pointed out here that if the Soviet Union —with less than half our national product—can afford to challenge the United States on land, on the seas, and in the air, in economic productivity, in technical innovation, in foreign aid and trade, in the struggle for the minds of men, it is tantamount to a declaration of national bankruptcy for us to act on the assumption that we cannot afford an adequate response to the Communist challenge. The issue which must for us overshadow all others is not how to save money but, first, how to survive and, then, how to emerge victorious from this contest. The nation which would persuade itself that it cannot afford the policies which will assure its survival and its victory would indeed have not only forfeited its claim to greatness but would sap the foundations of its very existence as well.

It is against this state of mind, permeating the Administration, that the 86th Congress must defend the interests of the nation. It is against its corrosive influence, against its infectious lure to escape from the hard and risky issues of history into the simple and certain world of accounting, that it must be on guard. For this state of mind, by taking our greatness and our survival for granted and by reducing the great issues facing the nation and mankind to a matter of dollars and cents, is in truth, as was its isolationist predecessor in the inter-war period, a prescription for disaster. Militarily, it spells mortal danger. Politically, it spells defense of an indefensible *status quo*. Economically, it spells chaos. And as the alternative presented by the opposition which controls Congress, it spells "moderation."

It is the mission of the 86th Congress, before it can even think of formulating concrete policies, to restore the lost sense of proportion to the Government by facing the great issues that threaten the nation. What are, in necessarily sketchy outline, these issues?

The military danger which the Russian earth satellites revealed in the autumn of 1957 has not been met by adequate action. The recommendations of the Gaither and Rockefeller committees have either not been implemented at all or else their implementation has been cut and slowed down by budgetary considerations. The sense of urgency which animated at least some public discussions more than a year ago has given way in Washington to a mood of wistful impotence. The possibility that the atomic deterrent may no longer be effective because of American weakness and vulnerability and the certainty that we are unprepared to fight a limited war are admitted, and so is the mortal danger that the so-called fourth-nation problem poses for mankind. But what can you or I do about it? Congress can do something about it in two different ways. It can elaborate a coherent defense policy of its own, going far beyond appropriating more money than the Administration had asked for, and while it cannot force the Administration to put such a policy into practice, by formulating it it erects a standard by which the performance of the Administration will be judged. Furthermore, it can mobilize public opinion in support of such a policy. A year ago some members of the Gaither committee met with the Vice-President, intent upon mobilizing public support for their recommendations; they must regret now they have allowed themselves to be dissuaded by the White House.

While our defense policy has been deflected from a bold, decisive course by the specter of an unbalanced budget, our foreign policy has been paralyzed by fear of the unknown. Here the need for innovation is obvious, and since Stalin's death many opportunities for novel policies have presented themselves. Yet far from at least exploring these opportunities, we have been content by and large to continue the military policies which had proven their effectiveness ten years ago and to extend them to regions and situations where they were bound to be ineffective. We have pursued an unqualified policy of the *status quo*, defined in narrow territorial and military terms. As the London *Economist* put it on November 29, 1958, in an article entitled "Stuck on the Status Quo": "It is not so much what Mr. Dulles does in a crisis as what he does not do in between them." However, the rationale behind Mr. Dulles' policy is valid: that any change in the *status quo* brought about by, or likely to lead to, the use of force can no longer be tolerated in the atomic age. The flaw which invalidates the policy is the refusal to recognize that not every *status quo* is defensible, that especially in Asia and Africa the *status quo* is inherently unstable, and that it is the task of statesmanship to create out of the ruinous heritage of the past a viable order which can be defended because it is considered worth defending.

The proper role of Congress in the formulation of foreign policy has since Washington's times been a subject of controversy. Yet in point of fact, the subordination of Congress to the initiative of the Executive is a matter of historic record. Congress can retard, modify, or even obstruct foreign policies of which it disapproves; it is incapable of initiating new foreign policies and forcing the Administration to execute them. But Congress does not need to be impotent in the conduct of foreign policy. It has three potent weapons at its disposal.

First, it can refuse to support foreign policies of which it disapproves. It can do so by witholding its moral support for which the Administration may ask in the form of resolutions or by withdrawing funds from the purposes of the Administration and diverting them to the purposes of Congress. Congress, if it had had a mind to, could have refused to approve, for instance, the resolutions concerning the defense of the offshore islands, the non-recognition of Communist China, and the Eisenhower Doctrine. The virtual or actual unanimity with which the Senate passed these resolutions, it can safely be assumed, reflected not so much the considered convictions of virtually all members of that body as the renunciation of its independent judgment and its subservience to the judgment of the Administration. Instead of going every year through the ritual performance of cutting off a certain percentage from the requested appropriations for foreign aid, a procedure which provides no alternative for the Administration's foreign-aid policy, Congress could indeed present the Administration with a foreign-aid policy of its own by appropriating funds only for purposes consonant with such a policy. If Congress could not compel the Administration to execute this alternative foreign-aid policy, it could, in the unlikely contingency of an extreme conflict, confront the Administration with the alternative of accepting the policy of Congress or having no policy at all.

Second, Congress can express its preferences through resolutions which, while they cannot bind the Administration, have a political weight which the Administration would have great difficulty in resisting. Congress has used in the past this political device for the support of Administration policies, and if its convictions counsel such a course this is as it should be. Yet does the new Congress really approve of our foreign policy, of its sterility and stagnation, of its boldness where it ought to be restrained, of its weakness where it ought to be strong, of its militarization where it is militarily useless and politically self-defeating, of its defense of an indefensible *status quo?* If it does not, it has an obligation to stop feeling ill at ease and seeking relief in attacking the Secretary of State and instead to go on record with a foreign policy of its own which presents the Administration, the American people, and the world with a recognizable alternative to the foreign policy of the Administration.

Finally, by thus establishing itself as the intellectual, if not the political counterfoil to the Administration, Congress can become the rallying point for a leaderless and, hence, ignorant and complacent public opinion. That ignorance and complacency, created and continuously nourished by the Administration and in some measure reflecting its own, have shut the American people off from the perilous political and military state of their affairs, on the one hand, and from the thinking of their best minds in Washington and elsewhere, on the other. In the long run, we are moving step by step, as in a helpless trance, toward the ultimate holocaust which will destroy all of us and all that Western civilization has created. In the short run, we are moving quickly into a zone of mortal danger created by the military superiority of the Soviet Union. Yet the American people live in the best of all possible worlds, and the voice of the individual, with no other mandate but his knowledge, judgment, and conscience, has no chance to make itself heard above the euphoric din of the chorus of delusion. Is it utopian to suggest that Congress, bridging the gap between the facts of life and a knowledgeable but ineffectual elite, on the one hand, and the people, on the other, constitute itself a kind of collective Demosthenes, explaining, warning, proposing, hammering away at the urgency of the dangers and the availability of the remedies?

The economic task which faces the 86th Congress is both more tangible and politically more delicate and difficult to execute than its tasks in the field of military and foreign policy. It is more easily taken hold of, but it requires great political courage and skill for its achievement. It requires a veritable revolution in our economic thinking and practices. For the first time in our history, our economic task does not arise from a domestic problem, such as monopolies or unemployment, nor from a limited foreign situation, such as currency devaluation, tariffs, or dumping. We are challenged, all of us, not just the watch industry or the cotton producers or the Treasury, and we are challenged not just as producers, distributors, and consumers of economic goods, but as representatives of a distinctive way of life, as members of a particular social system with principles, institutions, and arrangements of its own. The challenger is not a foreign industry or a foreign government pursuing hostile economic policies, but the social system of Communism in its totality, directed single-mindedly by a totalitarian government.

The Soviet Union has chosen the economic plane as the battlefield where Communism will win its decisive victory. Mr. Khrushchev has been explicit in his resolution to prove Marx and Lenin correct in their prophecy that capitalism is doomed. While Marx and Lenin believed that this doom would result from a series of world wars, fought primarily among the capitalistic nations themselves, Khrushchev has declared that capitalism will fall because of its inferiority in economic organization, technology, and productivity. He sees the Soviet Union destined to surpass the United States in economic productivity and well-being, and by demonstrating its economic superiority over the United States, the Soviet Union will set the example which the underdeveloped masses of the earth will want to emulate. They will choose the Soviet rather than the American way of life. Furthermore, this economic superiority will enable the Soviet Union to wage full-scale economic war against the United States by taking away its foreign markets and tying the underdeveloped areas of the world to its economic and political system. Thus, without firing a shot, the Soviet Union will triumph over the United States.

This total challenge, aimed not so much at our individual economic well-being as at our greatness as a nation, raises for all of us and, more particularly, for Congress the question of the viability of what we have come to regard as the American way of life in the economic sphere—that is, the competitive use, at home and abroad, of our resources and productivity primarily for purposes of private gain. The anachronism of our foreign-aid policies should have been obvious long ago; for, concerned as we have been with justifying foreign aid and the amount of money to be spent for it, we have never been of a mind to develop a rational, coherent policy of foreign aid derived from a carefully thought-out philosophy of purposes and methods which has stood the test of experience. Yet it is in the field of foreign trade that the Communist challenge touches the core of our economic traditions.

Ideally, foreign trade is carried on by private enterprise for the purpose of private gain. Actually, however, governments have time and again endeavored to use foreign aid as an instrument of national policy. The so-called dollar diplomacy is a case in point. It is not true, even though it is widely believed, that through it private enterprise gained the support of the government for its foreign commercial ventures. Quite to the contrary, it was predominantly the Government which used private enterprise abroad for the purposes of United States foreign policy. Yet while today, in view of the Communist challenge, the need for such use has become overwhelming, the Government, shackled by ancient shibboleths and parochial domestic interests, has not dared to develop a policy which would make foreign trade a potent instrument of American foreign policy, and these shibboleths and parochial interests have been powerfully supported by Congress. Traditionally, Congress had to be prodded by the Executive to face the issues of the day beneath the old labels and to subordinate parochial interests to the interests of the nation. Will Congress now be able to free itself from these shackles and give the nation an economic policy commensurate with its needs? In the absence of executive leadership and pressure, it can do so only if it develops out of its own membership a group of leaders with the vision, skill, and courage to persuade devotees of an outworn economic philosophy and representatives of parochial interests to support a veritable revolution in the relations between the Government and the economic sphere.

If Congress should rise to the occasion, it would have to ask itself not only whether the United States can still afford to have its foreign trade carried on exclusively by private enterprise for private gain and have the Government intervene by and large only for the purpose of maximizing exports and protecting the domestic producer against foreign competition. But it would also have to raise the much more fundamental issue of whether, in view of the total challenge of the Soviet Union marshaling all its economic resources to one end, the United States can still afford the enormous wastefulness of its economic production, distribution, and consumption. Can it still afford its Government-stimulated and paid-for agricultural over-production? Can it still afford the artificially induced annual obsolescence of its hard consumer goods? Can it still afford the production of scores of slightly different models of essentially the same merchandise, production which serves no economic need but only the whim of producer and consumer? What about a system of distribution which has in good measure become an end in itself, a ritual performing no valid economic function and being in some of its advertising manifestations hardly more than a respectable racket? And what about the consumer who has been conditioned not to use what the economy has produced for him until it can no longer be used, but to throw it away and tear it down when it is no longer as new as it is supposed to be? Finally, can we still afford the luxury of thinking about our economic problems in the obsolete terms of socialism *vs.* capitalism, spending *vs.* saving instead of facing the real issue: expansion *vs.* stagnation?

To these absurdities the Government could remain indifferent, or it could even allow itself to promote them, as long as, economically speaking, the United States was, as it were, alone in the world. The United States could then play havoc with its economic resources and still remain a great and powerful nation. Yet with the Soviet

Union using its economic resources as a sword aimed at America's greatness and with our whole economic life having thus become, to use a legal phrase, "affected with the public interest," how can our Government remain indifferent to the rate of growth of our economy having fallen behind that of the Soviet Union, to the misproportion between the resources available for advertising and for atomic submarines, to our policy of foreign trade defeating in good measure the purposes of our foreign policy? If the Government cannot remain indifferent to the political and military consequences of our economic policies, it must devise a comprehensive economic policy of its own which establishes the paramountcy of the public interest over private gain and convenience. With the leadership of the Executive branch in abeyance, the 86th Congress faces here a formidable task of innovation.

Even if it had the benefit of strong Presidential leadership, the executive branch of the American Government has become a cumbersome, slow-moving instrument of government which, short of being faced with disaster actual or impending, is incapable of swift, decisive action and radical innovation. It has become government by committee. Two facts—one structural, the other historic—are responsible for this development. The Constitution confers upon the President the fullness of executive powers and conceives of the other members of the executive branch as his advisers and the executors of his will. According to the Constitution, the President is head of state, Prime Minister, and the Cabinet in the British sense at the same time. In actual practice, the President has had, of course, to delegate many of his constitutional powers. Yet even the most influential member of the executive branch, as the least influential one, derives his power from the fullness of the President's executive powers. Thus, with the exception of the administrative agencies created by special acts of Congress, the executive branch is nothing but an elaboration and proliferation of the President's powers, lacking in that intermediate range of autonomous executive agents through which other constitutional systems have managed to assure responsible executive action.

This gap, created by the lack of a constitutionally provided executive hierarchy, we have filled by the extraordinary device of the committee system. The President delegates some of his executive functions to agency A, others to agency B, and others to agency C, and so forth a couple of times through the whole alphabet. Not subject to effective control by either the President or an autonomous agent below the President, these agencies tend to develop into semi-autonomous fiefdoms with vested interests of their own, which they jealously guard and ambitiously try to expand. Yet while these agencies are in their day-to-day operations probably less subject to central control than, say, a British ministry, they are devoid of the power of independent political decision, especially in so far as a decision, as the important ones generally do, impinges upon the interests of another agency.

With the President far away, functionally always and physically often, with no intermediate body, such as the Cabinet, having the power of decision, and with the business of government having to go on, the agency which wants to initiate a new policy must either seek the agreement of the other agencies concerned, or else it must do nothing. The latter is by far the safer and more convenient course; hence, the propensity of our Government to continue policies long after they have outlived their usefulness and even when they have become self-defeating. For the agency which insists upon a new policy must go to war with other agencies, allying itself with some, competing with others, and fighting others still. This struggle for power is brought to a halt by a peace treaty or, more often, an armistice agreement, issuing from a conference called an inter-departmental committee and being at worst an empty formula glossing over rather than settling the issue and at best a compromise among divergent views to be approved by the President. The new policy being the labored product of a faceless collectivity rather than due to the decision of one man, nobody in particular can be held to account for its results, and, being a compromise, its decisiveness is likely to fall victim to the cross-purposes and divergent interpretations of the different agencies having a hand in its formulation and execution. Thus if it is not stillborn, it is likely to come into the world with a weak brain and a mutilated body.

This system of government puts a premium on inaction and on the mechanical continuation of safe routines. The best it can achieve is a hesitant half-step forward, with one agency pushing and the other pulling back, taken after months of intrigue, bickering, and bargaining. There may have been times when we could afford this kind of government. The times in which we live require swift, decisive, co-ordinated action, instantaneous responses to sudden challenges. In terms of a single act, especially of a military nature, the President has proven himself capable of such a response. In terms of sustained policies, our system of government has proven itself incapable of it. As long as this system persists, whatever novel policies Congress might demand and be willing to support are likely to be delayed, corroded, and obstructed by that jungle of impersonal committee government. In the field of the arms race, the superior speed with which the Soviet Union has been able to transform basic science into technological application and the prototype into the operational weapon is obvious and menacing. The superior decisiveness with which it has been able to take the political and economic initiative is less obvious but no less menacing. The 86th

*The Last Years of Our Greatness?*

Congress will be little more than an ineffectual bystander in the realm of great policy if it does not restore to it, as a precondition for the substantive innovations and radical departures called for, individual initiative, personal responsibility, and co-ordination. Without that restoration, Congress, proposing new policies to the executive branch, will be like a man on the platform of a subway station during the rush hour suggesting to his friend wedged in the crowd of a local that he ought to take an express; the friend may be grateful for the suggestion, which, however, will do him no good if he isn't first helped out of the jam. Thus, the reform of the machinery of Government, in view of its ability to act decisively, responsibly, and in concert, is another urgent task of the 86th Congress.

Should and will the 86th Congress assume these tasks, and can it perform them? There can be no doubt that Congressional government is a poor way of governing a great nation in the most perilous period of its history. Both the spirit of the Constitution and political experience militate against it. Presidential government is vastly superior to it; the Constitution assumes that superiority, and political experience bears the Constitution out. I have myself time and again pointed to this superiority and called upon the last two Presidents to assume the kind of leadership which only they could have given. However, we must come to terms not with a Constitutional proposition or a political lesson derived from the past, but with the political conditions of the day. We have to choose, alas, not between Presidential and Congressional government, but between Congressional government and no effective government at all.

Will Congress make the choice which the situation demands? There is among the leaders of Congress a respectable hesitancy to take a firm hold of the reins of government which, in view of Constitutional principle and political experience, should be in other hands. There is among the leaders of Congress also a less respectable hesitancy which stems from that misunderstanding of the nature of bipartisanship and of the role of the opposition in a democracy, which we have discussed in these pages before. The watchword of that hesitancy is "moderation." Congressional moderation is indeed a political virtue if it acts as a counterweight and restraint upon the lack of moderation of one or the other branches of the Government. Similarly, Presidential or judicial moderation must from time to time counteract the policies of a Congress lacking in moderation. This mutual restraint is a necessary element in the political mechanics of our system of checks and balances. Moderation in Congress, then, presupposes lack of moderation elsewhere. There is obviously no point in telling a teetotaler to be moderate in the use of whisky. Where the executive branch is already moderate to a fault, Congressional moderation can only compound the evils of executive inaction and indecisiveness. In the presence of these evils, it is the task of Congress to push not to hold back, to lead not to follow, to go ahead not to stand still. Only thus will Congress restore the political balance which the lapse of effective executive government has impaired and upon which the American system of government rests.

Can the 86th Congress perform this task of leadership if it should be willing to assume it? It would be rash to deny that the odds, on organizational and political grounds, argue against the possibility of success. Yet in the absence of strong executive government, Congress has governed before; it is true, as Woodrow Wilson has shown, it has done so ineffectively, pettily, and on occasion unworthily. But it was then not faced with a supreme challenge to the greatness and the survival of the nation, which either it will meet or nobody will, and it could not draw then upon the abundance of fresh and exceptional talent which is the great asset of the 86th Congress; nor did the people then expect its leadership. Congress has never had the opportunity of proving itself, supported by a popular mandate, with such an asset against such a challenge. Thus we can find hope, and the 86th Congress can find confidence, in the words which Demosthenes addressed in the *Third Philippic* under similar circumstances to the Athenians, however in vain:

> The worst feature of the past is our best hope for the future. What, then, is that feature? It is that your affairs go wrong because you neglect every duty, great or small; since, surely, if they were in this plight in spite of your doing all that was required, there would not be even a hope of improvement. But in fact it is your indifference and carelessness that Philip has conquered; your city he has not conquered. Nor have *you* been defeated—no! you have not even made a move.

By the quality of that move, history will judge the 86th Congress.

# THE GREAT
# BETRAYAL[1]

THE VAN DOREN CASE is a great event in American history. It is the Hiss case of the academicians and the Dreyfus case of America. As the Hiss case pointed to the possibility of treason where it could least be tolerated—that is, in the foreign office—so the Van Doren case confronts America with the fact of mendacity where it can least be tolerated— that is, among the academicians—the professional guardians of the truth. Both cases, by bringing American society face to face with intolerable evil, test the moral judgment and fiber of America. As the Hiss case raised the specter of defenseless exposure to a foreign peril, so the Van Doren case presents us with the actuality of moral disintegration from within. As the Dreyfus case confronted French society with an inescapable moral choice, so does the Van Doren case American society, and as it was France and not Captain Dreyfus which was really on trial, so it is now America and not Professor Van Doren. Here, however, the analogy ends. For while the French institutions condemned an innocent man to be acquitted belatedly by public opinion, the American institutions have condemned a guilty man whom the preponderance of public opinion appears to acquit without further ado.

Thus the Van Doren case is a great event in the history of America in a dual sense. It brings to the fore certain qualities of American society, known before but perhaps

1 From *The New York Times Magazine*, November 22, 1959.

never revealed with such poignancy, and it poses a moral issue which goes to the very heart of American society. The confrontation of Van Doren with America illuminates with a sudden flash the social landscape: it makes the familiar intrude into the senses with a novel sharpness; it reveals the presence of things hidden and unsuspected; it proves the inescapable reality of things suspected but hopefully obscured. It poses a general moral problem in a peculiarly American context and, by doing so, confronts America with a fundamental moral choice and puts the moral sensitivity of the nation to a crucial test. The American reaction to the Van Doren case bears eloquent testimony to the moral values of America. In what America says about Van Doren, the moral fiber of America itself stands revealed. By judging Van Doren, America bears judgment upon itself.

This is not a case of political or commercial corruption, such as Tweed, Teapot Dome, or Insull. Pecuniary corruption in the political and commercial spheres must be expected. For since the ultimate values of these fields are power and wealth is a source of power, the abuse of wealth in the form of corruption is, as it were, foreordained by the very structure of these spheres; the ever present possibility of pecuniary corruption is built into them, however great or small the incidence of actual corruption may be in a particular period of history. Many politicians and businessmen are uncorrupted and fewer are uncorruptible, but they are all, by the very nature of their occupations, on familiar terms with corruption, encountering and skirting it even if they do not touch it.

Public reaction to political and commercial corruption is as predictable as the incidence of corruption itself. The familiarity of the fact evokes complacency, especially since many an onlooker preserves his virtue only for lack of opportunity to sin. The public rises in indignation only when the magnitude of the outrage exceeds the customary, when corruptive practices run counter to the political and commercial mores which are indifferent to some, such as implicit bribery, and condemn others, such as open blackmail, or when a prominent member of the other party or of the competition has been caught. The moral issue which political and commercial corruption poses is but the general issue of human fallibility. That fallibility was brought into the world by Eve and will be with us to the end of time. The best we can hope and strive for is to restrict its manifestations and mitigate its evil. In one form or other, we must live with it.

The Van Doren case raises an issue different and more profound than political or commercial corruption. It arose in a sphere whose ultimate value is neither power nor wealth but truth. The professor is a man who has devoted his life to "professor," and what he is pledged to profess is the truth as he sees it. Mendacity in a professor is a moral fault which denies the very core of the professor's calling. Power and corruption go together, as do wealth and corruption; pecuniary corruption is, as it were, their illegitimate offspring, preformed in their nature. Yet mendacity is the very negation of truth, the enemy which seeks its death. A mendacious professor is not like a politician who subordinated the public good to private gain nor like a businessman who cheats. Rather he is like the physician who, pledged to heal, maims and kills, or like the policeman who, pledged to uphold the law, assists the criminal in breaking it. He is not so much the corrupter of the code by which he is supposed to live as its destroyer. This is the peculiar enormity of his outrage, which sets his deed apart from the common corruption of power and wealth.

It is in view of the nature of the deed that the reaction of American society must be judged. There is nothing extraordinary in the deed itself. The truth is being betrayed every day by those who are supposed to uphold it. What is extraordinary in the Van Doren case is the spectacular and stark simplicity with which the issue has been presented to the moral forum of America. The issue, thus presented, must be met head on. The verdict must be "guilty" or "not guilty"; there is no room for a hung jury or for a Pontius Pilate washing his hands in skeptical abstention.

The two institutions concerned—Columbia University and NBC—have acted honorably, appropriately, and expeditiously. NBC put the finger on the crux of the matter when it cited as grounds for dismissal, aside from the original deception, the subsequent series of deceptions masking the original one. Yet the reactions of the public contrast strikingly with those of the institutions. Of the nine members of the House of Representatives who heard the testimony, five addressed Van Doren in laudatory terms, "commending" and "complimenting" him and expressing their "appreciation." Two Congressmen expressed the hope that he would not be dismissed from his positions at Columbia University and NBC, and the Chairman of the Committee delivered a peroration predicting "a great future" for him. Only one member of the Committee openly disagreed with the commendation of his colleagues. But even he did not convey awareness of the real issue, the scholar's special commitment to the truth.

Nor did the comments of most of Van Doren's students as reported by the press. One expressed "faith in him as a man" and called him "a fine gentleman," another thought that "what he did was not wrong," a third called the acceptance of his resignation "very unfair." The two students who are quoted as having approved of the acceptance justified it with the embarrassment Van Doren's continued affiliation would have caused the University. As one of them put it: "If Mr. Van Doren had remained, the school would have become associated with everything he had done." And a petition bearing the signature of 650 students demanded that he be rehired. None of the students whose reactions were recorded showed the slightest inkling of the moral issue raised by the case. And but a small minority of editorial comment and letters to newspapers did so.

How is this perversion of moral judgment, praising what deserves to be condemned and even at best remaining indifferent to the real issue, to be explained? The explanation of Congressional reaction is simple. The five members of Congress who approved Van Doren applied the standards of political behavior to the academic sphere. What they would have found pardonable and even praiseworthy in the politician they were unable to condemn in the scholar. Theirs was the fault of parochialism which elevates the standards applicable to a particular sphere into absolutes applicable to all men regardless of circumstances. They dealt with the Van Doren case as though it were just another case of political corruption to be dealt with tolerantly, understandingly, and even approvingly after the culprit had come clean and returned to the fold of fairly honest politicians.

However, the complacency of the politicians points to a more profound issue, a moral dilemma built in, as it were, into the very fabric of American democracy. This is the dilemma between objective standards of conduct and majority rule, between the compliance in thought and deed with standards which are true regardless of time and place, and accommodation to the standards prevailing in a particular society in a particular time and place. America was founded upon the recognition of certain self-evident truths which men do not create but find in the nature of things. Yet American society and, more particularly, American democracy have lived in good measure, and in even greater measure as time went on, by conformity to whatever values appeared to be accepted by the elite or the majority of the moment.

At the beginning of American history and in its great moments of heroic dedication, the moral relativism, if not agnosticism, of that conformist attitude was mediated and even at times overwhelmed by the intellectual awareness of those eternal verities and the compliance with them in deeds. Yet in our day-to-day collective life that tension between objective standards and the ever changing preferences of society tends to be resolved in favor of the latter. Mr. Justice Holmes' famous dictum: ". . . I have no practical criticism [with regard to laws] except what the crowd wants," is the classic expression of that resolution. It is also expressed in one Congressman's hope that Columbia University would not act "prematurely" and would at least wait to judge public reaction to Van Doren's statement.

The objective standards which constitute, as it were, the moral backbone of a civilized society are here dissolved into the ever changing amorphousness of public opinion. What a man ought or ought not to do is here determined not by objective laws immutable as the stars, but by the results of the latest public-opinion poll. What is expected of a man is not compliance with those laws, but conformity to the demands of society, whatever they may be. A man who has gotten into trouble because he is temporarily out of step with public opinion only needs to slow down or hurry up, as the case may be, in order to get back into line, and all will be all right again with him and the world. Moral judgment becomes thus the matter of a daily plebiscite, and what is morally good becomes identical with what the crowd wants and tolerates. The Congressional reaction to the Van Doren case, then, is easily understood in terms of the trend, deeply ingrained in American society, toward making conformity with prevailing opinion the final arbiter of moral worth.

The moral illiteracy of the student is less easily explained. For the students, so one would like to think, are apprentices in that noble endeavor of discovering and professing the truth, not yet compelled by the demands of society to compromise their convictions; they behold truth in all its purity; and they must look at a mendacious professor as a student of the priesthood looks at a priest that blasphemes God. How is it possible for a young man of presumably superior intelligence and breeding, predestined to be particularly sensitive to the moral issue of truth, to be so utterly insensitive to it? These men were not born morally blind; for, as I have said elsewhere, man "is a moralist because he is a man." These men were born with a moral sense as they were born with a sense of sight; they were no more morally blind at birth than they were physically blind. What made them lose that moral sense? Who blinded them to the moral standards by which they —at least as students—are supposed to live?

The answer must be in the same sphere which produced Van Doren himself: the academic world. There is profound meaning in the solidarity between Van Doren and his students, and that meaning is found in the academic sphere which made them both what they are as moral beings. While public opinion has pinned responsibility on television, advertising, business, or low teachers' salaries, nobody seems to have pointed to the academic system which taught both teacher and students.

A system of higher education, dedicated to the discovery and transmission of the truth, is not a thing apart from the society which has created, maintains, and uses it. This is especially true of a decentralized and largely private system such as ours. The academic world partakes of the values prevailing in society and is exposed to the social pressures to conform to them. Its very concept of what truth is bears the marks of the relativism and instrumentalism dominant in American society, and by teaching that kind of truth, it strengthens its dominance over the American mind.

Yet even its commitment to this kind of truth is bound to come into conflict with the values and demands of society. The stronger the trend toward conformity within society and the stronger the commitment of the scholar to values other than the truth, such as wealth and power, the stronger will be the temptation to sacrifice the moral commitment to the truth for social advantage. The tension between these contradictory commitments typically issues in a compromise which keeps the commitment to the truth within socially acceptable bounds—exempting, for instance, the taboos of society from investigation—and restrains social ambitions from seriously interfering with the search for a truth cautiously defined. In the measure that truth is thus limited and defined, the search for it is deflected from its proper goal and thereby corrupted. On either end of the spectrum, one finds a small group which either is subversive of the truth by telling society what it wants to hear, or else is subversive of society by telling society what it does not want to hear.

Contemporary American society offers enormous temptations for the academic world to follow the former path—that is, not only to corrupt the truth, but to betray it. In the process, the academic world tends to transform itself into a duplicate of the business and political worlds, with the search for truth subordinated to the values of these worlds. To the temptations of wealth and power held out by government, business, and foundations, the scholar has nothing to oppose but his honor committed to a truth which for him, as for society, is but a doubtful and for most of them at best a relative thing. He has his feet on an island of sand surrounded by the waves of temptation. The step from corruption to betrayal is big in moral terms but small in execution. What difference is there between receiving $129,000 under false pretenses from government, business, or a foundation, which has become almost standard operating procedure, and receiving the same amount under false pretenses from Revlon? The difference lies not in moral relevance but in the technique, which in the former case is discreet and elegant and remains within the academic mores while in the latter it is blatant, vulgar, and obvious. Van Doren and his students were formed by a world which makes it easier for some of its members to receive money than reject it and condones the betrayal of truth for the sake of wealth and power, provided the academic amenities are preserved. Van Doren is indeed a black sheep in the academic world, but there are many gray ones among the flock.

In the world of Van Doren, American society beholds its own world, the world of business and politics, of wealth and power. It cannot condemn him without condemning itself, and since it is unwilling to do the latter it cannot bring itself to do the former. Instead, it tends to absolve him by confusing the virtues of compassion and charity for the actor with the vice of condoning the act. Yet by refusing to condemn Van Doren, it cannot but condemn itself. For it convicts itself of a moral obtuseness which signifies the beginning of the end of civilized society. The Van Doren case is indeed the Dreyfus case in reverse. As France, by acquitting Dreyfus, restored itself as a civilized society ordered by the moral law, so must America by condemning Van Doren. Otherwise it will have signed the death warrant of its soul.

# EPISTLE TO THE COLUMBIANS ON THE MEANING OF MORALITY[1]

SOME OF YOU, students of Columbia University, have written me, commenting on an article on the Van Doren case which was published in *The New York Times Magazine* of November 22. Since your letters either raise identical points or express the same general philosophic position, I am addressing you collectively. By doing this in public, I am establishing already an important difference between your and my position. For all of you request that, if I *should* write on this topic again, I not reveal your names; and one of you asks that the content of his letter not be revealed either. You appear to shun the public debate of public issues and prefer to drop opinions into the confidential darkness of the mailbox. I believe that in a democracy which still possesses its vitality public issues must be debated in the public forum and that the citizens must be seen, heard, and counted in the interchange of ideas and the interplay of interests, out of which a new consensus will arise.

But what are you afraid of? Why do you feel you must hide your faces and muffle your voices? Your letters are

[1] From *The New Republic*, December 22, 1959.

courteous, decent, intelligent, literate, and moving in their concern about the moral problem and their anxiety to be on the right side of it. The opinions you express are eminently respectable and even conformist to a fault. You say what almost everybody says and you say it better and with greater erudition than most, but there is not a rebel among you. The only deviation which you allow yourselves is a criticism of the trustees of your University for having acted hastily in accepting Van Doren's resignation; but that indiscretion you had already committed when you signed the petition asking that Van Doren be rehired. If your letters were published and the identity of the writers revealed, it is inconceivable that you would suffer in even the slightest degree; for you have done nothing to be ashamed of, you have violated none of the mores of society, and you have much to be proud of by way of intellectual accomplishment and moral aspiration. Why, then, are you afraid?

I will tell you what frightens you. You are afraid of your shadows in the sunlight. You are afraid of the sound of your voices in the silence of the crowd. You are afraid of yourself. You are afraid to speak what is on everybody's lips as long as it is only you who would speak. Only when your voices merge into the chorus of the mass do you cease to be afraid. It is the protective anonymity of the crowd which gives you courage. To sign a petition in the company of 650 of your fellows, then, is one thing; to speak without assurance that you are not alone is quite another.

But imagine for a moment where man would be if his most intelligent, best-educated, and most secure children had throughout history hidden their faces and spoken only in whispers. The great men whose lives and works you study are remembered exactly because they were not anonymous, because they showed their faces above the crowd and spoke in a loud voice all by themselves. What they spoke was more often than not the opposite of what the crowd believed and wanted to hear, and many of them lived in prison or in exile and died in disgrace or on the cross. Have you ever heard of two German students by the name of Schell, brother and sister, who openly defied Hitler in the University of Munich and were hanged? Do you not remember the Hungarian, East German, Polish, and even Russian students who risked everything for their convictions and many of whom paid for them with their freedom and their lives? And you, risking nothing at all, refuse to speak above an anonymous whisper! Why are you so frightened by your own faces and your own voices? The answer to that question will become clear at the end of this letter; for it is intimately connected with the moral problem, to which we are turning now.

You are stung by my assertion that you are unaware of the moral problem posed by the Van Doren case, and you assure me that you disapprove of his conduct. But my point is proven by the very arguments with which you try to reconcile your disapproval of Van Doren's conduct with your petition to rehire him. The issue is for you confined in a three-cornered relationship among Van Doren, yourself, and Columbia University. Your concern is primarily with the misfortune of an attractive teacher, your regret in losing him, and the rigor of the University's decision. You support your position by five main arguments: the confession has swept the slate clean, Van Doren will not do it again, his teaching was above reproach, academic teaching is not concerned with substantive truth, and the University acted with undue haste. These arguments, taken at face value and erected into general principles of conduct, lead of necessity to the complete destruction of morality.

If confession, especially one which, as some of you conveniently forget, was not rendered by free moral choice but extracted by sheer necessity, can undo the deed, no evil could ever be condemned and no evildoer ever be brought to justice. If wrong could be so simply righted and guilt so painlessly atoned, the very distinction between right and wrong, innocence and guilt would disappear; for no sooner would a wrong be committed than it would be blotted out by a confession. Confession, even if freely rendered as an act of contrition and moral conversion, can mitigate the guilt but cannot wipe it out.

The argument that the morally objectionable act is not likely to be repeated assumes that the purpose of moral condemnation is entirely pragmatic, seeking to prevent a repetition of the deed; if what has been done once is not likely to be done again we might as well forget it. Yet while it is true that according to the common law a dog is entitled to his first bite, it is nowhere written that a man is entitled to his first murder, his first fraud, or his first lie. The moral law is not a utilitarian instrument aiming at the protection of society, even though its observance has this effect, but its commands are absolute and must be obeyed for their own sake. Oedipus did not think that it was all right to marry his mother once since he did not do it again. Or would you suggest that Leopold and Loeb should have gone free because it was most unlikely that they would repeat what they had done?

The arguments of the good teacher and of teaching not being concerned with substantive truth go together. You assume, and some of your academic experience may well support your assumption, that the teacher is a kind of intellectual mechanic who fills your head with conventionally approved and required knowledge, as a filling-station attendant fills a tank with gas. You don't care what the teacher does from 10 a.m. to 9 a.m. as long as he gives you from 9 to 10 a.m. the knowledge which he has been paid to transmit. You recognize no relation between a teacher's general attitude toward the truth and his way of transmitting knowledge, because you do not recognize an organic relation between transmitted knowledge and an objective, immutable truth. Yet the view that knowledge is but conventional—one conception of truth to be superseded by another—while seemingly supported by the radical transformation of physics, finds no support in the fields of knowledge dealing with man. If it were otherwise, Plato and Aristotle, Sophocles and Shakespeare, Montesquieu and Locke could mean nothing to us, except as objects for antiquarian exploration.

There is, then, in these fields an accumulation of knowledge, old knowledge being refined and added to, but not necessarily superseded, by new insights. The teacher of such knowledge is not only the recorder and transmitter of what goes by the name of knowledge in a particular time and place, but he is also and foremost the guardian and augmentor of a permanent treasure. This is not a part-time job to be performed during certain hours without relation with what goes on before and after. Quite to the contrary, this is a profession which requires the dedication and ethos of the whole man. Of such a man, it must be expected that he be truthful not only between 9 and 10 a.m. when he teaches, but always.

The last argument that the trustees of the University acted with undue haste is the most curious of all, and it gives the show away. One of you says that the trustees could not have evaluated the evidence during the four hours of their deliberations. Another mentions that the trustees acted before all the evidence was in. Still another argues that they wanted to wash their hands quickly of the whole business for fear of public opinion. And one advances the ingenious proposition that the students would not have protested if the trustees had waited a month or so with the acceptance of the resignation, pretending "however untruthfully," that they were investigating the case!

In truth, you do not mean any of these things, which are either patently at odds with the obvious facts or else absurd on their face. You look for reasons which justify your unwillingness to transcend that three-cornered relationship among yourself, your teacher, and your University and to judge the obvious facts by the standards of morality rather than adjust them for your and your teacher's convenience. You are sorry about losing an attractive teacher and you hate to see that teacher suffer; nothing else counts. But there is something else that counts and that is the sanctity of the moral law. Your Dean, in an admirable statement, which I have seen quoted only in your student paper, has formulated it thus:

> The issue is the moral one of honesty and the integrity of teaching. Appearing as a teacher, Mr. Van Doren engaged in an act of deception in professing to know what he did not know, and of dishonesty in accepting answers in a test of knowledge against an opponent he believed to be honest. Thereafter, he continued to act out the deception and continued to lie about his actions, even under oath, until after he had been subpoenaed by a committee of Congress. This behavior seems to me to have been contrary to the principles that a teacher stands for and undertakes to instill in his students. If these principles are to continue to have meaning at Columbia, Mr. Van Doren's ultimate offer to resign had to be accepted.

Here is indeed the nub of the matter.

You must have smiled indulgently or shrugged with impatience when you saw me refer to the sanctity of the moral law. Is not morality, so you might ask, a relative thing, the ever changing result of environment and circumstances? If this were so, let me ask you, how do you explain that we cannot only understand the moral relevance of the Ten Commandments, originating in a social environment and circumstances quite different from ours, but also make them the foundation for our moral life? How do you explain that the moral ideas of Plato and Pascal, of Buddha and Thomas Aquinas are similarly acceptable to our intellectual understanding and moral sense? If the disparate historic systems of morality were not erected upon a common foundation of moral understanding and valuation, impervious to the changing conditions of time and place, we could neither understand any other moral system but our own, nor could any other moral system but our own have any moral relevance for us. It is only because we as moral beings have something in common with all other men—past and present—that we are able to understand, and make our own, the core of the moral systems of others. What is it that all men have in common as moral beings?

All men—civilized and barbarian—in contrast to the animals, are born with a moral sense; that is to say, as man is by nature capable of making logical judgments, so is he capable by nature of making moral judgments. As I have said elsewhere, man "is a moralist because he is a man." Yourself, in your groping for a tenable moral position, in your anxiety to justify yourself in moral terms, bear eloquent testimony to the innate character of that moral faculty. Civilized man shares with the barbarian the faculty of making moral judgments, but excels him in that he is capable of making the right moral judgments, knowing why he makes them. He knows—as Socrates, the Greek tragedians (to whom one of you rather wistfully refers), the Biblical prophets, and the great moralists and tragedians of all the ages knew—what is meant by the sanctity of the moral law.

The moral law is not made for the convenience of man, rather it is an indispensible precondition for his civilized existence. It is one of the great paradoxes of civilized existence that—in contrast to the existence of the animals and barbarians—it is not self-contained but requires for its fulfillment transcendent orientations. The moral law provides one of them. That is to say, human existence, not in its animal but in its civilized qualities, cannot find its meaning within itself but must receive it from a transcendent source.

You are still in all likelihood closer to your birth than to your death, yet in the measure that your life approaches its natural limits you will become aware of the truth of that observation. For when you look back on your life in judgment, you will remember it, and you will want it to be remembered, for its connection with the things that transcend it. And if you ask yourself why you remember and study the lives and deeds of great men, why you call them great in the first place, you will find that they were oriented in extraordinary ways and to an unusual degree toward the things that transcend their own existence. That is the meaning of the passage from the Scriptures, "He that findeth his life shall lose it; and he that loseth his life for my sake shall find it."

This connection between our civilized existence and the moral law explains the latter's sanctity. By tinkering with it, by sacrificing it for individual convenience, we are tinkering with ourselves as civilized beings, we are sacrificing our own civilized existence. As Kant put it: "If justice should perish, man's existence on earth would have lost its meaning."

The issue before you, when you were asked to sign that petition, was not the happiness of a particular man nor, for that matter, your own, but whether you and your University could afford to let a violation of the moral law pass as though it were nothing more than a traffic violation. Socrates had to come to terms with that issue, and he knew how to deal with it. You did not know how to deal with it. And this is why you hide your faces and muffle your voices. For since your lives have lost the vital contact with the transcendence of the moral law, you find no reliable standard within yourself by which to judge and act. You are frightened by the emptiness within yourself, the insufficiency stemming fom a self-contained existence. And so you flee into the protective cover of the anonymous crowd and judge as it judges and act as it acts. But once you have restored that vital connection with the moral law from which life receives its meaning, you will no longer be afraid of your shadow and the sound of your voices. You will no longer be afraid of yourself. For you will carry within yourself the measure of yourself and of your fellows and the vital link with things past, future, and above.

# Index

*The concrete entries refer to America, if not otherwise identified.*

i

# A NOTE ABOUT THE AUTHOR

*HANS J. MORGENTHAU*, Professor of Political Science and Director of the Center for the Study of American Foreign Policy at the University of Chicago, was born in Coburg, Germany, in 1904. His university studies took him to Berlin, Frankfort, and Munich, and he did postgraduate work at the Graduate Institute for International Studies at Geneva. He was admitted to the bar in 1927, and was acting President of the Labor Law Court in Frankfort. A year before Hitler came to power, Dr. Morgenthau joined the faculty of the University of Geneva, where he taught from 1932 to 1935. The next year he lectured in Madrid.

In 1937 he came to the United States and in 1943 was naturalized as an American citizen. He has taught at Brooklyn College (1937–9), the University of Kansas City (1939–43), and since 1943 at the University of Chicago. He has served as Visiting Professor at Columbia, Harvard, Northwestern, Yale, and the University of California. Dr. Morgenthau also served as Consultant to the Department of State in 1949 and 1951 and has lectured at all of the United States War Colleges and the NATO Defense College. He was a member of the Institute for Advanced Study at Princeton, 1958–9, and an Associate of the Washington Center for Foreign Policy Research in 1959–60.

A member of the Missouri Bar, he is the author of many articles and books on international law, international politics, and political theory. Among them are: *Scientific Man vs. Power Politics* (1946), *In Defense of the National Interest* (1951), *Dilemmas of Politics* (1958), and *Politics among Nations* (1948; Revised, 1954, 1960).